CENTRAL ISSUES IN
JURISPRUDENCE

AUSTRALIA
Law Book Co.
Sydney

CANADA and USA
Carswell
Toronto

HONG KONG
Sweet & Maxwell Asia

NEW ZEALAND
Brookers
Wellington

SINGAPORE and MALAYSIA
Sweet and Maxwell Asia
Singapore and Kuala Lumpur

CENTRAL ISSUES IN JURISPRUDENCE

JUSTICE, LAW AND RIGHTS

Second Edition

N. E. SIMMONDS, M.A., LL.M., Ph.d.

Fellow of Corpus Christi College
Reader in Jurisprudence in the University of Cambridge

LONDON
SWEET & MAXWELL
2002

Published in 2002 by Sweet & Maxwell Limited,
100 Avenue Road,
Swiss Cottage,
London NW3 3PF
(http://www.sweetandmaxwell.co.uk)
Set by YHT Ltd, London
Printed and bound in Great Britain by
MPG Books Ltd, Bodmin, Cornwall

First edition 1986
   Second impression 1987
   Third impression 1990
   Fourth impression 1992
   Fifth impression 1994
Second edition 2002

British Library Cataloguing in Publication Data

Simmonds, N.E.
   Central issues in jurisprudence: justice,
   law and rights.
   1. Jurisprudence
   I. Title
   340′.1   K230

   ISBN 0 421 741 201

PREFACE TO THE SECOND EDITION

In the decade and a half since the first edition of this book was published, I have changed my mind about many things. I remain, however, firm in my conviction that lawyers should possess some understanding of the philosophical debates concerning the nature of justice, law and rights. Unfortunately, such an understanding is not easy to impart. The philosophical debates are irreducibly complex, and lawyers have many other subjects that they need to study.

When I wrote the first edition, I envisaged that the book would be read quickly, from cover to cover, in the first few days of the jurisprudence course, and then dispensed with: the point was to provide initial orientation, not deep insight. Experience has taught me that few students actually use the book in that way, preferring to employ it as a crutch throughout the year. I have also come to realise that the book is often read by lawyers who have never studied jurisprudence, but who are sufficiently intrigued by the intellectual aspects of law to wish to fill this gap in their education. Unfortunately, the first edition was rather lightweight for either of these roles. I have therefore completely re-written the book, and greatly expanded it, in such a way as to draw out the complexities of the subject more fully than was possible or desirable in the very short first edition. The book should still be fully accessible to complete beginners, assuming that they are prepared to exhibit a little resilience and determination.

I also hope that the book is sufficiently short to provide a stepping stone to other books, rather than being a self-contained substitute for them. With this in mind I have not hesitated to simplify issues quite considerably where I feel that such simplification serves the goal of getting the reader started in the subject, and where any potential misconceptions will naturally be corrected by wider reading.

An introductory book on a complex subject needs to be clear; but it also needs to stimulate and intrigue. These two goals can compete with each other. A book that is overly simple (as was, perhaps, the first edition) can create the misleading impression of deadlocked positions that look both simpler and more vulgar than they really are. Much of the fascination of jurisprudence springs from its endless richness and complexity, and from the way in which it is inextricably bound up with profound questions concerning the human condition and the nature of political communities. To convey some sense of this richness, one needs to indicate the contestability of all the positions one discusses, and one needs to draw the reader into deeper involvement with the uncertainties of the inquiry. My aim in the second edition has therefore been to provide a useful introduction that encourages active engagement with the arguments, rather than passive learning. A great deal of complex material is covered quite sketchily, but I have not avoided difficult questions when I have felt that they might excite the reader's interest and inspire further investigation.

The book has been completely rewritten, with only a few passages being cannibalised from the first edition. The sequence of chapters remains the same, except for the deletion of the old Chapter 9.

Some readers may regret the passing of the very brief first edition, and think that newcomers to jurisprudence need the kind of extremely brief preliminary orientation that that edition offered. They might like to look at my essay-length survey, "Philosophy of Law" in *The Blackwell Companion to Philosophy* edited by N. Bunnin and E.P. Tsui-James (Blackwell Oxford, 1996)

I have benefited enormously from many discussions with colleagues and students in Cambridge. Cambridge remains remarkably free from the tendencies towards dogmatism and discipleship that suppress creativity in so many academic institutions. One could not hope to work in a better university, or a more stimulating intellectual environment.

N.E. Simmonds
Corpus Christi College
Cambridge

CONTENTS

INTRODUCTION

"Jurisprudence" is the term normally used in English-speaking countries to refer to general theoretical reflections upon law and justice. "Philosophy of law" is an equally good label. Lawyers are mostly down-to-earth types, and mention of "philosophy" is likely to send them rushing for the exit. To most people, philosophers seem to spend their time asking unanswerable questions, or doubting obvious common sense. Why then should a lawyer need to know anything at all about philosophy?

The principal reasons for studying jurisprudence are intellectual: the object of the enterprise is to achieve a clear understanding, not to improve one's professional skills. Since plenty of otherwise intelligent and fairly well-educated people are quite devoid of intellectual interests, one should perhaps not expect them to enjoy studying jurisprudence. Yet, even for them, jurisprudence should occupy a necessary place in their legal education. Even in its most mundane aspects, the lawyer's business is a matter of argument and reasoning. It may be true that one can learn to engage in this practice by immersion and experience, without much intellectual reflection: but one is then simply the conduit for assumptions and understandings that one has never subjected to serious scrutiny. As we shall see in a moment, the taken-for-granted perspectives of practical men and women are sometimes but the residue of yesterday's philosophy.

It is a mistake to ground the importance of jurisprudence upon a set of claims about its practical implications. Nevertheless, the subject can have practical implications, and may even be increasingly likely to assume great practical importance. In periods of settled legal development, lawyers can operate with the assumptions that they absorbed while studying the standard doctrinal subjects. Having been adopted in this non-reflective manner, the relevant framework of ideas may be invisible to those who daily invoke it: it is like the air that they breathe. Even the air may come to occupy one's conscious attention when its supply is disrupted or polluted, however.

When the legal order confronts new challenges in a period of dramatic change, conventional assumptions may need to be identified, and their intellectual credentials examined. At such a time, the reflective detachment of jurisprudence makes a most vital contribution, as the most fundamental questions concerning law's nature and role must be addressed.

Lawyers with little interest in jurisprudence sometimes imagine that its exponents are claiming that the practice and application of law (in adjudication, for example) should be guided by philosophical theories. There are indeed theorists who take that view, but an acceptance of the importance of jurisprudence does not commit one to any such claim. Indeed, one of the central questions for jurisprudence is precisely the issue of how far law is a self-contained body of reasoning with its own autonomy or integrity, and how far the interpretation and application of law requires one to address open-ended questions concerning justice and morality: questions which cannot be resolved simply by reference to settled legal rules, and which traditionally fall within the province of philosophy. Some theorists believe that deep moral and political issues are unavoidably raised in legal argument and judicial decision; but there are others who deny this. Law is viewed by many as basically an exercise in rule-application, where reference has to be made to considerations other than the settled legal rules only in a small minority of situations. To decide whether adjudication needs to be guided by philosophy, we need to decide between these rival visions of law; and, in trying to decide between those rival visions, we are already engaged in philosophy.

Someone who denies the relevance of philosophical reflection to law is therefore entering the jurisprudential debate rather than rejecting it as irrelevant. The lawyer who argues that law has no place for broad philosophical theories is already adopting a certain philosophical understanding of the nature of law and of justice. To fully defend that position, such a lawyer would need to defend a series of general philosophical claims about the nature of law, the nature of rules, and the kinds of reasoning involved in the application of rules. Our supposedly "anti-philosophical" lawyer would soon find that he or she was engaged in philosophical discussion. To claim that, at bottom, legal practice is not a philosophical business is therefore not to oppose philosophy, but to adopt a philosophical position.

DOCTRINE AND THEORY

We usually think of law as requiring systematic study. We assume that law is not merely a long list of separate rules, or a jumble of unrelated decided cases, but an ordered body of standards exhibiting some degree of structure and system. Textbooks divide the law up into separate chunks that have a broad intellectual significance: thus, a book on contract might be divided into categories such as "formation", "vitiating factors", "discharge" and "remedies". Within each of these general categories, certain principles will be set forth, and the more specific rules will so far as possible be subsumed under general principles. The general principles will be invoked as a basis for interpreting and developing the more specific rules.

This way of thinking about law is so familiar to us that we tend to take it for granted. Yet it was not always so. Medieval legal writing did not take the form of a systematic treatise divided up into orderly categories and structured by principles. Right up until the eighteenth century, the main forms of legal writing (glosses, formularies and abridgements) were disorderly assemblages of legal information relatively untouched by any assumption that the law contained its own organising categories and principles. This prompts for us the question of why we make the assumptions that we do. Why do we assume that law will be structured by general principles, rather than simply being a long list of rules, enacted for enormously varied and unsystematic reasons?

Historically the assumed systematic character of law has been strongly influenced by the tradition of natural law theory, which argued for the existence of objective moral values binding upon the whole of humanity. It has been said that modern legal textbook writers are the heirs to the natural law tradition in so far as they seek to expound the detailed rules of law in relation to underlying principles and values. Certainly we can find legal writers of the seventeenth and eighteenth centuries invoking theories of natural law as a justification for their attempt to expound the law in ordered principles. Generally speaking, natural law theories in this period held that men have certain natural rights and duties, the enforcement of which makes organised social life possible. Courts and legal systems were viewed as defining and then enforcing these natural rights and duties. The law was capable of systematic study and exposition in so far as it was based on principles of reason and justice, since the various established rules could be related to underlying principles that they expressed, or rights that they protected.

Many of the modern debates in jurisprudence find their most immediate origin in the attack that was mounted on natural law theories, at the end of the eighteenth century, by Jeremy Bentham. Bentham argued that talk of natural law and of natural rights can settle nothing: there is no way of demonstrating what such laws and rights might be, and so the theory of natural law offers no determinate guidance on moral and political issues. The only proper basis for determining how we should live, what laws we should have, and so forth, is the principle of utility. This principle holds that one should always act so as to maximise the greatest happiness of the greatest number. The only good reason for a law is its tendency to maximise happiness: all talk of law as enforcing pre-existing natural rights is not only wasted breath but also positively harmful, as diverting men's attention from the real issue of the consequences for welfare of having this or that law.

Bentham's rejection of natural law and his adoption of the principle of utility led him to further controversial conclusions. As we have already noted, some of the great legal writers of the period tended to expound the law in terms of an underlying natural law theory. Thus, Blackstone's *Commentaries on the Laws of England* presented the major features of English law as an embodiment and protection of certain basic natural rights. Bentham objected to this approach because, he held, it confused the existence of a law with its merit or demerit. Whether or not a certain rule was an existing rule of English law depended upon whether that rule had been laid down. But whether or not it was a good law was an altogether separate issue, depending on the tendency of the law to maximise happiness. An approach that treated positive law expressly laid down in established rules as a manifestation of natural law was objectionable in that it confused what the law is with what the law morally ought to be. The theory of law that Bentham constructed admitted as part of the existing law only those rules that had been deliberately laid down by persons in authority (such as judges or legislators). All doctrinal arguments that were not concerned with the applica-tion of such rules were treated by Bentham as arguments about what the law should be, but not about what it is.

Bentham's critique of natural law theory gave rise to a number of problems that have continued to occupy the centre of the stage in modern jurisprudential debates. First and foremost is the question of the separation of the law as it is and as it ought to be. When we state that such and such a rule represents the law, are we making a kind of moral judgment about the justice or fairness or reasonableness of the rule? Or could we set on one side all such questions of justice and reasonableness, while nevertheless justifying our statement by reference to observable facts concerning the issuing of certain orders by persons in authority or the acceptance of certain standards by people more generally? In describing the law as imposing a duty, are we committed to saying that the law is morally right or morally binding? Those who wish to emphasise the separability of law from morality are generally called "legal positivists". Legal positivists do not wish to argue that morality does not influence the law, or that law is not subject to moral scrutiny and criticism; nor would they necessarily deny that we may have a moral obligation to obey the law. What they do wish to claim is that the mere fact that something is the law does not make it right. The concept of law, for positivists, is a concept with no intrinsic moral import. Whether a rule is morally good, and whether it ought to be obeyed, are questions quite separate from the question of whether that rule is part of the existing law.

Second is the question of how we are to conceive of the nature of legal standards. Does law consist entirely of rules that can be identified by their source of enactment (having been laid down in a statute or a specific case)? Or can the law be said to include principles that have never been expressly formulated, but which are believed to form part of the conception of justice on which the black letter rules are based?

Third is the principle of utility itself. We will see in Part I of this book that the principle of utility as an account of morality faces serious difficulty. It can be argued that adherence to the principle would lead to morally abhorrent action in certain circumstances. It can also be argued that general adherence to the principle would make social co-ordination impossible, since such co-ordination requires a framework of rules that are treated as binding, irrespective of the requirements of utility. It can be suggested that utility is strangely irrelevant to the problem of justice, since the principle of utility is indifferent to questions of distribution which are central to the concept of justice, and because justice is concerned with largely backward-looking considerations, not with the future consequences taken account of by utility. Later in Part I, we will consider some rival attempts to develop theories of justice. The theoretical problems of justice are important for the lawyer not only in themselves but also, as we shall see, for the bearing that they may have on the concept of law itself.

THE CENTRALITY OF JURISPRUDENCE

In his great work *The Philosophy of Right*, Hegel tells us that "the right of subjective freedom" is "the pivot and centre of the difference between antiquity and modern times."[1] Drawing upon this idea, we will find that it is possible to characterise modern political thinking in a way that makes jurisprudence seem central to the intellectual problems of a modern community.

One tradition of political philosophy, drawing its inspiration from Aristotle's *Politics*, begins by asking a series of questions about "the good". That is to say, it regards as fundamental the question of what counts as an excellent, valuable life for a human being. Having arrived at such a conception of excellence, a philosopher within this tradition will then describe the social and political institutions capable of fostering such excellent lives. The family, the forms of economic production, and the forms of governance will all be viewed from this perspective. Law is likely to play an important part in this type of political vision, for law can inculcate good habits of conduct, protect good citizens from the predatory conduct of others, and can help to sustain other valuable institutions such as the family and the market. Being centred upon the attempt to foster a conception of excellence, this tradition of thought tends to assume that an adequate political community will have a high degree of consensus upon values; those values will, of course, inform and guide legal judgment.

Political philosophies stemming from this tradition have continued to thrive in the modern world, on both the left and the right; but they have been opposed by a rival tradition giving greater centrality to what Hegel calls "the right of subjective freedom". These theories emphasise the importance of each individual deciding for him or herself upon what counts as a good or excellent life. The role of the state is not thought to be the fostering of this or that conception of excellence, but the

---

[1] Hegel, *The Philosophy of Right*, translated by T.M. Knox, (Clarendon Press Oxford, 1952), para.124.

provision of a framework within which each individual has an opportunity to choose and pursue his or her own conception of the good.

Within the Aristotelian type of theory, law occupies an important but not necessarily pre-eminent place. By contrast, law assumes absolute centrality within the later type of theory that emphasises the "right of subjective freedom". For individuals can be provided with the opportunity of pursuing their own conception of a good life only if they possess clearly demarcated domains of liberty within which they are free from interference: and it is the law that must demarcate such domains of liberty. In this way, political debate in such a community comes to be dominated by essentially juridical notions such as "rights", "justice" and "equality" (rather than by non-juridical notions such as "well-being", or "the common good").

If law becomes central in this way, it also becomes problematic. A political community that does not seek to foster a shared conception of excellence, but facilitates diverse individual choices, must contemplate a high degree of pluralism and diversity in the values espoused by its citizens and officials. How then is a shared set of rules going to be possible? Such a shared set of rules is *necessary* for the demarcation of domains of liberty, and it must be capable of being supported, understood and applied by people whose broader values are otherwise very diverse: but is this possible?

Jurisprudence has exhibited an intense concern with the nature of law partly in response to this problem. Can laws be identified with certain written texts (statutes and cases) established by authority? One problem here is that shared texts may not give us shared rules if we read the texts in quite different ways; and people with diverse values and cultural understandings may well reach diverse conclusions about the meanings of the texts. In any case, when judges apply the law they claim to discern its *true* meaning; and their conclusions frequently seem to be informed by the belief that the true meaning is that which renders the law most just. Can one really separate the meaning of the law from one's understanding of justice? Can one separate an understanding of justice from one's conception of "the good"?

In Part 1 of this book we will examine various theories of justice. Questions of justice must be addressed when we are making legislative decisions about the laws that should be enacted, and when we subject existing laws to criticism. Such questions may also arise in the context of interpreting and applying the law to specific cases. Is it possible for questions of justice to be addressed without reliance upon conceptions of excellence and well-being? Will not every proposed account of justice (and therefore every proposed body of laws) favour some conceptions of excellence at the expense of others? Or is it possible to develop theories of justice that are, in some sense, "neutral" between "conceptions of the good"?

In Part 2 we will turn to the question of the nature of law. What is the relationship between law and justice? Is genuine law necessarily just? Must it at least *claim* to be just? Must the interpretation of law always be guided by considerations of justice? Do we need to invoke theories of justice in order to identify the content of the law?

Finally, in Part 3, we will turn to the question of rights. The notion of a right might be considered central to the conception of politics as facilitating individual choices, or individual interests. Yet the concept of a right is very poorly understood. What exactly is entailed by the possession of a right? Are rights essentially concerned to protect choice? Or are they essentially concerned to protect our well-being, even independently of our choices? We will find that the various possible answers to questions of this sort are closely bound up with the issues of law and justice addressed earlier in the book.

INTRODUCTION TO PART 1

JUSTICE

In Part 1 we will examine a variety of philosophical theories of justice. Each of the rival theories seeks to offer an account of the principles of justice that should regulate our laws and political institutions. Some theories (those of Rawls and Nozick) maintain a distinction between questions concerning value or excellence (the good) and questions concerning justice. Rawls and Nozick propose particular visions of what a liberal society might be, wherein the society is able to exhibit pluralism and diversity at the level of conceptions of the good (ideas about what would be a worthwhile and valuable life) precisely because it espouses a conception of justice that is in some sense *neutral* between conceptions of the good. Both theories therefore set on one side all views about the worthiness or unworthiness of particular ways of life, and then seek to reach conclusions about justice in the austere intellectual landscape so created.

Another theory that we will examine is utilitarianism. Here the endeavour is not to construct an account of justice that is neutral between conceptions of the good, but an account of the good that judges different lifestyles solely by reference to the satisfactions that they yield, rather than by more traditional ideals of excellence or virtue. One might think of the theory as converting all goals and preferences into a single currency (of pleasure, or the satisfaction of preferences).

At the end of Part 1 we will examine a different type of theory that draws its inspiration from Aristotle and Aquinas rather than from the modern liberal tradition of political thought. This theory, expounded by John Finnis, proposes that we have good reasons for believing in the existence of certain objective goods that constitute "forms of human flourishing". Communities should be judged by their capacity to foster the flourishing of human beings. However, since there is a plurality of such goods, and they are "incommensurable", no single way of life can be said to be the best. Since one of the objective goods is to be found in our exercise of judgment and control over our own lives ("practical reasonableness"), the state will foster good lives most adequately when it provides a framework within which people can choose between the various possible good lives that are practically available. Thus Finnis avoids the implausible manouevres whereby theorists have sought for "neutrality", while he strives to avoid the potentially oppressive implications of a theory grounded in a particular conception of the good.

These modern debates trace out the lines of a major division between two traditions of political philosophy, one of which is represented by Aristotle, and the other represented by Kant. Aristotle begins with an account of excellence, and then seeks to explain the ways in which a political community can contribute to the realisation of excellent lives. Modern philosophers might describe Aristotle as making "the good" prior to "the right": that is he derives his account of justice and rights[1] ("the right") from a deeper account of what counts as a good or excellent way to live ("the good"). Kant, by contrast, seeks to establish principles of justice and rights that are grounded quite independently of any ideas about the excellence or worth of this or that way of life. In determining the content of justice and rights (as opposed to his account of an excellent life) Kant seeks to abstract the form of the will from its content: in other words, he seeks to set on one side all questions about the true merit (or unworthiness) of the goals that we choose to pursue, and to focus exclusively upon the question of how our actions impact upon the equal freedom of others. Kant therefore seeks to make "the right" prior to "the good".

While Kant's account of justice and rights has provided one of the major sources of inspiration behind modern liberalism, the same cannot be said of his account of "the good". Modern liberals tend to exalt individual "autonomy", understood as the capacity and opportunity to form and pursue preferences. For Kant, however, to act on one's desires or preferences is to act

---

[1] Some theorists would deny that Aristotle has any notion of individual rights. It is even suggested that ancient Greek contained no word that is translatable as "a right". Even if this is correct, however, it need not be taken to demonstrate a fundamental incompatability between the Aristotelian *tradition* and the idea of individual rights.

See Fred D. Miller, *Nature, Justice and Rights in Aristotle's "Politics"* (Clarendon Press Oxford, 1995) Chap.4; Brian Tierney, *The Idea of Natural Rights* (Emory University, Atlanta, Georgia: 1997).

heteronomously (such preferences result from a host of external influences and are therefore not genuinely autonomous). Kant would agree that a good life is an autonomous life; yet he holds that autonomous action requires, not the pursuit of one's desires, but willing submission to the requirements of the moral law. Such a conception of "autonomy as obedience" is unlikely to appeal to most present-day liberals, and will strike tyro philosophers as repugnant. Yet, it is easy to doubt whether the freedom to act on one's desires should be regarded as the epitome of self-governance (autonomy): what makes you desire a particular type of car or pair of sunglasses, for example? One question that liberals need to address concerns the legitimacy of detaching Kant's approach to the notion of justice (giving priority to "the right" over "the good") from his account of autonomy. Do our desires for the most part simply reflect external influences upon us? If so, should political philosophy not focus less upon freedom (the freedom to pursue one's desires) and more upon the nature and quality of the lives that people eventually lead?

Theories that give priority to the right over the good, together with utilitarian theories that convert all goods into the currency of preference-satisfaction, are generally thought of as composing the "liberal" tradition of political philosophy. Theories such as those of Aristotle and Aquinas, that proceed from some conception of excellence, represent an older, more classical, tradition. To think of a division between "liberal" and "non-liberal" theories can be dangerous, however, if it is taken to suggest that theories of the latter type are necessarily oppressive in their implications or fundamentally hostile to individual liberty. Whether they are so oppressive or hostile is a matter for substantive debate and is not to be settled in advance by an appeal to convenient labels that are inevitably crude and undiscriminating.

SUBJECTIVISM

While accepting that liberals may face substantial problems in defending their position on a philosophical plane, we should not be misled by some of the more superficial arguments that are frequently repeated by critics of liberalism. For example, liberalism is often accused of being grounded in "subjectivism", understood as the claim that moral and other evaluative judgments are merely expressions of a "subjective" attitude rather than an "objective" fact. The liberal's desire to refrain from enforcing or inculcating one particular way of life is thought to result from a belief that there is no objective ground for the choice between different ways of life: different people feel differently about them, but in themselves the alternative ways of living are neither worthy nor unworthy.

Subjectivism of this sort is often accepted uncritically by non-philosophers, but it is in fact less easy to defend than one might at first think. The matter is too complex to debate in this context. For present purposes, the question is not whether subjectivism is true, but whether liberalism is committed to a belief in its truth. For, if liberalism is indeed grounded in subjectivism, it proves to be self-subverting. The liberal wants to defend the claim that tolerance and political liberty are good, while intolerance and oppression are bad. If the defence of this claim must appeal to the idea that all moral judgments are subjective (and therefore neither true nor false), the alleged subjectivism must infect the claim itself: the thesis that tolerance is good will itself be a merely subjective assertion, neither better nor worse than its opposite (intolerance is good). Clearly a commitment to subjectivism will provide a poor way of defending liberalism, or indeed any other moral position.

Naive liberals often find themselves drawn to subjectivism because they believe it to be associated with tolerance. One who denies the existence of any moral truth, and views all moral claims as mere expressions of attitude or preference, is expected to be tolerant. As we have seen, this need not follow ("Personally," our subjectivist might say, "I prefer a spot of intolerance"). If anything, the connections run the other way. Only someone who believes moral judgments to be capable of truth and falsehood can admit the possibility that he may be mistaken in his moral views: if morality is simply a matter of personal commitment, it is impossible for my moral judgments to be false, and therefore impossible for me to be mistaken. One who accepts the possibility of moral truth is not necessarily claiming to have infallible access to that truth: their point may rather be to emphasise the possibility of error.

A belief in subjectivism is often the result of thinking that sound arguments must be conclusive and logically compelling: since morality seems to lack such arguments, the conclusion is drawn that it is not a matter of reasoned argument at all, but of emotional hot-air. Someone who is guilty of this error is for that very reason likely to think that those who reject subjectivism believe themselves to be in possession of infallible truths. In actual fact, a belief in the objectivity of morality can often accompany the realisation that arguments are very rarely conclusive and compelling: in morality, as in history or physics, one has to weigh different arguments, some of which are better than others, and the weighing process has an irreducible element of judgment about it. This realisation may itself contribute to a belief in tolerance: a realisation that our own conclusions have been reached by a process of weighing conflicting considerations in an often uncertain balance may help to sustain our respect for those with whom we disagree.

OTHER OPTIONS

It would be absurd to seek to reduce to a short list of alternatives the great variety of arguments that have been offered, within liberal political philosophy, as an underpinning for the liberal's commitment to individual freedom. It is, however, worth identifying two major alternatives (apart from the flawed option of subjectivism).

On the one hand, a liberal theory may be grounded in some conception of what is centrally important about being human. The liberal may extol our capacity to choose and pursue diverse conceptions of a good life, and may emphasise the great value that attaches to the freedom to make such choices. This approach reduces the intellectual distance between liberal and "classical" Aristotelian approaches, in so far as (like the Aristotelian view) it proceeds from a particular conception of excellence (in this case, a conception that emphasises the fundamental value of one's life being freely chosen). Consequently, it faces the difficulty of explaining why the value attaching to freedom of choice should *always* take priority over the values attaching to the different lives so chosen or rejected. If the content of the lifestyle one chooses is capable of being either meritorious or unworthy, why should some degree of free choice not be sacrificed so as to ensure that people generally choose better lives? Mere assertion that freedom must always take priority looks like dogmatism rather than reasoned argument.

On the other hand, the liberal may adopt a less ambitious line. Even though conceptions of excellence and value may not be *subjective*, it is nevertheless true (the liberal may claim) that we are unable to agree upon them. A political community therefore cannot regulate its affairs by reference to a shared conception of excellence. Yet an orderly and decent community needs some shared public conception of justice by reference to which laws, institutions and conduct can be evaluated and reformed. When we seek to construct such a public conception of justice, therefore, we should try to *abstract* from our differing conceptions of excellence and notions of a good life, to arrive at a theory that defines "the right" independently of "the good".

This line of argument has much appeal. Yet why should it be assumed that we will find it easier to arrive at a shared conception of justice than a shared conception of excellence or "the good"? Is it possible to construct a theory of justice that is "neutral" between different conceptions of the good?

NEUTRALITY

Attacks upon the alleged "subjectivism" of liberalism are rivalled in popularity only by attacks upon its claim to "neutrality". It is indeed true that certain influential modern versions of liberalism claim to be "neutral between conceptions of the good"; but the notion of "neutrality" is a slippery one that needs to be handled with care.

In the first place, it should be noted that theories that prioritise "the right" over "the good" are not claiming to be *morally* neutral. Rather, they are drawing a distinction *within* morality, between questions of justice and rights (the right) on the one hand, and questions of excellence, virtue or worthiness (the good) on the other. The claim that such a distinction can be drawn is a substantive moral claim, as is the claim that the content of justice should be worked out independently of questions about "the good". Laws that implement such a theory would make no claim to moral neutrality as such: only neutrality with regard to one aspect of morality.

Secondly, it would obviously be absurd to claim that a system of laws should make it equally possible for any conception of the good whatever to be pursued. The psychopathic killer has a conception of the good that involves terrifying and killing people, and the law of a liberal state will prohibit his activities without hesitation. It is true that the psychopath's pursuit of his "good" will interfere with the ability of others to pursue their own conceptions of the good, but it is a mistake to suggest that prohibition of the psychopath's activities could be justified by the need to maintain equal opportunities to pursue the good. It will commonly be the case that one person's pursuit of the good will impact upon another person's pursuit of their own good. If our object is to secure *equal* chances for everyone, outright prohibition of an activity will never be justified: we will somehow have to give the psychopath an equal chance of enacting his desires. The impossibility (as well as the undesirability) of equalising such chances is surely obvious, and it seems reasonable to conclude that this is not what liberals intend by their espousal of neutrality.

Those liberals who believe in "neutrality between conceptions of the good" intend to exclude considerations of excellence or value from the justification for the law's prohibitions: they are not suggesting that the law can or should be neutral in its *effects*. The object is not to give everyone an equal chance of pursuing their conception of the good, regardless of its content. Rather, the point is to ensure that, when conduct is prohibited, the prohibition is justified by reference to considerations that are independent of our opinions about the unworthiness of the goal that the conduct pursues. The psychopath's activities would be prohibited, not because we consider his actions to be lacking in value (even though we may so consider them), but because (for example) his actions impact unreasonably upon the interests or liberties of others. We might claim, for instance, that the psychopath's actions violate the rights of others. The next step in the argument would then be to show that the existence and content of such rights can be established without invoking considerations of "the good" of the type that the theory of "liberal neutrality" seeks to exclude. Different liberals seek to achieve this exclusion in different ways: Nozick derives his system of rights from a basic right to exclusive self-ownership (see Chapter 3); while Rawls derives his system of rights from the principles that rational persons would agree to in circumstances where they did not know the content of their own conception of the good (see Chapter 2).

Chapter 1

UTILITARIANISM

While philosophical reflection upon law and justice has a history extending back to the Greeks, many of the central themes of modern jurisprudence assumed their present form (at least for the English-speaking world) in the work of Jeremy Bentham. Bentham put forward a positivist theory of law (such theories will be considered in Part 2 of this book) and an incisive analysis and critique of rights (rights will be considered in Part 3); but the central foundation of Bentham's jurisprudence was his advocacy of utilitarianism. It therefore makes good sense for us to begin Part 1 by considering the moral and political philosophy of utilitarianism.

Actually, there are a great many different moral and political theories which fall under the general heading of utilitarianism, and it will obviously not be possible to discuss all of them, or even a representative selection of them. For the purposes of this book it is enough to isolate certain features which are common to the majority of such theories, and to indicate in brief terms some of the major divergencies and alternative lines of development that have been pursued in different individual theories. The classical utilitarian theories (of Bentham, J. S. Mill and Henry Sidgwick) took the fundamental basis of morality to be a requirement that happiness should be maximised: the basic principle of utility required us to weigh up the consequences, in terms of happiness and unhappiness, of various alternative actions, and choose that action which would, on balance, have the best consequences, in the sense of producing the largest net balance of happiness. Applying the principle of utility involves "trading off" the benefits accruing to some against the harms accruing to others, and deciding upon the course of action that produces the largest net benefit. Later theories have sometimes abandoned the notion of happiness in favour of other notions (such as the idea of "preference attainment", for example) or have modified the account of how exactly the principle of utility is to be brought to bear on individual actions. I shall describe some of these modifications in general terms later in this chapter.

Since all utilitarian theories are concerned with making people "better off" in some sense, I shall use the term "welfare" as a general label which does not distinguish between happiness and other values that replace that notion in more modern theories.

It is helpful to distinguish between various separable features of utilitarianism, as follows:

1. Utilitarianism is *monistic*, in that it proposes one supreme principle (the principle of utility) as governing all moral questions. Non-utilitarian theories, by contrast, can sometimes be pluralistic in that they may hold there to be a number of distinct principles or values that must be weighed against each other. For example we would usually think of liberty, equality, and economic efficiency as values that are important but different, and that may come into conflict with each other. When they do conflict, we may feel it is necessary to "strike a balance" between them, without any determinate principles to guide us. The utilitarian will treat all of these values as important only insofar as they bear on the maximisation of welfare, and will handle apparent conflict between them simply by applying his supreme principle.

2. Utilitarianism is monistic in another respect also: its basic principle (the principle of utility) requires us to maximise a single goal, although the goal may be conceived of differently in different versions of utilitarianism (for classical utilitarianism the goal is happiness, understood as the balance of pleasure over pain). Philosophers sympathetic to utilitarianism have sometimes tried to incorporate qualitative distinctions into their "maximand" (the goal to be maximised): thus J.S. Mill sought to distinguish between "higher" and "lower" pleasures. It is, however, generally assumed that the maximising structure of utilitarianism permits only quantitative distinctions to be made: if one is to speak of "maximising" pleasure, one must ask "how much pleasure?" and not "what type of pleasure?". Hence the utilitarian must not only advocate a single supreme moral principle, but also a single goal that the principle requires us to maximise. (We will see in Chapter 4 that it is possible to question this conventional view).

3. Utilitarianism is a version of *consequentialism*. Consequentialist theories claim that the moral rectitude of an action is a function of its expected consequences. Utilitarianism is

exclusively future-looking, in the sense that it evaluates actions solely by reference to their likely consequences and not at all by reference to past events, except in so far as those events have a bearing on the future. We ordinarily assume that I may be morally bound to do something because of a promise that I made: but a utilitarian will argue that in itself the promise cannot constitute a reason for action of any kind. If I am morally bound to keep the promise this is not because of the bare fact of having made it, but because of the harmful consequences that my act of promise-breaking is likely to cause. Many of these harmful consequences will only occur because I made the promise in the first place, *e.g.* some people may have been induced to rely on me, and may be harmed as a result of my failure to keep my word: but the past event of the promise is relevant only by virtue of such consequences, and not in itself.

4. Utilitarianism is also individualistic, in the sense that it judges actions, laws and institutions by their impact upon the lives of individuals. Collective goals such as (for example) the creation of a flourishing sense of national identity or fraternity will be accepted by the utilitarian as genuinely valuable only to the extent that they have positive consequences for the lives of individuals. Utilitarians disagree about how those positive consequences for individuals should be conceived (as a surplus of pleasure over pain? as the attainment of the individual's preferences?, etc.). For the moment we will ignore such differences, and will speak of all utilitarians as being concerned with the "welfare" of individuals.

WHY BE A UTILITARIAN?

Philosophers have been led to adopt utilitarian positions for a great diversity of reasons; but two broad lines of thought have played an influential part, and can be briefly outlined here. One line of thought urges the merits of utilitarianism as a general moral philosophy, while the other sees utilitarianism as proposing a principle that is especially appropriate to the decisions of public bodies such as legislatures and courts, even if it does not form the ultimate basis of morality in general.

1. Why do we have moral rules at all? What is their point? One

answer might be that they alleviate the human condition: things would go worse for us generally if we did not share certain moral rules. If this is the point of having moral rules, however, we could say that all soundly based moral rules are expressions of a concern for welfare. What at first may seem to be unrelated prohibitions upon conduct turn out to be expressions of a single principle: that welfare should be maximised.

This line of thought can be opposed in a variety of ways. Some critics of utilitarianism have resisted the idea that the betterment of the human condition can treated as the maximisation of some single value such as "welfare": they have argued for a plurality of values, and have claimed that such plurality undercuts the aggregative structure of utilitarian theory (see Chapter 4). Others have pointed out that one cannot move from the claim that morality is intended to have good consequences to the conclusion that we should maximise such consequences in aggregate, because this ignores the importance of how the good consequences are distributed amongst persons: perhaps equalising welfare is more important than maximising it, for example. Finally, some distinguished philosophers have resisted the very idea that morality might have a "point" in any straightforward sense: for such thinkers (Kant and Kierkegaard are examples) morality represents a wholly autonomous and self-contained perspective upon life, that is irreducible to other terms (such as "happiness" or "welfare").

2. Utilitarianism may be thought to be a suitable principle to guide the decisions of those who exercise public power (including judges and legislators) even if it is not the fundamental principle of morality as a whole. It may be said, for example, that utilitarianism possesses two virtues that are highly desirable in public decision- making. In the first place, utilitarianism seems to make each issue turn upon a question of *fact*: in each case we will be asking what will actually serve to maximise welfare. Thus the theory seems to offer the attractive prospect of decisions based upon hard evidence and firm criteria (an appearance that may well be misleading). Secondly, utilitarianism can claim to treat conflicting interests with absolute equality: everyone's interests are taken into account and are given equal weight;

the decisions that result simply reflect the neutral results of the calculus of losses and gains in utility.

Since we expect public officials to act upon the basis of evidence and objective criteria that treat everyone's interests equally, we may feel that the principle of utility is the appropriate guide for their decisions. Here, the principle of utility is not being offered as a philosophical explication of the basis of morality, but as a public conception of justice that is recommended by some of our specific moral beliefs regarding the proper role and responsibilities of public officials.

The idea that utilitarianism is recommended by its egalitarian character is sometimes invoked as a basis for amending or rejecting the doctrine. Ronald Dworkin has argued that utilitarianism attempts to implement a basic value of "equal concern and respect", but does so in an inadequate or misguided way. Equal concern and respect finds a more adequate expression, Dworkin holds, in a theory of individual rights.

LIBERALISM, UTILITY AND MORAL NEUTRALITY

The contrast between utilitarianism as a moral philosophy and as a theory to guide public decision (a public conception of justice) can be deepened a little by comparing utilitarianism with the Aristotelian approach to ethics and to politics.

The Aristotelian tradition of ethical and political thought was characterised earlier as giving priority to "the good" over "the right". That is to say, the tradition begins by offering an account of what counts as an excellent and valuable way for an individual to live, and then recommends those political and social institutions that will tend to foster such excellent lives. Conceptions of law, justice and rights are presented as reflecting the desirable form of political community. We will study a modern version of this type of position in Chapter 4. For the present, however, we should notice that one of its significant difficulties is to be found in the contentious nature of the theory's starting point. Different people may be expected to have different conceptions of what an excellent and worthwhile life might be: for example, I may consider a life dedicated to the acquisition of wealth to be shallow and unworthy of an intelligent person, while you admire the ruthless pursuit of money, and consider me to be a pathetic and self-deluding fool.

Given the fact of such disagreements, it is at first hard to see how the Aristotelian approach can overcome the contentiousness of its starting point.

Utilitarianism resembles the Aristotelian approach in so far as it gives priority to "the good" over "the right"; but its conception of "the good" seeks to overcome problems of contentiousness by being pitched at a higher level of abstraction. It might be proposed, for example, that you and I do not really disagree about our ultimate goals in life, but only about the best means to those goals: perhaps we both seek happiness, and you feel that this is to be found in the acquisition of wealth, while I feel that it is to be found in some other, less acquisitive, way of life. Disagreement about the good at one level might therefore be thought to conceal a deeper level of agreement on the more general goal of happiness. Impartial moral concern for others, therefore, need not take the form of seeking to impose or encourage a contentious version of the good that many would reject: it may instead take the form of an attempt to maximise the general happiness.

When advocated on this basis, utilitarianism is being proposed as a theory of morality generally: it is being suggested that our seemingly diverse concerns for different ways of life and different values reflect an underlying agreement that the point of life is to be "happy", or to attain "pleasure". When advocated as a public conception of justice, however, the theory can be framed rather differently. Accepting that people do in fact disagree about the good, and pursue irreducibly different goods, the utilitarian may propose that it is nevertheless necessary to find some fair and uniform way of handling such diverse preferences at the level of public decision-making. The language of "welfare", "pleasure" or "happiness" may then be proposed as (in effect) a neutral currency into which diverse conceptions of the good can be converted.

This is not a book on moral philosophy but on jurisprudence. Even if we are ultimately persuaded that utilitarianism makes a poor job of providing a philosophical underpinning for morality, it may nevertheless provide a very suitable guide for law-making, and for the interpretation and application of laws in adjudication. After all, we noted earlier in the book the general division between ancient and modern approaches to political thought, and the special importance of law within the modern liberal conception of a political community. If the state aims, not to foster some particular way of life that is conceived to be meritorious, but to sustain a framework within which various life-plans may be chosen and pursued, law will play the central role in demarcating the entitlements within which such choices and projects can be pursued without interference. But, if a modern political community is to contain within itself a high degree of moral diversity, what standards are to guide the enactment of laws?

Viewed against this background, utilitarianism might be regarded as an attempt to construct a suitable public conception of justice for a morally pluralistic society. Thus, the theory avoids the privileging of any particular moral ideals: ways of life are judged, not by their worthiness or unworthiness, but simply by the pleasure or satisfaction that they yield. At the same time, the diverse moral viewpoints of the populace are accommodated within the theory, where they feature as preferences to be weighed and balanced against other conflicting preferences.

The founding father of utilitarianism, Jeremy Bentham, thought of his theory primarily as a guide for law-making rather than private ethical reflection; and we will see in due course that, by keeping this in mind, we can discern some plausible lines of reply to many standard criticisms of the theory.

Bentham himself seems (at least intermittently) to have adopted the view that human agents should be regarded as always acting out of self-interest; his argument is constructed from the viewpoint of rational self-interest.[1] Rational self-interested agents will find that things go better for them on the whole if they can establish a system of rules. Each such agent would prefer a set of rules that advances his preferences at the expense of everyone else; but the best he can hope for is a set of rules that serves the aggregate welfare. Although it may be in my interest to see that such a set of rules is established, it will not always be in my interest to comply with the rules; hence the rules can only be made effective if they are backed by sanctions.

A different type of argument might reject the Benthamite

---

[1]   Rational self-interest need not be thought of as a matter of selfishness in any conventional sense. The rational self-interested agent can be thought of as seeking to advance his or her own projects: but these may include projects to benefit other people. Rationality, on this view, consists in the efficient pursuit of one's goals: the goals themselves are neither rational nor irrational. The fundamental point is that rational agents are not *assumed* to be altruistic: altruism is not viewed as a requirement of reason, but as a matter of variable preference.

emphasis upon self-interest, preferring to appeal to certain very general moral or political conceptions that might be shared even by those who hold otherwise very diverse moral viewpoints. Suppose, for example, that it could be agreed that an orderly society that is governed by law requires certain general standards (a public conception of justice) to govern the making of laws and their application in adjudication. It might then be possible to agree upon certain general and formal characteristics that such a conception of justice should possess. It should, for example, employ criteria that are objective, in the sense that they are accessible to everyone: situations should be evaluated by reference to observable facts. Also, the criteria should be even-handed in their treatment of diverse moral positions. A public conception of justice that could satisfy requirements of this sort might be supported by people of diverse moral persuasions, in spite of its failure directly to express their own moral viewpoint (their moral views would feature as preferences to be balanced against other, competing, preferences). This would be because one part of that moral viewpoint led them to accept the need for such a shared conception of justice, given the existence of moral diversity; and because the particular conception in question satisfied formal requirements that could be independently specified and felt to be appropriate.

In evaluating criticisms of utilitarianism, therefore, one needs to distinguish between utilitarianism as a moral theory and as a political or jurisprudential theory. When construed as a moral theory, utilitarianism is an attempt to clarify the philosophical basis of our moral concern by setting forth a supreme principle that, supposedly, serves as the ultimate criterion for what we morally ought to do. When contrued as a political or jurispru-dential theory, on the other hand, utilitarianism does not seek to elucidate the basis of our morality, but proposes the principle of utility (in one guise or another) as a suitable public conception of justice for a morally diverse liberal society. The principle is recommended, not on the basis that it captures the fundamental bedrock of morality, but on the basis that it is supported by a number of diverse considerations such as its neutrality and objectivity, combined with the need for some such shared criterion of public justice.

The possibility of achieving such a separation of political or juridical principles from moral principles will be discussed somewhat further in relation to the later writings of John Rawls. For the moment it will be assumed to be a realistic possibility. In considering the more familiar criticisms of utilitarianism, we will focus chiefly upon the principle of utility as a fundamental moral principle, but we will note in passing those criticisms which might miss their target when aimed at utilitarianism as a more narrowly political or jurisprudential theory.

UNCERTAINTY

Bentham was inclined to recommend the principle of utility on the basis that it offered a determinate guideline by comparison with the uncertainties of conventional moral opinions which Bentham took to reflect the arbitrariness of "sympathy and antipathy". In fact, the claims of utility to offer highly determinate answers are not very convincing: evaluating the net welfare yielded by a law, policy, or individual action is an inherently uncertain and speculative enterprise.

In the first place, the notion of maximising welfare seems to require that we have some way of measuring quantities of welfare (conceived, let us say, as the balance of pleasure over pain) as they accrue to different people (some way, that is, of making "inter-personal comparisons of utility"). Suppose, for example, that one is administering a limited supply of painkillers to the injured victims at an accident, and that one seeks to do so in a way that will maximise welfare. Suppose that you have to deal with two victims, one having suffered extensive and severe burns, and the other having suffered a minor cut. In this case, practical people will say that the victim of the burns is suffering most pain, and is therefore most in need of the pain-killer. But what if giving all of the available painkiller to the victim of burns would deprive of any relief a large number of victims of cuts? Might the aggregate suffering of the victims of cuts outweigh the suffering of the burn-victim? In requiring us to maximise welfare in aggregate, utilitarianism appears to require that we should be able to answer questions along these lines. Many economists and philosophers doubt whether it makes any sense to engage in such "inter-personal comparisons of utility".

In addition to the problem of inter-personal comparison there is also the more obvious problem of predicting the consequences of an action, law or policy. Attempts to address serious social problems by means of state intervention have frequently served to demonstrate that the consequences of such action can be hard to predict, and can often be counter-productive. Some utilitarians favour deliberate attempts at social engineering in the interests of overall welfare. Others are more daunted by the difficulty of predicting the consequences of such interventions; they tend to adopt the conservative stance of saying that sticking by tried and trusted rules and institutions is the best way to serve human welfare. In this way the seemingly radical posture of utilitarianism can become conservative in its implications when confronted with the complexities and uncertainties of the real world.

CONSEQUENCES

Utilitarianism holds that, in deciding what we should do, we should consider only the consequences of our actions: an action cannot be justified purely by its relationship to past facts. An example will make this clearer.

Suppose that I am stranded on a desert island with one other man, who is dying. In his last hours he entrusts me with a large sum of money and asks me to give it to his daughter if I ever manage to return to England. I agree to this arrangement.

Eventually I am rescued and arrive back in England. I find the man's daughter and I discover that she is already fabulously rich. The money I have for her, which seemed a large amount to me, will scarcely be noticed by her. I begin to wonder whether I would not do more good by giving most of the money to charity, rather than by giving it all to the castaway's daughter.

Now, according to utilitarianism, I am at least asking the right question: I must consider whether breaking my promise would do more good than keeping it. The utilitarian will insist that I should not assume that this question is easy to answer. The system of making and keeping promises has itself great value for human welfare, and acts of promise-breaking will tend to undermine that system and so have adverse effects on welfare. If people come to hear of frequent acts of promise-breaking, like the one I contemplate, they will be less inclined to rely on promises in the future; and, even if I keep the facts completely secret, my decision to break the promise may weaken my own propensity to keep promises in the future. These are the possible consequences of my actions, and I must weigh them against the benefits of giving the money to charity.

It can be argued that utilitarianism misses the central feature of the whole situation: that is, that I have promised to give the money to the castaway's daughter. The reason why I ought to give the money to her is not some future consequence of my action but a past fact: the fact of my having promised. After all, we may say, it is odd that I should feel free to decide for myself what will be the best way of doing good with the money: for the money was not given to me to do good generally but for me to give it to a specific person. The very evaluation of consequences required by the utilitarian approach is, on this view, one that I have no right to engage in.

The utilitarian will insist that he does take account of the past fact of the promise, but only insofar as it affects the total consequences of the contemplated act of giving away the money. His opponent will argue that all the claims about general weakening of the system of promise-breaking are not only artificial and tortuous, but also immoral in that they suggest that secret promise-breaking may be justifiable when open and declared promise-breaking would not. Opponents of utilitarianism face a difficulty at this point however. Very few people would hold that the duty to keep promises is absolute: most of us would feel that it may be overridden in certain circumstances. Suppose, for example, that I have promised to take you to the theatre for the evening, but quite unexpectedly my help is needed at an emergency. We would generally feel that the duty to help in the emergency overrides the duty to keep my promise and that I act properly in breaking that promise. Yet how can that be, if the morality of keeping promises is not ultimately based on a calculation of consequences? The utilitarian can explain such situations quite easily (perhaps too easily) but an approach which treats the act of promising as taking away the right to evaluate the pros and cons of keeping the promise will have much more difficulty.

Suppose we argue along the following line. When I made the promise to take you to the theatre, you could not have thought that I was promising to do so come what may. If, for example, I had myself been seriously injured you would not expect me to struggle out of hospital in a wheelchair in order to take you. This is because (we might argue) the promise was made subject to certain implied and unspecified exceptions. When I helped with the emergency instead of taking you to the theatre, I was not really breaking my promise but relying on an implied exception to it.

The notion of an implied exception to a promise, of unspecified extent, and covering eventualities that I did not contemplate for one moment at the time of making the promise, may be thought to be a nonsense. It would be wrong, however, to jump to this conclusion. To say that I meant this or that by my promise need not imply conscious advertence on my part. As Wittgenstein points out, if I ask someone to "show the children a game", and the person requested teaches them gambling with dice, I may truthfully say that I did not mean that sort of game, even though the possibility of their being taught such a game had never occurred to me. Similarly I may say that when I promised to take you to the theatre I did not promise to do so come hell or high water and I never intended that the promise should apply to emergency situations. The truth of my statement would not be affected by the fact that I never even contemplated the possibility of an emergency arising.

The "implied exception" approach may, however, go too far, for it suggests that, properly understood, my act of helping at the emergency was not a breach of the promise I made to you at all. That promise, it is argued, did not apply in these circumstances, and so I did not break it. But we may feel that this is a misguided approach. Although I have done nothing wrong, I have broken my promise to you and perhaps I should do something to compensate. Neil MacCormick has argued that there is an obligation to compensate for the effects of certain actions which are not themselves wrongful acts, and a breach of promise in these circumstances would be a good example.[2] The utilitarian on the other hand, with his exclusive focus on consequences, will argue that whether or not one should be required to pay compensation for a breach of contract (or to buy a bunch of flowers as compensation for a missed trip to the theatre) should be evaluated by the overall consequences of requiring such compensation, just as the rightness or wrongness of breaking the promise itself is to be evaluated by reference to its consequences.

I have used the example of promising not only because it casts light on the exclusive concern of the utilitarian with the future consequences of actions, but also because it should help the student to see the possible bearing that these arguments may have on an area of law like the law of contract. Arguments about the nature of implied terms, the basis of the doctrine of frustration, the basis of damages in contract and the general rationale of the distinction between private law damages and criminal law penalties are inextricably intertwined with the

---

[2]   Neil MacCormick, *Legal Right and Social Democracy*, (Clarendon Press Oxford, 1982), Chap.11.

philosophical problems we are discussing. It should not be assumed, however, that the relationships between moral philosophy and jurisprudence are always straightforward. For example, one might reject utilitarianism as a moral philosophy precisely because one rejects its exclusively forward-looking focus (one regards the past promise as a moral reason for action in itself); yet, at the same time, one might regard it as inappropriate for the law in a liberal society to seek to enforce such private moral beliefs, and one might think that the principle of utility (with its forward-looking focus) provides the most acceptable guide for lawmaking and for the interpretation of legal doctrine.

Equally, reversing the picture, we might imagine someone who accepts utilitarianism as a moral philosophy, but believes that welfare will best be maximised if citizens and judges act upon general rules that exclude consideration of future consequences. Such a utilitarian will think it desirable that there should be a rule requiring the keeping of promises, and desirable that people should follow that rule regardless of their estimate of the consequences of doing so. Hence, at the level of choosing general rules, one would take the principle of utility as a guide; but in applying and following such rules, one would ignore future consequences. This is a matter to which we shall return shortly.

UTILITY AND DISTRIBUTION

Questions of law and justice are quite commonly thought of as questions about how wealth, resources and opportunities should be distributed. Should the distribution of such things be equal? Or in accordance with need? Or with merit? One objection that is sometimes made to utilitarianism is that it shows no concern whatever with questions of distribution, and therefore cannot be an acceptable theory of justice, or an adequate guiding principle for the law.

It is quite true that the utilitarian is not concerned with how welfare is distributed: his concern is with the maximisation of welfare, with how much there is in total. If the utilitarian is faced with a choice between two societies in one of which welfare is equally distributed (or distributed according to need, or merit, depending on your favourite theory) and in the other of which gross inequalities of welfare exist, he will regard as morally preferable that society in which the sum total of welfare is higher. To demonstrate this point clearly it is necessary to speak as if welfare could be quantified in a numerical fashion. Let us therefore imagine individuals as having so many "units of welfare" and let us compare the situations represented by the following two schemes:

Situation 1					
Individuals:	A	B	C	D	E
Units of Welfare:	10	10	10	10	10
Situation 2					
Individuals:	A	B	C	D	E
Units of Welfare:	2	2	2	2	95

In situation 1, everyone has an equal level of welfare, and the total level of welfare may be expressed as 50 units of welfare. In situation 2, by contrast, welfare is unequally distributed: E enjoys a very high level of welfare, whereas A, B, C, and D all have a comparatively low level. But the total level of welfare in situation 2 is 103, much higher than in situation 1. Being concerned to maximise welfare, a utilitarian will prefer situation 2 to situation 1. If we found ourselves in situation 1, and if it were possible somehow to move to situation 2, a utilitarian would advocate that change. This demonstrates two points about utilitarianism: that it is genuinely not concerned with the question of how welfare is distributed, but only with how much welfare there is in total; and, secondly, that utilitarians may sometimes have to advocate policies that would make many people, or even most people, worse off, if those policies will produce for others benefits which are large enough to outweigh the adverse effects.

However, it is a mistake to conclude that because the distribution of welfare does not concern him, the utilitarian is also not concerned with questions of how wealth, resources, and opportunities should be distributed. On the contrary, the utilitarian is not only concerned with such issues, but can argue that he alone has a convincing explanation of why we should be concerned with such issues. His basic argument is that a more equal distribution of opportunities, wealth and other resources is desirable because, and in so far as, it will maximise welfare. (For simplicity's sake I shall include wealth and opportunities under the general heading of "resources" in what follows.)

The utilitarian is provided with a good argument in favour of a more equal distribution of resources by the theory of diminishing marginal utility. Expressed very simply, this theory entails that an additional £1 given to a millionaire will make a negligible contribution to his welfare, whereas £1 given to a very poor man might be a significant contribution to his welfare, enabling him, say, to buy a meal that he could not otherwise afford. The £1 will therefore maximise welfare more effectively if placed in the hands of a poor man than if placed in the hands of the millionaire. If we aim to maximise welfare, we therefore have good reason to transfer resources from the rich to the poor.

If diminishing marginal utility were the only factor we needed to consider, the utilitarian would be a very strict egalitarian, believing in an equal distribution of resources, perhaps modified only to accommodate special needs. But there are other factors against which the argument from diminishing marginal utility must be balanced. For example, it is widely held that high productivity requires a structure of incentives to encourage people to work hard, to invest, and so forth. If this is true, strict equality of resources, by robbing individuals of strong and immediate incentives to work hard, may in the long run bring about a fall in productivity and an overall decline in welfare. Similarly it can be argued that the maintenance of an equal distribution of resources will require constant interference with the market on a scale that is unprecedented and that is bound to impair economic efficiency, thereby leading to a fall in welfare.

We are now in a position to see the strengths of the utilitarian attitude towards distributive issues. First, the utilitarian can claim that his theory explains the way in which we do in fact trade-off equality against productivity and economic efficiency. This trade-off is neither arbitrary nor hypocritical: it reflects the fact that the underlying concern is with the maximisation of welfare, that being a goal to which both redistribution and higher productivity can contribute. Secondly, the utilitarian can argue that he alone has offered a plausible explanation of why redistribution matters. When we take money from the rich and give it to the poor, he may argue, we do this because we believe it will do more good relieving poverty than being spent on trivial comforts. In holding that it will "do more good" we mean that the loss in welfare for the rich will be minimal but the gain in welfare for the poor will be substantial. What other reason for redistribution could there be?

One answer to this question might suggest that utilitarianism is misguided in taking aggregate welfare as its focus. The concern for aggregate welfare might sometimes justify reducing the welfare of some to a very low level in order to sustain a high level for others: the sole question for the utilitarian would be how the sums come out to produce the greatest aggregate. Instead of adopting this approach, we might treat the attainment of a certain minimal level of welfare for everyone as a prior goal. Only when everyone had been brought up to the minimum level could we legitimately concern ourselves with aggregate welfare; and aggregate welfare could not be advanced by means that would reduce someone below the minimum level. Even making full allowance for diminishing marginal utility, utilitarians find it hard to accommodate this type of reasoning. They can legitimately point out that bringing the poor up to a minimum level will often be the easiest way to maximise welfare overall; but they cannot rule out the possibility of small gains for a large number of relatively affluent people outweighing substantial welfare losses incurred by a minority of the poor.

Many critics of utilitarianism believe that all persons should be guaranteed a certain minimum level of welfare, so that all such claims to the minimum would have to be fully satisfied before considerations of aggregate welfare could be pursued. Thus, a policy that increased aggregate welfare at the cost of reducing the welfare of some individuals (the losers) would be permissible only if it did not reduce the welfare of the losers below the minimum level. This sounds, on the face of it, an attractive position. On closer examination, however, it looks more problematic. After all, there are limits to the amounts of money that communities are prepared to spend on health care or road safety; yet the failure to receive appropriate treatment, or the suffering of avoidable injury, may well reduce one's level of welfare below any acceptable minimum. Perhaps many serious road accidents would be avoided if we all drove at 15 m.p.h. Can a seriously injured pedestrian complain that their welfare has been reduced below an acceptable minimum level, simply in order to improve journey times for the rest of us?

The utilitarian's lack of concern with how welfare is distributed has a further implication. Since he is only concerned with the overall maximisation of welfare, there is in principle no limit to the harm that the utilitarian will be prepared to inflict on individuals, provided that the harm is balanced by an even greater increase in welfare for others. Thus, it is argued, there is literally nothing that the utilitarian might not be prepared to do, given appropriate circumstances: killing the innocent, torture, lying, promise-breaking, might all in some circumstances be necessary if overall welfare is to be maximised. How can the utilitarian respond to this claim?

The most obvious line of defence would be to deny that torture, murder, and other such actions ever would actually maximise welfare. This defence raises questions (about the probable effects of actions in hypothetical situations) which are virtually impossible to answer. We may certainly say that the utilitarian has no grounds for confidence that the principle of utility would, in no circumstances, justify murder or torture.

The utilitarian has a better defence in a more aggressive response, for he can plausibly argue that we would all (or nearly all) hold killing and torture to be right in circumstances where it clearly did maximise welfare overall. For example, in the Second World War, the fight against the Nazis may have required us to kill innocent persons in Germany and elsewhere. But we regard such killing as justified by the need to destroy an evil regime. Similarly, if a madman had hidden a nuclear device which was set to destroy the whole of South-East England at a pre-set time, we might feel justified in torturing him if this really was the only way of discovering the location of the bomb so as to defuse it. Thus the utilitarian will claim that we are all prepared to set aside our basic feelings of revulsion about such acts as torture when we are sure that welfare will be maximised most effectively by such an act.

The opponent of utilitarianism, however, may point out that these situations of the Second World War and the nuclear madman are cases where a catastrophe of immense proportions is threatened. While the killing or torture of innocent persons is indeed of the greatest moral seriousness, it is here done in order to save far greater numbers from equally severe infringements upon their welfare. Since the utilitarian deals in aggregates, he must be prepared to do anything which will increase welfare by however small a degree. Torture to save the lives of many may be acceptable; but what of torture to secure an incremental improvement in the standard of living for millions of already comfortable and affluent people?

In any case, it may be a mistake to focus too much upon problems posed by welfare-maximising acts of torture or killing: acts of a much less extreme character may nevertheless strike us as wrong when performed without the consent of the victim, even if the act does increase welfare overall. Suppose for example that someone derives enormous pleasure from inflicting merely slight discomfort on his victims: say, by boring them with his holiday snaps or with lengthy descriptions of his new Volvo. Does that make his activity justifiable, even though it is done without the victim's consent (the victim is, let us say, strapped into a chair, or locked in a garage with only the Volvo to look at and hear about)? Surely, we may feel, people are not entitled to use us, without our consent, simply because they can in some way derive pleasure from us. From this point of view the pleasure and pain flowing from the sadist's activities is an irrelevance. His act, being done without our consent, is a violation of our rights and that is what makes it wrong.

As we shall see in Chapter 2, John Rawls argues that utilitarianism makes the mistake of defining the right in terms of the good. He means that the utilitarian starts with an account of what is good (pleasure, happiness, obtaining one's preferences, etc.), and then says that an action is right insofar as it maximises that good. Against this approach, Rawls argues that rules of justice are prior to the good. We can arrive at certain principles of justice which are independent of any particular conception of what is a good or worthwhile life. Such principles provide a framework within which people's conception of the good must be pursued. We can therefore only decide whether positive moral value attaches to a certain form of pleasure when we know how it is related to the basic principles of justice. For this reason, Rawls would regard as valid the objection that the sadist's pleasure must be discounted, and no positive value should be attached to it, because it is obtained in violation of basic principles of justice.

Some utilitarians would agree with Rawls about the importance of rights, but would disagree about their basis. Rather than being (as Rawls puts it) "prior to" questions about "the good", rights might themselves be consequences of the principle of utility. Thus a utilitarian might agree that the sadistic Volvo owner should not be permitted to lock me in his garage, even for a very short period (and even though my discomfort is minor while his pleasure is very great): for a society will maximise aggregate utility best when it accords people certain rights (such as the right not to be falsely imprisoned) and does not permit encroachments upon those rights even where the individual encroachment might itself seem to be welfare-maximising. The possibility of the utilitarian recognising and protecting such rights depends upon the viability of what is called "rule utilitarianism", to which we now turn.

ACT AND RULE UTILITARIANISM

It can be argued that a society will maximise the welfare of its members only if those members do not themselves act upon the principle of utility. For example, it is in everyone's interests that there should be a developed commercial system, but this is possible only where people can rely on the promises of others. A society of utilitarians, it can be argued, will be a society where promises are frequently broken and cannot be relied upon: a society of utilitarians will therefore fail to maximise utility.

To take another case, it might be in everyone's interests to have public gardens with beautiful lawns, but this will require everyone to refrain from walking on the grass. Now suppose that I am a utilitarian, I am alone in the garden, and am wondering whether I should walk on the grass. Walking on the grass will give me pleasure and will not affect the grass to any perceptible degree. Since I am alone, my act of walking on the grass will not encourage others to walk on the grass or make it more likely that they will do so. My act will benefit me and harm no-one: it will therefore maximise utility, and I will (as a utilitarian) decide to walk on the grass. If everyone is a utilitarian, everyone will, in similar circumstances decide likewise. Very soon the beautiful lawns will be damaged and scarred by footpaths marking popular short-cuts across the grass. Once again, a society of utilitarians will inevitably fail to maximise utility.

Various solutions to this problem can be offered by utilitarians. Bentham's answer was to emphasise the importance of sanctions for a utilitarian society: the promise-breaker and the grass-walker should be encouraged to keep their word and keep to the pavement by coercive penalties. A more popular answer significantly modifies the general utilitarian standpoint, and is usually called "rule-utilitarianism". The rule-utilitarian holds that one should not decide upon individual actions directly by reference to the principle of utility. I should not ask myself whether breaking the promise or walking on the grass would have the best consequences overall. Rather I should regulate my actions by reference to general rules, these rules being themselves justified by reference to the principle of utility. Two versions of rule-utilitarianism may be distinguished for present purposes. "Ideal" rule-utilitarianism holds that I should regulate my actions by those rules that would maximise welfare if they were generally observed. "Actual" rule-utilitarianism holds that I should comply with those rules actually accepted and observed in my society, in so far as the general acceptance of the rules maximises utility.

There are many complex objections to rule-utilitarianism. I will briefly summarise three such objections. First, ideal rule-utilitarianism appears to be irrational in that it requires me to act as if something were the case when I know that it is not the case: observing the rule would maximise welfare if the rule were generally observed, but I know that it is not generally observed. Secondly, actual rule-utilitarianism is either conservative, or it fails to give one any determinate guidance: either we interpret it as requiring general compliance with accepted social rules, or as requiring such compliance only when the accepted rules are perfect from a utilitarian point of view. In the latter case, the theory fails to tell me what I should do when the actual rules are dis-utilitarian. Thirdly, all forms of rule-utilitarianism contain the following paradox: whilst presupposing that the whole point of the rules is a utilitarian one, they require one to comply with rules even where compliance in this instance will not maximise utility. If they do not require compliance in such circumstances, the theories do not differ from "act-utilitarianism" of the conventional type, which applies the principle of utility directly to individual acts.

It has been argued that the best society from a utilitarian point of view would be a society where rules are chosen by an elite group of utilitarians, but the bulk of the population remain un-enlightened non-utilitarians, who obey the rules without reflecting on the tendency of their actions to maximise or diminish welfare. This has aptly been described as "Government House utilitarianism". We tend to feel that such a society of manipulators and the manipulated would be profoundly objectionable, even if it did maximise welfare. Why should we feel that? One reason might lie in the belief that the manipulated would have no safeguard against being manipulated for the benefit of the manipulators, rather than for the greater good. But suppose we could assume that the governors were genuinely benevolent utilitarians, motivated solely by a concern for aggregate welfare? We might still feel troubled, but our worries would have to be framed in different, and essentially non-utilitarian terms. We might feel, for example, that rational moral agents should regulate their conduct by principles that are fully transparent to their own understanding. To act upon the basis of standards that are accepted without question, or the intellectual basis of which is misunderstood, is to fail to be a fully autonomous and reasonable moral agent. If the only thing that matters is happiness, being a "fully autonomous moral agent" may be of no intrinsic importance. Does that give us a reason for rejecting utilitarianism, or a reason for feeling comfortable with the dictats of Government House?

RULE UTILITARIANISM AS A JURISPRUDENTIAL THEORY

We have seen that rule-utilitarianism exhibits some serious defects when it is offered as a position in moral philosophy. We saw above, for example, that "actual rule-utilitarianism" is either unduly conservative or fails to offer guidance at all; while "ideal rule-utilitarianism" invites me to act in a way that would maximise utility if circumstances were quite different from the actual circumstances (*i.e.* if the ideal rule were generally followed). A further difficulty with "ideal rule-utilitarianism" is that it may in fact be indistinguishable from act- utilitarianism. This is because there is no limit to the number of qualifications that can be built into our imaginary "ideal" rule.

The rule-utilitarian hopes to demonstrate that acts such as torture or the punishment of the innocent will not be prescribed by the principle of utility, since that principle should be used only to select rules, while individual actions should be judged by reference to the rules so selected. While individual acts of torture (for example) might, in unusual circumstances, maximise utility, rules providing for or permitting such torture never would have such utility-maximising consequences. If, therefore,the principle of utility is employed solely in the selection of rules, and individual actions are judged by reference to the rules, the principle of utility will never lead to acts such as torture or the punishment of innocent persons.

However, if there is no limit to the complexity of the rules that may be recommended by rule-utilitarianism, it will always be possible to tailor a proposed rule so precisely (by building in numerous qualifications and exceptions) that it will in fact allow for torture or other seemingly abhorrent acts in all of the circumstances where those acts would have been required by direct application of the principle of utility. Without some inherent limitation upon the complexity that can be tolerated in a rule, there will be no real difference between act utilitarianism and rule utilitarianism.

Once we turn from utilitarianism as a moral philosophy to utilitarianism as a jurisprudential theory, however, the picture changes. For, if the principle of utility is being employed as a critical guide to the selection of *legal* rules, there will be certain built-in limitations upon the complexity that can be tolerated in the rules recommended by that principle. Legal rules both prescribe conduct and enable citizens to form reliable mutual expectations. I can know what is legally required of me, and also know how others are likely to behave in certain circumstances, by consulting the law. This will not be possible, however, if the law consists of rules that are so hedged in with qualifications and exceptions that they are of staggering complexity; or subject to provisos formulated in very general terms (*e.g.* "always keep promises, unless breaking them will maximise utility"). The need to select rules that will be reasonably simple, concise and formulated in specific terms, places a constraint upon the selection of rules, and thereby gives a real content to rule-utilitarianism that it might otherwise lack.

When utilitarianism is viewed as a guide to lawmaking, rather than as a basis for private ethical reflection, it can neatly sidestep certain other standard objections. Critics sometimes argue, for example, that utilitarianism proposes too suffocating a view of morality, insofar as it requires us to be constantly acting in a way that will maximise welfare overall: we can never simply get on with our own lives and our own concerns, because the principle of utility requires us to be always acting for the greater good.[3]

The problem is avoided, however, when we view the principle of utility as a guide to lawmaking rather than as a guide to private conduct. Indeed (as explained earlier) one strong strand of Benthamite utilitarianism sees individuals as motivated by self-interest, rather than by impartial concern for the greater good. It is in their self-interest to establish a system of laws, enforced by sanctions, to serve the greater good; but they will not and need not view themselves as required to act for the greater good when the requirements of such laws have been satisfied.

Does this really overcome the problem? If laws are to be selected by reference to the principle of utility, why not enact as

---

[3]   For one version of this familiar argument, see Ronald Dworkin, *Law's Empire* (London, 1986) Chap.8.

law the principle of utility itself? We would then be under a legal duty to be constantly maximising welfare. How is this possibility to be excluded? An adequate answer to this question must draw upon several strands of thought. In the first place, one way in which the law contributes to aggregate welfare is by helping to co-ordinate conduct. Road traffic laws are a good example: if we were simply told to drive in a way that would maximise welfare overall, we would maximise welfare less effectively than we do by obeying specific rules about driving on the left, observing certain procedures at roundabouts and priorities at junctions.

Secondly, we advance our own welfare, and that of others, by pursuing medium to long-term projects; to do this, we must be able to form reliable expectations about how other persons (about whom we will generally know nothing) will behave; we can form such expectations only if we can have recourse to a body of tolerably specific rules that those persons can be assumed to follow. You, for example, may currently be studying jurisprudence in the expectation that your university will in due course organise examinations and award degrees. You feel justified in this expectation because you believe there to be a body of rules that will be followed by the administrators of your university, and those rules require some such form of assessment. Your expectations would seem far less well-grounded if you thought the university administrators were guided only by the simple injunction to do whatever they think will maximise welfare: perhaps they will consider that welfare will be maximised by giving you all a break from exams this year? or by protecting the public from you by refusing to let you qualify as lawyers at all, regardless of your deep jurisprudential insight?

It might, however, be said that we have only demonstrated that we need laws with a more specific content than the general injunction to maximise welfare: we have said nothing to exclude the possibility of enacting such a general injunction as a residual provision that would apply when all of the more specific laws had been fully complied with. Certain areas of liberty might be left after all the specific legal duties were taken account of, and it might be precisely such areas of liberty that could be replaced by a general legal duty always to act for the greater good.

Such a law, however, would be unworkable. The great bulk of acts that clearly fail to maximise utility would almost certainly fall within the scope of some more specific prohibition. In relation to the residue, it would be well-nigh impossible to prove that the defendant's actions had failed to maximise utility. The costs of prosecution and trial would therefore be large, and the outcomes uncertain. Since the outcomes would be inherently uncertain, the deterrent impact of such a law upon non-welfare-maximising behaviour would be very minimal.

Pragmatic considerations of this type may not be fatal objections to an argument within moral philosophy (an impractical theory may still elucidate the basis of our moral concerns even if it offers us little practical guidance) but they are fatal flaws in a more jurisprudential or political theory that presents itself as a way of coping with the problems of a modern community. By enabling us to invoke such pragmatic considerations, the jurisprudential version of utilitarianism can give plausible responses to many standard objections.

LIBERALISM AND PREFERENCES

When the utilitarian calculates the likely consequences of his actions in terms of welfare or happiness, he takes account of everyone's interests. Indeed, the claim to weigh everyone's interests equally may be thought to form an important part of utilitarianism's appeal. It may be that, in extreme cases, the utilitarian might approve of actions that seriously harm particular individuals: but this will not be because the interests of those individuals have been ignored. Rather, their interests will have been considered and given equal weight along with the interests of everyone else. If the infliction of harm is justified it is justified because its beneficial consequences for the general welfare outweigh its harmful ones. To refuse to harm the individual even when that will serve the general welfare may be said to fail to attach equal importance to the interests of everyone: it is (it could be argued) to allow this individual's interests to weigh more heavily than do the interests of others.

This can seem a convincing argument. If we find it plausible, we may conclude that the utilitarian accords equal respect to everyone in the only way that such equal respect can ever be accorded. But before we reach that conclusion we should pause to consider some deeper problems.

Suppose that it is, in one sense, true that utilitarianism allows each person's interests to count equally. Does utilitarianism also exhibit respect for persons in constructing its account of what constitutes each person's interests? The utilitarian begins, it would seem, with an account of welfare, and then seeks to maximise welfare as so defined. He may, for example, regard happiness or pleasure as the most important thing, and then seek to increase the sum total of happiness in the world. Or he may offer some other account of the "good" that is to be maximised. Could it be said that a theory that is constructed in this way does not attach sufficient importance to the capacity of each person to decide for himself on a conception of "the good"? Utilitarianism appears to choose one goal or ideal in terms of which it assesses everyone's interests. Thus, for the classical utilitarian, an artist's wish to paint is of moral importance only insofar as it will yield happiness for the artist or his customers. But the artist might not accept this characterisation of his aim. Happiness, for him, might not be the point.

Is there a way in which the utilitarian can avoid imposing one conception of the good on everyone, including those who do not accept it? The question becomes especially prominent if we think of utilitarianism as an attempt to address some of the jurisprudential problems of morally diverse liberal societies. For, if a community incorporates many different and often conflicting moral viewpoints, what standards should it adopt in selecting its laws? Must the law always of necessity implement the moral viewpoint of the majority (or of whoever else happens to be in power)? Or is it possible to set forth standards for lawmaking that are in some sense "neutral" between different moral perspectives?

One possibility is represented by what I shall describe as "preference-utilitarianism". This theory holds that one should seek to maximise, not happiness, but the extent to which people can attain their own preferences, whatever those preferences may be.

Preference-utilitarianism has the virtue of being close to the liberal spirit of the classical utilitarians such as Bentham and Mill. Their theories took happiness or pleasure as the goal, but they also assumed that each individual is the best judge of his or her own interest. In other words, it was assumed that if X wants a fast, shiny sports car or wants to swim the Channel, this is because these things will make her happy, and she is the best judge of that. Adherence to this maxim ensured that the classical utilitarians attached overriding importance to people's preferences, and would not seek to ignore those preferences by invoking a superior conception of the good.

One problem with this classical approach is that the maxim that each person is the best judge of his own happiness is quite possibly false. What if we were convinced that the maxim was false, and that we were the best judges of what would increase the happiness of some other person: would we feel justified in ignoring that person's expressed wishes and "doing him good" even without his consent? The assumption that each person is the best judge of his own interests seems too insecure and inappropriate a basis on which to rest our concern with human liberty and the autonomous choices of others. It is for reasons of this kind, amongst others, that many utilitarians have abandoned the classical emphasis on happiness in favour of a version of utilitarianism that attaches central importance to preferences.

Preference-utilitarianism raises a number of problems. In the first place, there will be severe practical problems in identifying the content and intensity of people's preferences. Theorists sympathetic to economic approaches have sometimes proposed a demonstrated willingness to pay as a reliable indicator of preferences: preferences would count only when they were backed up in the market by money or its equivalent. One problem with this suggestion is that willingness to pay would reliably indicate the intensity of one's preferences only against a background of equal wealth. In the absence of such a background, willingness to pay may say more about one's disposable income than it says about the intensity of one's preferences: rich people may pay large sums for the gratification of quite mild preferences, while poor people may find it hard to pay more than a modest sum even for their heart's desire.

There are also troubling questions concerning the variety of preferences that are to be admitted to the utilitarian calculus. For example, are we to attach positive importance to objectionable preferences such as the preference of a racist for a society where black people are confined to subordinate and badly paid positions? The utilitarian need not be committed to *satisfying* such preferences, since they may be outweighed by other preferences of other people (including, of course, the black people directly affected): but he does seem to be committed to *taking account* of such preferences when he is calculating the probable utility of a proposed action. It may be argued against the utilitarian that racist preferences should not be taken account of in this way. The fact that people hold preferences does not provide even the weakest of arguments in favour of a system that satisfies those preferences.

Some preference-utilitarians try to distinguish between personal and external preferences. Personal preferences are preferences about what you acquire or what you are able to do. External preferences are preferences about what other people acquire or are allowed to do. Thus, a white racist may have personal preferences for a big car and lots of money; he may also have an external preference that blacks should not drive big cars and have lots of money. It can be argued that the utilitarian should take account only of personal preferences, and should not attach importance to external preferences. Assuming that the personal/external distinction can be clearly drawn (which we may doubt) this would deal with the problem of the racist. We should note, however, that this approach would also exclude other preferences that we may consider less objectionable. Suppose that Sophie wishes to live in a community of caring and compassionate persons who enjoy sharing and communal life generally. She therefore advocates laws and institutions that will foster mutual concern. Sophie's preferences incorporate preferences about other people's behaviour (other people should be caring, should share things, should live communally, etc.), and would therefore be excluded from consideration as external preferences. In this respect her preferences do not differ from those of a racist, who wishes to live in a community where white people possess all the wealth and power. It seems therefore, that the external preferences approach cannot exclude objectionable racist preferences without excluding people's political views quite generally.

Perhaps the most serious problems with preference-utilitarianism, however, spring from the notion of "preference" itself. Suppose that, in your innocence, you want to drink sulphuric acid because you believe it to be a harmless and pleasurable drink. Is this "preference" to be respected by the utilitarian? Or might we rather say that the preference should not count because you would not have it if you did not have certain false beliefs? Your *real* preference is for harmless and pleasurable drinks, and this would be better satisfied by giving you a glass of fruit juice.

Once we have taken the step of distinguishing people's *real* preferences from their actual or expressed preferences, however, it is hard to know where to stop. Could we say that racist preferences should be disregarded, because they too depend upon false beliefs? This is not so easy, because it is not easy to identify a discrete set of false beliefs upon which racist attitudes depend. What if we focused upon the preferences that people *would* have had, had they been brought up in a society free from racism? But then, the racist might argue that your non-racist preferences should be disregarded on the same basis: if you were not the product of a liberal middle-class culture (they might say), but had grown up on the streets of the inner city, you too would be a racist.

Some slaves may feel contented with their slavery, but we would not regard that as a justification for slavery: we would feel that contented slaves have simply *adapted* their preferences to what seems to them an unalterable situation. If the slaves could experience freedom (we may feel) they would see its superiority. We are therefore inclined to disregard their expressed preference for the secure hierarchy of the plantation. Yet, how does our attitude to the contented slaves differ from the attitude that some would adopt towards modern consumerism? What if I feel that modern consumer culture generates an endless series of "preferences" that yield little real fulfillment? If only people could once experience the joys of working for the common good on the collective farm, and spending their evenings singing Party songs with their comrades: then they would view their current preferences for junk food and T.V. game shows as utterly misguided. How is one to respond to this argument? To say that we should be guided by expressed preferences and not hypothetical ones will leave the contented slaves on the plantation. To say that consumerism is good, and Party collectivism is bad, abandons any connection with preferences, and simply asserts the superiority of one way of life over another. In the end "preference utilitarianism" can find it hard to avoid an autocratic disregard for people's actually expressed preferences, so that its talk of "preferences" becomes an empty shell within which a particular conception of the good life is imposed.

RIGHTS AND UTILITY

Much of the recent opposition to utilitarianism has focused on the apparent preparedness of the theory to prescribe the infliction of serious harm on individuals if that maximises the general welfare. To inflict great harm on a small minority in order to achieve a marginal increase in the welfare of the overwhelming majority seems wrong, even if the small gains (when added up) outweigh the harm inflicted. Some people articulate this view as a belief that individuals have "rights", and that such rights override considerations of the general welfare.

Is a belief in individual rights really inconsistent with a commitment to utilitarianism? The rule-utilitarian might well deny this, for it could be argued that rules conferring and protecting such rights would serve the general welfare in the long-run. It may be true that this particular act of torturing an innocent person might maximise general welfare; but, if the principle of utility has to be employed in the selection of general rules rather than specific actions, a different picture emerges. For a rule prohibiting torture may advance welfare more than would a rule permitting torture in certain circumstances. The compatibility of rights and utility therefore hinges upon the debate about rule-utilitarianism, discussed earlier.

The distinction between "personal" and "external" preferences has also assumed great importance in this context. Ronald Dworkin has argued that the utilitarian should exclude "external" preferences from consideration, but can do so only by recognising individual rights that operate to "trump" considerations of utility. According to Dworkin, the basis of utilitarianism's appeal lies in the notion of equality: by weighing all interests together in the calculus of utility, the utilitarian appears to treat everyone as equal. This, however, is a poor interpretation of equality, according to Dworkin, because it ignores the difference between external and personal preferences. In working out what will maximise welfare, the utilitarian will not only have regard to people's personal preferences, but also to their external preferences. This Dworkin believes to be wrong: racism does not become right even if most people hold racist external preferences. To exclude the influence of external preferences from our political deliberations, we need to treat people as possessing "rights" that protect those areas of conduct most likely to be affected by the external preferences of others. Thus, we should have a right to free speech, because we know that people often have external preferences concerning the free speech of others. Such rights would override, or in Dworkin's words, "trump" considerations of utility.

Selected reading

* Probably the best introduction is:
J. J. C. Smart and B. Williams, *Utilitarianism: For and Against* (1973).
The classic texts are:
J. Bentham *An Introduction to the Principles of Morals and*

Legislation (1789)
J. S. Mill, *Utilitarianism* (1863)
H. Sidgwick, *The Methods of Ethics* (1874)

- Further reading:
D. Lyons, *Forms and Limits of Utilitarianism* (1965).
D. H. Hodgson, *Consequences of Utilitarianism* (1967).
D. H. Regan, *Utilitarianism and Co-operation* (1980).

Chapter 2

RAWLS

INTRODUCTION

In the middle decades of the twentieth century, philosophical reflection upon the nature of justice had fallen into a sad condition of neglect. Many philosophers thought that varying opinions about justice simply reflect differing subjective preferences which do not lie open to rational scrutiny or evaluation. Some even argued that invoking justice is equivalent to banging the table to reinforce one's demands: one thereby adds nothing to the content of one's assertions, but simply indicates the emotional intensity with which they are put forward.[1] Few people believed that disciplined philosophical argument could provide us with reasons for choosing one particular view of justice in preference to rival positions. The great tradition of philosophical thinking about justice, running from Plato and Aristotle to Kant and Hegel, seemed to have run its course and expired in the sand.

Thinking about law and politics tended, in this period, to be informed by two main strands of thought. One of these was utilitarianism, which suggested an image of politics wherein the collectivity confronts an array of conflicting preferences and seeks to maximise overall satisfaction of those preferences, without passing judgment upon the soundness or worthiness of the preferences in terms of their content. A rival position rejected the monism of utilitarianism, and postulated a number of widely accepted political values, such as equality, liberty, and material prosperity: there was held to be no single and supreme principle that regulated the relationship between these different values; consequently, conflicts between the values (between, say, greater equality and greater material prosperity) could be resolved only by balancing the values against each other in an intuitionistic manner.

In 1971, John Rawls published his massive book *A Theory of*

---

[1] Alf Ross, *On Law and Justice*, Chap. 12, (Stevens London, 1974).

Justice, having earlier developed some of its main ideas in influential essays stretching back to the 1950s. Rich in themes and densely packed with argument, the character of the book cannot easily be conveyed in a brief discussion such as this. We can, however, endeavour to trace the major themes and issues in a way that will assist the reader in his or her efforts to study the book itself. It will help if we think of Rawls as responding to the intellectual situation that confronted him prior to the book's publication. As we have seen, that situation was one of widespread scepticism about the possibility of any philosophical account of justice, combined with a general and somewhat uncritical acceptance of utilitarianism, or alternatively of an intuitionistic pluralism.

REFLECTIVE EQUILIBRIUM

How can one construct a philosophical theory that will yield conclusions about justice? One approach might be to try to deduce conclusions about justice from a starting point from which rational agents could not dissent. Suppose, for example, that we could be shown to be committed to standards of rationality that we could not coherently deny or reject; and suppose that we could demonstrate that certain principles of justice were entailed by the standards so established. We would then have produced a very powerful and well-grounded philosophy of justice. Many philosophers have pursued this ambitious course, but it is unclear whether any of them have succeeded.[2]

Rawls does not seek to deduce a set of conclusions about justice from some incontestable bedrock of logic or of rational agency. His argument operates entirely upon the plane of what we already believe about justice: our "considered convictions of justice". We should seek to achieve a state of "reflective equilibrium" in those considered convictions.

The nature of reflective equilibrium is best explained in the following way. Suppose that I have a great many opinions about what is just and unjust: I think, for example, that it is unjust that the innocent should be criminally punished, or that people

---

[2]   For an example that approximates to this approach, see Alan Gewirth, *Reason and Morality* (Chicago, 1978). For the flaws in Gewirth's position, see Kramer *In the Realm of Legal and Moral Philosophy*, (London, 1999) Chap.10.

should be enslaved; just that contracts should be performed and wrongful injuries should be compensated; and so forth. I must now ask myself whether there is any coherent and appealing set of principles that would serve to justify those moral judgments concerning justice. Unless I am a quite unusually consistent person, I am likely to find that there is no plausible set of principles under which all of my initial judgments might be subsumed. I must therefore go back to reconsider those judgments. Some of them I may discount because I find that, on reflection, I lack confidence in their soundness; others I may discount because my own interests are too closely bound up with them, thereby raising the suspicion that they reflect my self-interest rather than my moral understanding. Having discounted some such judgments, I will once again ask myself whether the revised set can be subsumed under any coherent and appealing general principles. If, once again, the answer is "no", I may have to reconsider further judgments. I will also have to consider various alternative sets of principles, and the general arguments that might be offered for them. In this way I will work backwards and forwards between relatively specific judgments and possible general principles under which they might be subsumed. All the time I will be seeking to achieve a coherent set of moral judgments that I am prepared to live by and that could be justified by reference to attractive moral principles. When I have achieved this happy state I can offer an account of my moral judgments as "considered in reflective equilibrium".

The ultimate test for Rawls' theory of justice is the test of reflective equilibrium. That is to say, he hopes to persuade us that his theory represents the best available attempt to articulate our own considered judgments "when considered in reflective equilibrium". This is not to say that we already accept the views he puts forward, even before we have read his book. Rather, the point is that we will be persuaded by those views as, in reading his book, we go through the process of trying to order and reflect upon our initial intuitions.

The search for reflective equilibrium is not unstructured. Rawls' general strategy is to try to work from unambitious and relatively uncontentious premises towards stronger and more contentious conclusions. In this way he hopes to persuade us that the more contentious conclusions flow naturally and reasonably from weaker assumptions that we are initially inclined to accept. His device for achieving this is an imaginary situation that he calls "the original position".

It is obvious that, upon a host of issues, we disagree about justice. You, for example, may believe that income and resources should be distributed equally, while I may believe that they should be proportioned to need, or distributed in accordance with desert. Yet, in spite of such disagreements, there may be certain more abstract or general propositions about justice upon which we could agree. We might agree, for example, that principles of justice should apply to people impartially: there can't be one set of principles for Simmonds and another for Smith, for example. We might also agree (after a little philosophical explanation and persuasion) that questions of justice presuppose both limited resources and some degree of self-interest. If I care just as much about you as I care about myself, I will not care whether you get the pay increase or whether I do: hence, no question of justice will arise between us.

Such general, formal ideas about justice might be said to constitute our "concept" of justice. A number of philosophers have pointed to a distinction between the formal structure of the notion of justice, and its substantive content. Justice requires (it is said) that like cases should be treated alike and different cases treated differently. We might all agree to that proposition (which is sometimes called "the principle of formal justice"), but would nevertheless disagree when it came to offering an account of the substantive criteria for likeness and unlikeness. Thus one person might regard need as a relevant criterion for the distribution of income, while another might deny the relevance of need and insist upon the exclusive relevance of desert. We might agree that there must be some set of principles to regulate competing claims, while disagreeing about the precise content of those principles: we would then (to use Rawls' terminology) have a shared *concept* of justice, but disagree in our various *conceptions* of justice.

The philosophical task that Rawls confronts is therefore one of choosing between various alternative conceptions of justice. In addressing this task we should, he believes, work so far as possible from unambitious but widely shared premises to stronger (and therefore more contentious) conclusions. The relatively settled framework of ideas constituting the "concept" of justice does not in itself dictate any particular favoured conception. Suppose, however, that we could combine such formal ideas into a perspicuous and enlightening model: they might then (in conjunction with other philosophical claims which can be evaluated as they are introduced) point to one conception of justice rather than another as being the most reasonable choice. The object is to show that, by combining relatively uncontentious assumptions about justice in a fruitful and enlightening way, we can be led to see that Rawlsian conclusions follow in a natural and plausible way from relatively uncontentious starting points.

THE ORIGINAL POSITION

Rawls invites us to imagine a group of rational individuals who have to agree on a set of principles that will govern the basic structure and institutions of their society. They are to choose these principles on grounds of rational self-interest and in the knowledge that the principles chosen will be binding upon them. But their choice is constrained by the fact that they are deprived of certain types of knowledge about themselves: they are to choose, as Rawls puts it, from behind a "veil of ignorance ". Rawls hopes to persuade us that the conditions imposed upon the choice are fair ones; and that, when a rational choice is made under such fair conditions, the resulting principles will be just. The value of this strategy depends in large part upon the idea that we may be persuaded of the fairness of the conditions of choice when we would not otherwise have felt persuaded by the principles of justice that are chosen as a result: by showing that the latter follow from the former, we are deriving strong and contentious conclusions from weak and relatively uncontentious premises. The idea that principles of justice are those that would be chosen in conditions of fairness explains the name that Rawls gives to his theory: "justice as fairness".

Essentially, the veil of ignorance excludes knowledge of all those features that distinguish one person from another. Thus the rational persons in the "original position" (as Rawls calls the basic choice situation) do not know their own identities; they do not know what they do for a living, nor how intelligent they are, nor what their abilities might be; most importantly, although the persons know that they have their own conception of a good life (and that it may differ from the conceptions held by others) they do not know what that conception is (what their personal ideals and values may be).

Rawls believes that the veil of ignorance represents a set of conditions that it is fair to impose upon the choice of principles of justice. When we argue for this or that moral principle we regard it as proper to set on one side our personal interests and to judge the matter from a more impartial point of view. Utilitarianism achieves this impartiality by attaching equal weight to the welfare of each person. Rawls seeks to achieve it by erasing from the discussion all knowledge of features that distinguish one person from another. The veil of ignorance also attempts to ensure that Rawls' theory of justice will be neutral between different conceptions of the good. Since the persons in the original position do not know what their own conception of the good is, they will choose principles that do not seek to reflect or embody any one particular conception, but provide a framework within which the pursuit of differing ideals is possible.

Strictly speaking, the device of the original position forms a part of the broader method of reflective equilibrium: it is a technique which enables us to structure our considered judgments, and to combine in a fruitful way those beliefs (bearing upon the fairness of the conditions of choice) that are widely shared and relatively uncontentious. Much of the time, Rawls' arguments are aimed at convincing us that the conditions imposed upon "the original position" are reasonable, and that his favoured principles of justice would indeed be chosen in that situation. However, because he offers this as only one part of a broader argument of reflective equilibrium, he also feels entitled, from time to time, to offer more general arguments supporting the attractiveness and plausibility of his favoured principles of justice.

CRITICISM OF UTILITARIANISM

I explained at the start of this chapter that the intellectual climate addressed by Rawls was characterised by the influence of utilitarianism on the one hand, and by a pluralistic intuitionism on the other. Rawls has little to say about intuitionism: he believes that his own theory offers a set of ordered principles enabling us to overcome the ad hoc balancing of distinct values (equality and liberty, for example) of the kind contemplated by intuitionism, and he suggests that it is only by producing such principles that one can refute the intuitionist. Utilitarianism, on the other hand, forms a focus of attack for Rawls, and his criticisms of utilitarianism go to inform the structure and assumptions of his own theory.

Rawls rejects utilitarianism on two main grounds. Utilitarianism, he argues, ignores the distinctness of persons, and it defines the right in terms of the good. These criticisms may be explained as follows.

i. *Ignoring the distinctness of persons*
    When we are making decisions about our own welfare, we consider it rational to make short-term sacrifices in order to achieve long-term gains. We suffer the dentist in order to get rid of the toothache, for example. Utilitarianism extends this form of decision-making to decisions concerning the welfare of society as a whole. The principle of utility rests on the assumption that, just as rationality requires us to make small sacrifices for larger gains, so it requires us to trade-off the welfare of some against the welfare of others. Just as the pain of a visit to the dentist may be justified by the increase of welfare resulting from the removal of the aching tooth, so the pain inflicted on one section of the population may be outweighed by the happiness accruing to the remainder. According to Rawls, utilitarianism goes astray here in simply extending to society as a whole a principle of rational decision that is appropriate only for individuals. When I go to the dentist, the pain that I suffer at his hands is outweighed by the pleasure that results from the cessation of my toothache. But the utilitarian is prepared to contemplate hardships inflicted on one person or group that are compensated by gains to others, and here the pleasures and pains are experienced by different individuals. There is no reason why the same principle should apply to decisions of individual prudence and decisions which must adjudicate between different individuals. In effect, Rawls suggests, utilitarianism treats people as lacking any distinctness, but as receptacles in which welfare is to be maximised.

ii. *The right and the good*
    Utilitarianism defines the right in terms of the good. That is, it begins with an account of what states of affairs are valuable or desirable and defines right action as action that leads to such valuable states of affairs. Classical utilitarians count happiness as the thing that ultimately matters, and regard an action as morally right or wrong according to its tendency to increase or diminish happiness. This approach requires us, for example, to take account of the happiness

accruing to slave owners as a positive factor tending to justify the institution of slavery. It does not follow, of course, that the utilitarian will regard slavery as justified: for it seems highly likely that the harms inflicted upon the slaves will greatly outweigh any benefits accruing to the slave-owners. Even if the utilitarian reaches the right result here, however, he seems to reach it by the wrong route. For we may feel that the slave owner's happiness should be ignored because it is unjustly obtained. Perhaps the utilitarian goes wrong in assuming that happiness is always a good thing, and that justice is a matter of maximising such good consequences. Perhaps we can only say whether someone's happiness counts as a good thing after we have determined whether it was justly obtained. Thus, in Rawls' view, questions of justice are prior to questions about the good, because it is only when we know a desire or pleasure to be just that we can regard it as having any positive value: the pleasures of sadists who prey upon non-consenting victims, for example, would have no merit on Rawls' approach in so far as those pleasures are obtained by violating principles of justice.

This points us to a deeper sense in which Rawls' theory treats "the right" as prior to "the good". Rawls wants to construct an account of the principles of justice that does not presuppose a particular conception of a good and worthwhile life. Rawls wishes to offer a theory that is, in a sense, neutral between different ideals and aspirations, differing personal ideas of what makes life valuable. The principles of justice represent a framework within which different individuals have a fair opportunity to pursue their own goals and values.

The two ideas on which this critique of utilitarianism turns form key elements in Rawls' theory. We can see this very clearly in the way that the veil of ignorance excludes knowledge of conceptions of the good, thereby seeking to ensure that principles of justice are settled prior to any questions about the good. It is in this way that Rawls embodies in his theory the priority of the right over the good.

The notion of the distinctness of persons has a role within the theory that is both fertile and complex. Rawls rejects the direct application of criteria of rational prudence to social choice, because such a direct application ignores the distinctness of persons. In other words, while it may make sense to think of an individual's well-being as composed of the sum of his pleasures and pains across time, it is less clear that social well-being may be construed in an analogous way, by summing pleasures and pains across individuals. Yet Rawls cannot simply reject the criterion of rational prudence in favour of some other conception of rationality, for he wishes to work from weak and widely accepted criteria, and there is no uncontentious conception of rationality available, apart from that of rational prudence. He therefore seeks to rely upon the conception of rational prudence, but within a framework that renders it appropriate for social and not just individual choice. We are to imagine the persons in the original position choosing principles of justice on grounds of self-interest, but from behind a veil of ignorance. Criteria of rational prudence guide their choice, but the choice is one that leads to unanimous agreement amongst a plurality of individuals, and is not one within which losses to some may simply be traded off against gains to others.

It follows from the distinctness of persons (according to Rawls) that one cannot with propriety speak of maximising welfare across individuals: it is, as he puts it, "impossible to maximise with respect to more than one point of view".[3] This raises the question of how we should interpret the conventional understanding within democratic societies that public power should serve the common interest: how is the notion of the "common interest" to be construed if we cannot equate it with the aggregate welfare of citizens?[4] Rawls regards his theory of justice as providing an answer to this question.

Utilitarians since Bentham have often sought to promote their theory (either as a moral philosophy or, more commonly, as an appropriate public standard for law-making) by claiming that the principle of utility offers a relatively determinate guideline for decision-making when compared with the principles proposed by other philosophies. It is worth noting, therefore,

---

[3] J. Rawls, *Theory of Justice*, revised edition, (Oxford 1999) p.280.

[4] Whereas Rawls emphasises the impossibility of maximising across a plurality of distinct persons, Finnis emphasises the impossibility of maximising a plurality of distinct goods. Both theories then seek to construct more convincing, non-maximising, accounts of the "common interest" or "common good". See Chap. 4 below.

that Rawls devotes some space to an exposure of the indeterminacy and uncertainty of the principle of utility.[5] This indeterminacy springs from the basic problem of measuring aggregate welfare, a problem for which Rawls believes there to be no adequate solution. He recommends his own theory as offering a more workable set of guidelines.

THE THIN THEORY OF THE GOOD

Rawls' theory of justice is a theory for the justice of what he calls "the basic structure" of society. That is to say, it is meant to give us a set of principles with which we can evaluate the justice of the way in which the major social institutions distribute liberty and other resources. The rational agents in the original position are to choose principles for the basic structure of their society, and they are to choose them on grounds of self-interest. The principles so chosen will be binding upon the individuals once the "veil of ignorance" is lifted and they are restored to the normal conditions of social life. Thus it is important to appreciate that persons in the original position are not asking a question along the lines of "which principles are truly just?"; they are asking "which principles will best serve my self-interest?". The justice of the resulting principles is secured by the conditions (of the veil of ignorance) in which the choice is made, not by the content of the choice itself.

This model is intended, amongst other things, to enable us to answer the intractable philosophical question of justice by addressing a more manageable question about rational self-interest. There is a difficulty, however. Rawls seeks to secure the priority of "the right" over "the good" within his theory by excluding, behind the veil of ignorance, the parties' knowledge of their own conceptions of the good. Each of them knows that they have a conception of the good (an idea of what is valuable and worth pursuing in life) and that it may be different from the conceptions held by other people: but they do not know its content. How then are they to choose principles of justice on grounds of self-interest? If I do not know what I consider to be valuable and worth pursuing, how can I know what will serve my self-interest?

Rawls relies at this point on what he calls "the thin theory of

[5] J. Rawls, *Theory of Justice* pp.281–285.

the good". This theory holds that there are certain things which it is rational to want whatever else one may want, because of the role that they can play in the pursuit of any particular conception of the good. Liberty, opportunity, income and wealth would all be examples, according to Rawls, for they will help me to carry out (or will not hinder) any plan of life that I may have in mind. Persons in the original position, having no knowledge of their personal conceptions of the good life, will therefore seek these more neutral goods. Goods such as liberty, opportunity, income and wealth are distributed by the basic structure of society, and Rawls therefore refers to them as "social primary goods".

The objection to Rawls' argument at this point is that the "thin theory of the good" is inherently biased in favour of bourgeois, individualist conceptions of the good life. Liberty and money are important constituents of the good life for some people, but play a much less central part in the conception of the good held by many others. Suppose, for example, that Jack wants a life devoted to driving fast cars and eating in fashionable restaurants: money and liberty will be very important constituents of the good life for him. Jim, on the other hand, wants a life devoted to meditation, in a community of like-minded others. Money and liberty will not hinder the pursuit of Jim's project, and may assist it; but they are not central constituents of that life, as they are for Jack. Does this denote an inherent bias in the Rawlsian approach in favour of individualistic (and possibly acquisitive) ways of life, and against more communitarian notions of the good?

I pointed out earlier in the book[6] that the legal order of a liberal society cannot claim to be neutral in the sense of allowing everyone an equal opportunity to pursue his or her own conception of the good life, for what would we say of the conception of the good pursued by a psychopathic killer? The neutrality of a liberal legal order is neutrality at the level of justification, not of effect. We must therefore ask, not whether Jack and Jim will find it equally easy, under a Rawlsian regime, to pursue their differing conceptions of the good; but whether the justification for the thin theory of the good is itself neutral, or whether it assumes that some conceptions of the good (such as Jim's) are inferior to others (such as Jack's). The goods identified by the Rawlsian thin theory would be of assistance to both Jack and Jim. If Jim faces greater difficulty than Jack in pursuing his

---

[6] See pp.14–15 above.

conception of the good, that is principally because he requires the co-operation of other like-minded people. In requiring that such co-operation be voluntary, a liberal regime may well be less favourable to his interests than would an illiberal regime committed to his particular set of communitarian values; but it may be more favourable to his interests than would an illiberal regime committed to a different form of orthodoxy, for such a regime might prohibit Jim's commune entirely. This explains why liberalism is often thought to favour individualistic (and possibly acquisitive) personal values. The man who wishes to pursue life in a certain type of community has preferences that extend to the behaviour of other persons. In a liberal society, he will be able to satisfy these preferences only with the consent of those persons. The man with purely acquisitive values has preferences that relate solely to what he gets and not at all to how other people behave. The man with materialistic goals is in a better position here, for he does not depend in the same way on other people sharing his idea of a good life.

Given such differences in our conceptions of the good, Rawls seeks to step back to a higher level of abstraction: instead of asking what would serve to advance this or that conception of the good, we ask what would be chosen by people who do not know what their conception of the good might be; instead of regarding principles of justice as implementing an overall conception of excellence, we are to regard them as establishing a fair scheme of co-operation for persons who hold diverse ideas of excellence.

TWO PRINCIPLES

According to Rawls, rational persons in the original position will choose two principles of justice. For present purposes, we will consider a very simplified formulation of those principles:

> The first principle holds that each person is entitled to the most extensive system of basic liberties that is compatible with a similar system for everyone else.

> The second principle holds that social and economic inequalities are just only in so far as they work to the advantage of the least advantaged people in society.

The first principle takes priority over the second in that it is only when the first principle is completely satisfied that we can apply the second principle at all. The meaning of the two principles will become clear as we discuss them in detail.

THE DIFFERENCE PRINCIPLE

"The difference principle" is the name that Rawls gives to the second principle of justice as I have formulated it above. The principle requires that inequalities in the distribution of social primary goods must be justified by reference to the interests of the least well-off.

To understand the significance of this principle, we must think of the basic structure of society (the major institutions of property, the market, the family, the tax and welfare systems, and so forth) as representing a scheme of social co-operation that distributes the benefits and burdens of that co-operation. Under any particular scheme of distribution (other than strict equality) some will receive more than others. The difference principle holds that any such inequalities are justified only if, in the absence of the inequality, the disadvantaged would receive even less than they do under the scheme that includes the inequality. Thus, suppose that the basic structure tends to yield higher incomes for managerial workers than those received by some low-paid group, such as unskilled labourers. This inequality is justified only if it can be shown that, were managers to be paid less, the economic consequences would be such that labourers would be worse off than they are under the present arrangement. It might be the case, for example, that we could equalise the incomes of managers and labourers; but the consequences of doing so might be to put both groups upon a level of real income that was lower than the income enjoyed by the low-paid prior to the equalisation. This might be the result if, say, high earnings were necessary to attract able people into management, and a fall in their earnings would result in a loss of management talent, a decline in efficiency, and a corresponding decline in the economy, making everyone (including labourers) worse off. If, on the other hand, the differential between highly-paid and low-paid workers could be reduced without a fall in the real income enjoyed by the low-paid, this would show the high earnings of the managers to be unjustified under the difference principle.

The difference principle thus allows for a trade-off between economic efficiency and strict income equality in a somewhat similar way to the principle of utility. The difference is that, whereas the principle of utility judges differential earnings and incentives by their impact upon the general or overall welfare, Rawls will allow such inequalities only when they are necessary to increase the resources of the least advantaged.

Rawls argues for the difference principle in two main ways. On the one hand, he tries to demonstrate that it would be chosen by his rational persons in the original position: if one agrees that this is so, and one agrees that the conditions of the original position are fair conditions for the choice of principles of justice, then the difference principle is a reasonable implication of those fair conditions. At the same time, and to some extent independently of his claims about the original position, Rawls argues that the difference principle is an independently attractive principle. This double strategy reflects the fact that the argument from the original position is but one aspect of a broader argument of reflective equilibrium. In other words, Rawls seeks to demonstrate that his two principles are the best available attempt to order our intuitive judgments about social justice; the device of the original position is merely one device whereby we can be led to see that this is indeed so. In this section we will examine one of Rawls' principal claims for the independent attractiveness of the difference principle; in the next section we will examine his argument that the principle would be chosen by persons in the original position.

One interesting and important argument offered by Rawls is aimed at demonstrating an intellectual instability in some commonly espoused views about justice, and at suggesting the difference principle as the best way of resolving that instability. He assumes that few people would be attracted by an unrestricted free market in which the distribution of assets over time is shaped by morally arbitrary factors such as inherited wealth: it is widely felt that people's life-chances should not be fundamentally determined by such factors as the wealth or poverty of their parents. Many people are therefore attracted by the idea of "equal opportunity". This conception of justice seeks to ensure that people's prospects are determined by their natural talents and the amount of effort they put in to using those talents: their prospects should not be determined by the accident of social class and fortune. But, Rawls argues, this position, though superficially attractive and very influential, is unstable. For, once we have come to regard social class and fortune as arbitrary factors that are irrelevant from the point of view of justice, we can have no good reason for not regarding natural talents and abilities in exactly the same light. We no more deserve our talents and abilities than we deserve our parents' fortune: both are equally irrelevant from the point of view of justice. Accordingly, it is just as wrong for a person's prospects to be determined by his talents and abilities as it is for his prospects to be determined by his parents' wealth.

The difference principle embodies this view of natural talents in the following way. If I am a talented individual in a Rawlsian society, I will be allowed to increase my "social primary goods" only if, in doing so, I also indirectly increase the social primary goods of the least advantaged. Thus my talents are not resources that I may exploit for my own benefit alone: they are to be regarded as common assets that must be exploited for the benefit of everyone.

The intuitive appeal of the difference principle has been doubted, however. Rawls argues that the arbitrary nature of the natural distribution of talents should lead us to regard talents and abilities as resources to be exploited for the benefit of everyone. But, as Robert Nozick has observed, why should the same argument not be applied to bodily organs? After all, some people have two healthy kidneys and two eyes and others do not. This difference is not deserved, and is arbitrary from a moral point of view. So why should kidneys and eyes not be regarded as common resources? Why not parallel the coercive redistribution of wealth with a coercive redistribution of eyes and kidneys?

Nozick's argument forms part of a wider theory that, like that of Rawls, attaches considerable importance to the notion of "the distinctness of persons". Nozick, however, finds within that basic notion a set of implications quite different from those outlined by Rawls. He regards it as ironic that Rawls should offer a principle that, in effect, gives persons rights in the talents of other persons: according to Nozick, if "the distinctness of persons" has moral significance, it indicates that persons are the exclusive owners of themselves. Setting on one side this general issue, however, we may feel that Nozick's analogy with the distribution of eyes and kidneys does not do justice to Rawls' argument. For it must be kept in mind that Rawls is speaking of the way in which the benefits of social co-operation are to be distributed: he is not proposing principles for re-distributing the benefits and disbenefits of nature. We can arrange our social affairs in a variety of ways. Some schemes of social co-operation will mean that the differences in natural talents and abilities are directly reflected and even magnified in the distribution of the benefits of society; other schemes of co-operation will tend to compensate for differences in talent and ability. Rawls is suggesting that because we do not *deserve* our natural talents (our possession of those talents is neither just nor unjust), those natural talents give us no particular claim to a social system that would reward us for possessing them. In the absence of such an entitlement to reward, we should choose social arrangements that do not reinforce and exaggerate the inequalities stemming from such talents. Rawls is not suggesting that our possession of differential natural talents is unjust and should therefore be rectified (although his sometimes incautious formulations of the argument can foster this impression); he is suggesting that our possession of those talents in itself gives us no claim to a larger share of the benefits of social co-operation.

CHOOSING THE DIFFERENCE PRINCIPLE

According to Rawls, rational persons in the original position would choose the difference principle as a basic principle of justice to regulate their society. They would choose this principle, in preference to other alternatives such as the principle of utility, because they would base their choice on very conservative and cautious criteria of rational decision. From behind the veil of ignorance, the rational persons are faced with a very difficult problem. They must choose principles of justice which will regulate the basic structure of their society, and so will fundamentally affect their own prospects in life, the resources and liberty that they will enjoy. They know that any principles so chosen will be binding upon them when the veil of ignorance is lifted, but they do not know the position that they will occupy in such a society, nor do they have enough information to form a meaningful estimate of how probable it is that they will be among the better-off or the less well-off. Given the seriousness of the choice and the paucity of information on which the choice must be based, the rational persons will make their decisions according to the "maximin" rule. The maximin rule holds that alternative options should be ranked in terms of their worst outcomes. Imagine, for example, that I am trying to decide whether I should become a civil servant or a bank robber, and assume that my one concern is with how much money I will acquire in my chosen profession. If

I am a very successful bank robber I might make £20,000,000 per annum (the best outcome), but if I am an unsuccessful bank robber I might make nothing (the worst outcome). If I am a civil servant I might be promoted to a job where I earn £100,000 per annum (the best outcome), or I might remain on a salary of £25,000 (the worst outcome). If I choose according to the maximin rule I will choose to be a civil servant, since I will rank the alternative occupations by their worst outcomes, and being a civil servant has the best worst outcome.

It is not difficult to see how the maximin rule would lead to the choice of the difference principle in preference to the principle of utility. Under either principle the best outcome would be finding that I am in the most advantaged group in society, and the worst outcome would be finding that I am in the least advantaged group. Now, since the difference principle permits increases in social primary goods only when these benefit the least advantaged group, it is necessarily true that (in these two alternatives) the difference principle is most favourable to the interests of the least advantaged group. It therefore has the best worst outcome (and satisfies maximin) from the point of view of the original position.

We may agree with Rawls that if the choice is made according to maximin, the principle chosen would be the difference principle; but choice according to maximin only has a claim to rationality so long as we are ignorant of the various probabilities. In the choice between bank robbery and civil service, it would be irrational to choose according to maximin in circumstances where I know that as a bank robber I am virtually certain to make £20,000,000 per annum, and that as a civil servant it is most improbable that I will make more than £25,000. Rawls does not allow his persons in the original position sufficient knowledge to form an estimate of probabilities: but is he justified in so restricting their knowledge? After all, such a restriction does not seem necessary in order to secure the impartiality and fairness that we feel should characterise the choice of principles of justice, since the knowledge of probabilities would be the same for everyone and equally available to everyone. Moreover, the utilitarian regards it as an important part of his case to argue that the principle of utility is in fact most unlikely to lead to the justification of institutions such as slavery: but Rawls's exclusion of probabilities has the effect of disallowing all such appeals to the probable results of applying different principles.

Rawls seeks to justify the exclusion of a knowledge of

probabilities by appealing to a number of separate ideas. He tells us, for example, that the principles of justice chosen must be "capable of serving as a public charter of a well-ordered society in perpetuity", and for this reason their validity must not be dependent upon the particular circumstances of this or that society.[7] Once detached from the particular features of this or that society, however, probabilities would become incalculable and imponderable, and one is consequently justified in excluding them. Utilitarians frequently argue that those liberties and entitlements to which we attach great importance would be protected by the principle of utility, since they generally serve to advance aggregate welfare and it is unlikely that welfare would be advanced by encroachment upon them: it is this type of argument that makes the consideration of probabilities so important for the utilitarian. In Rawls' view, however, the utilitarian leaves too much to such arguments from general facts and probable consequences: this reliance upon conjectures that could possibly be false is a weak spot in utilitarian theory. The persons in the original position would not choose to render their vital interests dependent upon such speculations, but would prefer to protect those interests more directly in the principles of justice that they chose. They would also be concerned to choose principles that were straightforwardly applicable without reliance upon complicated theoretical arguments.[8]

We might well wonder, however, whether Rawls' own theory satisfies this latter requirement: can the difference principle be applied without relying upon complicated theoretical arguments? The effects upon the least advantaged group of changes in wage levels, tax levels, and welfare benefits will surely be immensely difficult to establish; yet we would need to understand such effects, and attribute them to specific causes, before we could judge an inequality to be justified or condemned by the difference principle. If probable ease of application is an appropriate criterion for choosing theories of justice, the Rawlsian theory might not be the best choice.

Perhaps Rawls' best argument against the choice of the principle of utility concerns the possible difficulty of compliance with that principle. Persons in the original position are to envisage a society which will be governed by the principles of justice that they choose. The principles will be understood by all

---

[7] J. Rawls, *Theory of Justice* p.114.
[8] J. Rawls, *Theory of Justice* pp.138–139; pp. 281–285.

citizens, and the citizens must be prepared to comply with the relevant principles: Rawls does not envisage a society where the principles of justice are enforced purely by coercion. Persons in the original position, when choosing principles of justice, must therefore avoid choosing principles with which they might (in certain circumstances) be very unwilling to comply.

Let us imagine a situation where I believe that choice of the principle of utility will very probably advance my interests better than would the difference principle. I must nevertheless bear in mind that, when the veil of ignorance is lifted, I may find myself in some disadvantaged group which might conceivably fare very badly under a utilitarian regime: suppose, for example, that overall utility is increased by maintaining a small group of workers on very low rates of pay, and I happen to find myself in that group. Could I willingly comply with principles of justice that sacrifice my interests to advance those of other persons? Will it be enough for me to tell myself that those same principles might have worked to my advantage had things worked out differently? If I believe that compliance with such principles will be impossible for me in circumstances of this type, I cannot conscientiously choose them in the original position.

GREATER EQUALITY?

Utilitarians regard the Rawlsian difference principle as unreasonably obsessed with the position of the least advantaged, and insist that a straightforward concern to weigh everyone's interests equally would lead to the principle of utility instead. Unlike Rawls, they would accept inequalities that served to advance the general welfare, and not simply those that improved the resources of the least advantaged.

Rawls also has to face attack from another direction, however. Some radical egalitarians see his theory as legitimating inequality in an unacceptable way. They would urge the justice of complete equality of resources (or perhaps of welfare) and would see the difference principle as wrong in so far as it contemplates the possibility of some inequalities being justified.

At first this type of objection to Rawls can seem puzzling. The difference principle leaves off redistributing in favour of the least advantaged only at the point at which further redistribution would make the least advantaged worse off; so why would anyone want to continue redistribution beyond that point? To make the more advantaged worse-off even at the cost of reducing the resources of the least advantaged seems at first to be a clear instance of the politics of envy gone mad.

Suppose, however, that a radical egalitarian were to make the following point:

"Redistribution beyond the point at which the difference principle ceases to redistribute will make the least advantaged worse-off in terms of what Rawls calls 'social primary goods' (as identified by the 'thin theory of the good'); but they may be *better-off* in *other* terms. A society characterised by inequality of resources will exhbit a number of defects: personal relations will be distorted by envy, for example; people will focus too much on what others have and not enough on the most meaningful and valuable way to conduct their own lives. Only a society characterised by strict equality of resources will be able to sustain transparent and mutually compassionate relations between fellow citizens. Thus, a truly worthwhile and valuable life can be lived only in a society of equals."

The factual assumptions from which this argument proceeds might strike you as naive (or at least as unduly optimistic), but let us overlook such worries. The important point is this: the radical egalitarian argument, as we have imagined it, invokes a particular conception of a good life, involving the transparency and warmth of communal relations. Not everyone, however, shares this conception of a good life; and Rawls is looking for principles of justice that will govern the relationship between people who hold diverse conceptions of the good. His argument for the difference principle (as opposed to some more radically re-distributive principle) depends directly upon his claim to have found, in the "thin theory of the good", a basis for judging the interests of rational individuals that is neutral between conceptions of the good. We saw above, when we examined that part of the Rawlsian theory, that the claim to neutrality here is contestable but not devoid of merit.

THE FIRST PRINCIPLE OF JUSTICE

Rawls' first principle of justice holds that "Each person is entitled to the most extensive system of equal basic liberties compatible with a similar system of liberty for all." The principle enjoys "lexical priority", so that it must be fully satisfied before the second principle can be applied at all. In this way Rawls seeks to ensure that all citizens will enjoy a set of basic liberties that cannot be encroached upon simply in order to improve the welfare of the majority, or the resources of the least advantaged. As Rawls expresses it at one point:

> "A basic liberty covered by the first principle can be limited only for the sake of liberty itself, that is, only to insure that the same liberty or a different basic liberty is properly protected and to adjust the one system of basic liberties in the best way."[9]

It might, at first sight, be tempting to equate this principle with the classic liberal principle that liberty may be restricted only in order to maintain equal liberty, and some of Rawls' formulations tend to invite such an equation. This classic principle of equal liberty holds that the law is justified in interfering with conduct only when that conduct threatens the liberty of other persons: the sole aim of the law must be to maintain equal liberty. The classic principle exhibits some serious defects. One is that it tends to make all political issues dependent upon the definition of "liberty": since that notion can be interpreted in a great many different ways, the principle offers less guidance than might at first be apparent. A second problem stems from the fact that there is no way of measuring the *extent* of liberty: when my trumpet playing interferes with your studying, the instruction to "equalise liberty" between the two of us tells us nothing. In fact, as we shall see, the Rawlsian first principle differs from the classic liberal principle; but while this might rescue Rawls from some difficulties, it leads him into others.

Some political theorists would reject the distinction between "liberty" protected in the first principle, and the social and economic resources regulated by the second principle, since lack of money and material resources can restrict one's range of available options, and therefore (it is argued) one's liberty. Rawls, by contrast, prefers to distinguish between "liberty" and "the worth of liberty". Persons enjoy "liberty" for Rawls when they are protected by law from the interference of government and other persons with their performance of certain activities. The opportunities thereby provided are not, however, equally

[9]   J. Rawls, *Theory of Justice* p.179.

valuable to everyone, since poverty and ignorance may diminish the worth of liberty for some. This lesser worth of liberty is, Rawls argues, compensated for by the difference principle. Thus, while the first principle confers equal liberties on everyone, the second principle seeks to maximise the worth of those equal liberties for the least advantaged.[10]

At this point in his argument, Rawls appears to deal in a somewhat cursory way with a most intractable difficulty. It is far from clear that poverty can be treated as affecting the "worth of liberty" rather than liberty itself, so that equal liberty may be compatible with inequality in material resources. After all, one who possesses an item of property has available to him a certain range of actions that are not available to non-owners of the property; the liberty to perform these actions will be protected by law from the interference of third parties. The more property one owns, it would seem, the more such actions one has available; whereas to own no property at all is to find oneself subject to the restrictions that flow from the ownership of others, while enjoying none of the freedoms that flow from such ownership. It is therefore not easy to see why "equal liberty" should not entail "equal property".

The sense that Rawls has dismissed an important line of argument here stems from the tendency to equate his first principle with the classic liberal principle of equal liberty. In fact, Rawls' first principle of justice is considerably less stringent, for his theory as a whole is not exclusively concerned with liberty, but (in the second principle) with equality as well. If the first principle of justice really corresponded to the classic principle of equal liberty, there would never be any scope for the application of the second principle. The first principle takes priority over the second, in the sense that we may only set about rectifying inequalities in accordance with the second principle when the first principle has been completely satisfied. Now (if we accept Rawls' distinction between liberty and "the worth of liberty") any rectification of inequality by the compulsory redistribution of wealth involves an interference with liberty: namely, the liberty to retain one's property. If the first principle protected all forms of liberty it would protect this liberty, giving it priority over the redistributive concerns of the second principle. The result would be that the compulsory redistribution of wealth to foster greater equality could never be justified. Since Rawls

---

[10] J. Rawls, *Theory of Justice* p.179.

clearly does contemplate the compulsory redistribution of wealth, he cannot intend his first principle as a defence of liberty in general.

The first principle of justice differs from the classic liberal principle in that it protects, not liberty in general, but certain specific liberties. These are the conventional civil liberties of freedom of speech, freedom from arbitrary arrest, freedom of conscience and freedom to hold personal property. Such liberties cannot, in Rawls's view, justifiably be interfered with even where this would make for greater equality: it is in this sense that the first principle takes priority over the second. Rawls's rational persons would attach this great importance to basic liberties because they must choose the principles of justice without knowing their own conception of the good. They know that they have such a conception, and that its pursuit will be very important to them, and that their conception may differ from that held by others in their society. In these circumstances the only safe thing to do is choose a principle which gives strong protection to liberty, thereby protecting the individual from the intrusive and oppressive effects of the disapproval that others may feel for our own idea of a good life. It is in this way that Rawls seeks to make his account of justice and right prior to an account of the good.

We may well ask, however, why the rational persons in the original position regard some liberties as more important than others? Taxation, for example, interferes with a person's liberty to dispose of his property as he chooses: in order to pay my employee £20,000 I may also have to pay the Inland Revenue £4,000; in order to give my friend a large sum of money I may have to pay tax to the Inland Revenue; I am not free simply to give people what I like, without restriction. Now, why should people in the original position value freedom of speech so highly, but not freedom to dispose of their property? What justifies Rawls' choice of just those basic liberties? Rawls tells us that the favoured liberties enable citizens to exercise their sense of justice, and pursue their conception of the good.[11] Yet this surely depends upon what their conception of the good might

---

[11] Rawls addresses these issues at length in his essay "The Basic Liberties and their Priority", which appears as Lecture VIII in John Rawls, *Political Liberalism* (Columbia University, New York Press 1993). For brief statement of his position, see John Rawls, *Justice as Fairness: A Restatement* (Harvard, 2001) p.45.

be. One must be forgiven for suspecting that, in the end, Rawls could not avoid reliance upon his own preferred conception of a good and worthwhile life. Is it the case that Rawls assumes a life of public concern and participation to be superior to a life of material acquisition? If so, he sacrifices his claim to have offered a theory of justice as prior to particular conceptions of the good.[12]

POLITICAL LIBERALISM

We have so far been discussing the arguments presented in Rawls' great book *A Theory of Justice*. We must now turn to his later book, *Political Liberalism*, for (at the very least) it adds some further complexities of argument that we cannot afford to ignore, even in an introductory work of this kind. Unfortunately, *Political Liberalism* is a much more difficult book than *A Theory of Justice*, and it is possible to construe its significance in a number of different ways. The complexities and uncertainties are increased by the fact that Rawls himself offers an account of the relationship between the two books that is at odds with the way in which many of his readers construe that relationship.

Many readers see the later book as an attempt by Rawls to respond to criticisms of his earlier work, particularly those offered from what has come to be called a "communitarian" perspective. Communitarians have tended to attack Rawlsian liberalism for its alleged neglect of the importance of concrete human communities with their various complex traditions and institutions. After the publication of *A Theory of Justice*, two such lines of criticism achieved particular prominence. One line of argument[13] attacked the abstraction of Rawls' method, and suggested that appropriate conclusions about justice could only be arrived at by consulting the traditions and practices of concrete political communities. Another, closely related, argument[14] attacked the metaphysical conception of the person that was said to be implicit in Rawls' theory, in so far as Rawls appears to treat persons as having an identity which is prior to any of their goals or values. It is possible to regard *Political*

---

[12] *cf.* Ronald Dworkin, *Sovereign Virtue* (Harvard, 2000) p.138.
[13] Associated primarily with Michael Walzer, *Interpretation and Social Criticism*, (Harvard 1987); *Spheres of Justice* (Oxford, Blackwell 1983).
[14] Michael Sandel, *Liberalism and the Limits of Justice*, (2nd ed., Cambridge 1998).

Liberalism as offering concessions to these two lines of criticism, insofar as Rawls now insists that his theory is itself drawn from the concrete traditions and practices of actual liberal polities (thereby meeting the first attack) and that (precisely in relying upon such established traditions) the theory avoids any commitment to any contentious philosophical positions on such issues as the nature of the person.

Rawls, however, does not see the book as a response to communitarian criticisms, but as an attempt to overcome a problem in *A Theory of Justice* that he had not originally discerned. The problem concerns the possibility of a stable liberal society ordered by the Rawlsian principles of justice. In *A Theory of Justice* Rawls had taken the view that it was possible to have a society wherein the great bulk of citizens accepted the two principles of justice as what Rawls calls a "comprehensive philosophical doctrine". He later came to feel that such a degree of consensus would be incompatible with the freedom of speech and thought that should characterise a liberal society. Such a liberal society is bound to contain a variety of reasonable but incompatible philosophical and religious doctrines, since such a plurality is the normal result of reasoned reflection operating within the context of free institutions. Consensus upon a single philosophy could be maintained, if at all, only by repression.

This does not lead Rawls to abandon his argument about the original position, the veil of ignorance and the two principles.[15] Rather, it leads him to offer a complex new interpretation of the *status* of the earlier argument. The theory is now offered, not as a "comprehensive philosophical doctrine" but as a "political" theory that can be supported by persons espousing different philosophical and religious doctrines.

We have already encountered a related idea, in Chapter 1, when we saw that utilitarianism could be construed *either* as a moral philosophy, *or* as a specifically jurisprudential theory concerned with the principles that should underpin our laws. Someone might reject the idea that the principle of utility is the fundamental principle of morality, while accepting that it is an appropriate standard to be followed in the enactment of legal rules. One reason for taking this view might be a sense that

---

[15] There are, however, numerous changes of detail and of emphasis which are ignored in the above discussion. In the main part of this chapter I have focused upon the argument as originally presented in *A Theory of Justice*.

utilitarianism embodies an attitude towards the interests and preferences of citizens (taking account of all of them, and weighing them equally) that is specially appropriate to legislative choice: moral and religious issues about which we might disagree are simply treated as differing preferences, to be weighed in a supposedly neutral calculus. Citizens in such a utilitarian regime might accept that their personal moral concerns (*e.g.* for saving whales, or persecuting homosexuals) should be treated in the public realm as simple preferences, to be weighed one against another.

While having a broad structural similarity to this position, the argument of Rawls' *Political Liberalism* is rather different (and of considerable complexity). The basic question to be addressed concerns the possibility of a liberal society that is ordered by a shared public conception of justice, while nevertheless exhibiting within the society's background culture a diversity of broader philosophical and religious positions. How can the followers of various secular moral philosophies, and the adherents of diverse religions, all support public institutions based upon a single theory of justice? What would the content of such a conception of justice be? How should its content be determined?

One strategy for constructing a shared public conception of justice in such a pluralistic society would be a search for compromise, through a process of give-and-take. Adherents of each philosophical or religious position would make certain concessions to their opponents, so that a set of compromises that all could support would result. Rawls says that such a process would be inappropriate, for its content would simply reflect the current balance of power between the different groups, and the relative extremity of their various demands. The appropriate way to construct a political theory of justice is not by compromise but by abstraction. Instead of the adherents of various religious and philosophical views seeking to construct compromise positions, they should abstract from the *content* of their views entirely. They should ask themselves, for example, what principles would be agreed to by rational persons who knew that they held a comprehensive philosophical doctrine, but who did not know its content. In short, they should approach the question of justice by means of the model of the original position.

It was explained above that Rawls' earlier work had been criticised for its apparent reliance upon a metaphysical conception of the person as having an identity that is prior to the person's goals and values. We can now see how the later book offers Rawls a way of responding to this criticism. The response is summarised by Rawls' phrase "political, not metaphysical": the conception of the person embodied in the original position is not chosen because it represents our ultimate essence in terms of some comprehensive philosophical doctrine, but because it constitutes an appropriate way in which persons should be represented in our attempt to construct a public conception of justice. Such a public conception of justice seeks to abstract from the differences in moral and religious viewpoint that will inevitably characterise a liberal society: the representation of persons as capable of holding a conception of the good (a philosophical doctrine, or a set of moral or religious values), but as not knowing its content, is not an attempt to express a deep philosophical truth: it is simply a reasonable way of performing this necessary move of abstraction.

What of the other "communitarian" criticism of Rawls that was mentioned above? This criticism, it will be recalled, attacked the abstraction of Rawls' theory, and claimed that the appropriate way to construct an argument about justice was by reference to the particular practices and traditions of the community in question. Here Rawls' response is to suggest that, in substance, he is already working from established traditions, rather than from philosophical conceptions: his arguments are, in effect, a philosophical interpretation of the established traditions and practices of established liberal democracies. The degree of abstraction that the arguments exhibit is not a consequence of any belief that the appropriate way to tackle questions of justice is by detachment from such traditions and practices; rather, it results from the fact that concrete traditions can be interpreted in diverse ways, so that the attempt to reach a shared interpretation itself forces a certain move into abstraction. Abstraction in argument is, according to Rawls, "a way of continuing public discussion when shared understandings of lesser generality have broken down."(p.46)

Many ardent admirers of Rawls' first book have been disappointed by these responses to communitarian criticisms. Some theorists feel, for example, that detachment from the features of our particular traditions and practices is the appropriate path for political philosophy whether or not our "shared understandings" have broken down: for the point of political philosophy, on this view, is to test the soundness or validity of those shared understandings. A theory of justice should enable us to evaluate societies as just or unjust, and this it cannot do (it is argued) if the theory draws its standards from the practices of our own society: for why should we assume that those practices are themselves just? However, it should be remembered that, right from the start, Rawls' theory has been grounded in an appeal to our moral intuitions "considered in reflective equilibrium." Such intuitions are highly likely to reflect the familiar political institutions with which we have grown up. While certainly providing some critical leverage upon individual aspects of those institutions, the "reflective equilibrium" approach is poorly placed to evaluate our shared understandings from an external perspective. Those who hanker after a theory that engages in such a strong form of external evaluation may have to search for an approach that Rawls has never offered, and that may not be available at all.

Similarly, many liberals hold that our capacity autonomously to choose a personal conception of the good is our morally most significant feature, outstripping in significance the content of the conception so held. Liberalism so conceived is opposed to cultural outlooks that emphasise the importance of submission to the authority of tradition, and the undertaking of unchosen roles and responsibilities: for the liberal, such roles and traditions are valuable only when and in so far as they have been freely chosen. Liberals of this type believe that Rawls should have proffered his theory as a universal one that seeks to capture fundamental moral truths about the human condition, and energetically defends the superiority of liberal society to its alternatives. Instead, they feel that Rawls has offered an argument that has nothing to say to those who reject liberalism outright, since the theory assumes a pre-existing commitment to liberal pluralism and the institutions of liberal democracy.

Political Liberalism is best seen as seeking to avoid contentious philosophical claims about what is or is not our morally most significant capacity. This is of some significance as liberalism strives to accommodate cultural groups that do not endorse the most self-confident version of liberalism, with its exaltation of individual free choice and autonomy. Groups that find value in the undertaking of traditional roles and responsibilities can feel threatened by a public culture that emphasises the centrality of autonomous choice, for they do not regard the value of their traditions as conditional upon those traditions having been endorsed as a matter of free choice. Moreover, such groups will find little to command their allegiance in a version of liberalism that is at odds with their own outlook. It is therefore important to appreciate that Rawls is claiming that the institutions of liberalism need *not* rest upon the assumption that our most important and admirable feature is our capacity to choose our own path in life. In Rawls' opinion, liberalism can ground itself upon the reasonableness of *abstracting* from such differences in outlook. His theory of the veil of ignorance does not implicitly assert the superiority of an autonomous way of life: it asserts the possibility of our reaching agreement once we abstract from all such differences concerning conceptions of the good or comprehensive philosophical viewpoints. Groups wedded to a philosophy of tradition and submission can support the institutions of liberalism once they see that those institutions rest, not on the value of autonomous choice, but on the need for us to abstract from such differences in outlook if we are to find principles of justice that are reasonably acceptable to all.

Commentators sympathetic to communitarianism might at first be pleased by Rawls' apparent concessions to that latter view. This would, however, be a mistake. For Rawls is not in any sense seeking to incorporate the intellectual strengths of those positions that oppose liberalism. His intention is simply to set on one side all difficult philosophical questions, so far as that is possible. He sees his task as the *practical* one of proposing a public conception of justice that people of diverse viewpoints will be able to endorse, and he hopes to show that this can be done without answering any difficult and fundamental philosophical questions. The question can therefore be asked (and has been asked) whether Rawls is still doing philosophy at all, or is simply pursuing a practical political project aimed at addressing and eliciting the support of his fellow citizens, without making any broader claims to truth.

Rawlsian "political liberalism" depends upon a division between the public realm of politics and the constitution, and the private realm within which citizens are free to pursue their own philosophies and conceptions of the good. There is therefore a large and intractable set of questions concerning the viability of such a distinction. Institutions such as the family have a dramatic impact upon the life prospects of individuals, and are therefore rightly regarded as a part of the "basic structure" of society, to which Rawls' theory is intended to apply; yet the family is also thought of as a central feature of the private realm within which people seek their own satisfactions and personal visions of the good life. To prevent the structures of the family from producing injustice in the public realm the state may need to intervene in such private domains: for example, if (within the family) daughters are encouraged to believe that they are less valuable than sons, the result may be adult women who are unwilling to exercise the full powers and rights of citizens. But how can the state address such problems without eroding the capacity of the private realm to sustain comprehensive doctrines distinct from the doctrines of political liberalism?

Selected reading

J. Rawls, *A Theory of Justice*, revised edition (1999).
J. Rawls, *Political Liberalism*, (1993).
J. Rawls, *Justice as Fairness: A Restatement*, (2001).
N. Daniels (Ed.), *Reading Rawls*, (1975): an extremely valuable collection of articles on Rawls.
R. P. Wolff, *Understanding Rawls*, (1977).
S. Mulhall and A. Swift, *Liberals and Communitarians*, second edition, (1996).

Chapter 3

NOZICK

Robert Nozick opens his book *Anarchy, State and Utopia* with a striking assertion. "Individuals have rights," he tells us, "and there are things no person or group may do to them (without violating their rights)." To some this starting point seems extraordinarily arbitrary: still more so when Nozick goes on to spell out the content of the basic rights that he has in mind. "How do we know that individuals have rights?" such critics ask, "And how can we establish the content of any such rights?". Nozick seems on the face of things to offer no argument for the sweeping propositions from which his theory proceeds.

In fact, as we shall see, Nozick's starting point is undeveloped, but considerably less arbitrary than it might at first appear to be. Before we turn to such matters, however, it will be helpful to sketch the path that his theory follows from its initial assertion.

Many political philosophers have placed questions about the justification of the state at the heart of their inquiry; but, in the middle decades of the twentieth century, philosophers tended to assume the existence of a legitimate and justified state as the background for their reflections upon distributive justice. Nozick restores the question of the state's legitimacy to a central position within the discipline. This is because he perceives that inviolable individual rights might seem to render *any* state illegitimate: the belief that individuals have such rights might contradict the belief that states may be legitimate. States claim a monopoly on the use of force: the state may use force and coercion in the enforcement of its laws, but similar force or coercion engaged in by citizens would constitute a crime. Perhaps the enforcement of that monopolistic claim is itself a violation of individual rights.

In the first third of *Anarchy, State and Utopia* (which will not be examined in this chapter) Nozick addresses this question concerning the state's legitimacy. He argues that the existence of individual rights is compatible with the existence of the state: rights do not require anarchy, for a minimal state, aimed at the protection of property rights and the prohibition of force and fraud, could arise without any violation of individual rights. The upshot of the first part of the book is that the minimal or "night-watchman" state is justified: the state may prohibit the use of force and fraud, may protect property rights, and may enforce contracts. In the second part of the book (which will concern us in the present chapter) Nozick goes on to argue that no state *more* extensive than the night-watchman state can be justified: in particular, the state is not justified in redistributing wealth or other resources in order to achieve some favoured share-out, whether that be an egalitarian or a meritocratic one. Resources should be distributed by the operation of a free market: the resulting distribution is just if it results from a series of voluntary transfers of legitimate entitlements.

The argument leading to this conclusion has a remarkably simple structure, which can be briefly outlined. Nozick tells us that each person has a basic right of exclusive self-ownership. That is to say, each person is the owner of him or herself and cannot be used (without consent) for the purposes of others, no matter how admirable or worthy those purposes might be. Self-ownership gives rise to property rights in other resources by individuals "mixing their labour" with unowned resources. If I am the exclusive owner of myself, I am the exclusive owner of my own labour; by mixing that which I own (my labour) with an unowned resource, I can acquire ownership of that resource. Having acquired such ownership, I can transfer the resource to others, who thereby acquire ownership in turn. Hence, the justice of a distribution of resources depends upon the series of transactions by which it came about: if each step in the process was just, the resulting distribution must be just, regardless of where the resources have ended up. A series of individually just transfers might result in a few people owning the great bulk of the resources, while the majority of people have very little. Given a just history, however, the inequality of such a resulting distribution would not amount to an injustice.

Theories of social justice often seem to imagine that the total wealth of society can be regarded as a cake and the problem of justice can be seen as a question about how the cake should be divided up. It is not surprising, in view of this approach, that equal distribution has strong supporters, with distribution according to need coming a close second. Some theories emphasise that the way the cake is distributed will affect the size of future cakes, while other theories play down this fact. In Nozick's view, the whole approach is misguided. There is no one who is entitled to treat society's total wealth as a cake to be divided up as we please. Much of the the wealth is brought into existence by individuals, and (Nozick argues) they already have rights attaching to it.

Understanding the general drift of this set of claims is a relatively simple matter; evaluating the soundness of the various steps in the argument is more difficult. We must begin with the most problematic step of all: Nozick's basic theory of rights.

AN ARBITRARY STARTING POINT?

The most common objection to Nozick's theory insists that his starting point is arbitrary, and therefore his entire theory is devoid of merit. We must, however, be careful to identify the precise nature of the alleged arbitrariness. Some commentators appear to object to the ungrounded assertion that individuals have rights; while others accept that individuals have rights, but object to Nozick's particular choice of rights.

When Rawls began to develop his theory in the 1950s, utilitarianism was still very influential; but, by the time Nozick produced *Anarchy, State and Utopia* in 1974, utilitarianism was deeply unpopular. Criticisms of utilitarianism tended to centre upon the objection that an act might lead to an increase in overall welfare (and so be prescribed by the principle of utility) even though it involved the infliction of serious harm upon particular individuals. It was thought that there *must* be limits to what might justifiably be done to innocent individuals, even in the name of the general welfare; and this sense of there being inviolable limits to what may permissibly be done was frequently articulated as the idea that individuals have certain basic *rights*.

When Nozick opens his book with the assertion that people have rights, he has in mind this general background of the rejection of utilitarianism. He is himself a critic of utilitarianism; and he takes the rejection of utilitarianism to be amply justified, for reasons that he develops in the early part of his book. If we reject utilitarianism partly because we believe that there are limits to what may justifiably be done to individuals in the name of the general welfare, then we are likely to believe that "Individuals have rights, and there are things no person or group may do to them (without violating their rights)."

This does not, however, explain how Nozick comes to choose the rights that in fact form the basis of his theory. In particular, the fundamental right from which all else follows in Nozick's argument is the right of self-ownership: each person is the exclusive owner of himself, his body and his labour. Why, we may ask, is *this* our fundamental right? Why not a right to a basic level of welfare, or to a degree of equality?

Nozick's argument at this point is not easy to reconstruct with confidence; but it seems to run along the following lines. He distinguishes two ways in which rights might feature in a moral theory: rights could be conceived of as "goals" or as "side-constraints". As an example, consider a right not to be intentionally killed. If rights are conceived of as goals, the right not to be intentionally killed would require us to strive for a state of affairs where the overall number of intentional killings is reduced. When thought of as a goal, such a right would not prohibit (indeed, it might prescribe) the intentional killing of one person in order to reduce the number of intentional killings overall. The concept of "a right" features here as a way of characterising the state of affairs that we are trying to achieve by our actions.

When, by contrast, rights are thought of as side-constraints, they do not require us to pursue any particular state of affairs, but remove certain options from the repertoire of actions that we have legitimately available to us. If, for example, the right not to be intentionally killed is conceived of as a side-constraint, it requires us at all costs to avoid intentional killing, even if our failure intentionally to kill one person may result in more intentional killings overall: rights on this model constrain our ability to pursue whatever goal we are pursuing, be that goal good or bad.

Suppose, for example, that you are the Minister of Justice in a country that has recently been plagued by violent street assaults, some of which have resulted in death. So far, none of the perpetrators have been caught, and the evidence suggests that more and more people are taking to such street crimes, encouraged by the manifest impotence of the police and the criminal justice system. By selecting one innocent citizen, then framing, convicting and executing him, you might bring a halt to the rising tide of street killings: although killing someone yourself, you would minimise the number of killings overall. If rights are goals, you might consider such a course of action, for the overall number of rights-violations would thereby be reduced. If, on the other hand, rights are side-constraints, you could not contemplate such an action: for you would regard the right not to be intentionally killed as absolutely prohibiting your killing of an innocent person, regardless of the goal you hoped to achieve by the killing.[1]

If rights are viewed as goals rather than side-constraints, it seems, all of the main problems of utilitarianism (such as its willingness to sacrifice individuals for the "greater good") are reproduced: one has, in effect, a utilitarianism of rights. If we reject utilitarianism, therefore, we should regard rights as side-constraints. Yet, if rights are side-constraints, they have the effect of sometimes prohibiting us from performing actions that would save lives on balance or serve the greater good in other ways. So our belief in rights as side-constraints demands an explanation.

In explanation of the status of rights as side-constraints, Nozick points out that we attach central moral importance to our capacity to lead our own lives according to some overall conception of the life we wish to lead. What matters to us is not simply that we should have good experiences, nor that we should have at any particular moment the freedom to choose between different options. We also want to lead a life that has some overall coherence, and that we consider to be valuable and worthwhile. This we can do only to the extent that we are not used as instrumentalities in the projects of others. Hence, our basic rights are rights not to be interfered with: rights of exclusive control over ourselves; in short, rights of self-owner-ship. It is because each of us is the exclusive owner of himself that we cannot be used for the purposes of others or of the collectivity, no matter how worthy those purposes may be. The notion of the right of exclusive self-ownership is therefore offered as a plausible way of elucidating the status of rights as side-constraints. Nozick argues from the rejection of utilitarian-ism to the idea of rights as side-constraints; and from the formal idea of rights as side-constraints to the substantive idea that our basic right is a right of exclusive self-ownership.

Nozick's argument here is loosely structured, but not devoid of merit. Those who accuse him of proceeding from an arbitrary starting point appear to have missed the point.

---

[1] Nozick allows exceptions in situations where the consequences of respecting the right may be "catastrophic". I do not propose to discuss this qualification, although it could represent a serious dilution of the theory.

COMPARISON WITH RAWLS

It will be recalled that Rawls mounted certain criticisms of utilitarianism, and Nozick's argument for the basic right of self-ownership is not unrelated to those criticisms. Rawls attacked utilitarianism for (i) ignoring the distinctness of persons by treating the losses accruing to one person as compensated by the gains flowing to another; and (ii) for giving priority to the good over the right, by defining justice as the maximisation of good consequences. An adequate theory of justice, Rawls argued, should work out principles of justice (of "right") that do not simply trade-off losses and gains in the service of aggregate welfare, and that do not rely upon any particular conception of the good.

Nozick shares with Rawls a desire for a theory of justice that rests upon no particular conception of the good, and the idea of exclusive self-ownership seems on the face of things one possible way in which we might seek to construct such a theory: self-owners would be entitled to pursue whatever conception of the good they chose, provided only that their pursuit of that conception respected as side-constraints the rights of self-ownership possessed by others. The intuitive idea behind such an approach is that we might be able to construct principles derived from the notion of self-ownership, and demarcating domains of liberty within which people are free to choose and pursue their own notions of the good. Conduct would then be constrained only when it threatened to encroach upon the similar domains of entitlement enjoyed by others. In this way, Nozick might hope to avoid many of the problems associated with Rawls' "thin theory of the good", and with his selection of particular liberties for protection under the first principle (aspects of Rawls' theory that are hard to reconcile with his claim to develop his principles of justice independently of any conception of the good).

The idea of the distinctness of persons leads Rawls to reject the straight trade-offs of utilitarianism: one person's losses cannot be compensated by another's gains. Yet perhaps Rawls' theory does not depart as dramatically as one might assume from the utilitarian calculus: concern for the general welfare is abandoned in favour of concern for the "least advantaged", but losses imposed upon the better-off will nevertheless be justified when they improve (or do not diminish) the primary social goods of the least advantaged. There might therefore seem to be a sense in which Rawls continues the utilitarian practice of licensing trade-offs: he simply judges those trade-offs from a different perspective. Indeed, because he believes that justice should seek to correct the social inequalities stemming from the arbitrary natural distribution of talents and abilities, Rawls invites us to regard such natural talents as resources to be exploited for the benefit of everyone. This, in effect, gives persons rights in other persons, and seems a direct violation of the notion of "distinctness".[2] Nozick, by contrast, builds upon the distinctness of persons in a very straightforward way: each person is distinct in so far as each person is the exclusive owner of himself, and has no rights in other persons. No trade-offs at all are permitted in this theory of justice: the question is always solely one of whether your action has impinged upon my rights of self-ownership.

PRINCIPLES OF ACQUISITION

Nozick's theory is grounded in the right of self-ownership. But how does he pass from self-ownership to ownership of external resources? Nozick holds that an adequate theory of justice would include "principles of acquisition" that determine how one may acquire ownership of an unowned resource. This is done by mixing one's labour with the resource. As exclusive owner of myself, I own my own labour; if I mix my labour with an unowned object, I acquire a property right in the object. Having acquired ownership of the object, I can transfer the ownership to someone else. Property is justly held when it was acquired in accordance with the principles of acquisition and of transfer.

Nozick himself acknowledges some of the difficulties in his argument about the mixing of labour. For example, he notes that, if I spill my can of tomato juice into the sea, I have not acquired ownership of the sea, but have lost my tomato juice: so why should mixing one's labour be any different? When I mix my labour with an unowned resource, why do I acquire the resource? Why have I not just wasted my labour?

John Locke (the seventeenth-century philosopher from whom

---

2   Appearances may be misleading. Rawls' assertion of "the distinctness of persons" is probably not intended to condemn all trade-offs between the interests of persons, but to assert the importance of distributive issues, as against the utilitarian's exclusive focus upon aggregates.

Nozick borrows much of his argument) added a proviso that there must be "enough and as good left over for others" before I can acquire ownership of an unowned resource. Locke's proviso helps to overcome some of the difficulties that Nozick perceives. Suppose that I hunt and kill a deer in the wilderness. If there are "enough and as good" deer left over for you to hunt, but instead you appropriate the deer that I have killed, you are, in substance, appropriating of my labour. For the only difference between *this* deer and those remaining in the wilderness is that I have "mixed my labour" with this one. In choosing to take this one rather than hunt one down for yourself you take the benefit of my hard work.

Nozick sees a problem with Locke's proviso, however. Suppose there is only one deer left in the wood. Then I cannot acquire ownership of it, because I will not be leaving "enough and as good" for others; but then (Nozick thinks) it follows that I cannot acquire ownership of the penultimate deer either, for my appropriation of that deer would not leave any deer available for appropriation (the last deer not being open to appropriation). If, however, I cannot acquire the penultimate deer, I cannot acquire any deer at all, for the argument will "zip back" to encompass every single deer (if you do not see why, think about it!).[3]

In consequence of this argument, Nozick adopts a weakened version of the "Lockean proviso". He reconstrues the proviso to require that my acquisition must not make others worse off than they would have been in a state of nature devoid of any property rights at all. Nozick assumes that private property and the market will be far more productive than would a simple economy based on the common exploitation of unowned natural resources. Consequently, it will be rare for acquisition of property to make others worse-off than they would have been in such a state of nature. It will not, however, be impossible: thus I could not acquire ownership of the only waterhole in a desert,

---

[3]   The argument may founder on the difference between claiming exclusive rights in the deer, and simply using it (by consuming it): appropriation of the penultimate deer leaves one left for consumption, even though one could not acquire ownership in it. As an *ad hominem* argument against Locke, however, the argument works, because Locke is himself guilty of confounding the appropriation of a resource by consumption with the claim to exclusive rights in that resource.

For an incisive analysis of Locke's argument, see M. Kramer, *John Locke and the Origins of Private Property* (Cambridge, 1997)

and claim to exclude from access to the water supply the other inhabitants of the desert.

The difficulty with this revised version of the proviso is that it undercuts Locke's basis for treating the "mixing of labour" as the acquisition of a resource, rather than the simple expenditure of labour. We can no longer say that in taking the deer that I have killed you simply steal my labour: for (under Nozick's version of the proviso) there may be no other deer left for you to take from the wilderness.

We might ask why the mixing of labour gives one ownership of the *whole* resource, rather than just the value added by one's labour. For example, oil and gas (being scarce resources) have an economic value while they are still in the sea-bed. Before they can be utilised, however, they must be raised to the surface, and this involves labour. If I expend my labour in extracting the oil and gas, I may be entitled to the full value of my labour. But why should I be entitled to the full value of the oil and gas, including the value that they had simply as scarce resources and quite independently of my labour? Nozick suggests that wealth should not be regarded as a big cake to be divided up: wealth is brought into existence by the efforts of individuals. But this is not true of natural resources: they simply exist and are not brought into existence by anyone. Of course, individual labour may be necessary before the resources can be used, but I am not denying that individuals are entitled to the value of labour expended. There is no reason why their labour should give them an exclusive right in resources that they did not produce (from a utilitarian point of view, such a right in resources might be offered as an incentive to useful effort: but an argument of this sort is clearly not available to Nozick). Thus it may be that Nozick's argument goes astray at this point and that, from his basic premises, he should have reached different conclusions. Maybe he should advocate something like a resources tax which would tax people on the basis of the quantity of natural resources that they are consuming. The proceeds of such a tax might be distributed equally, on the basis that no one can have a better right than anyone else to natural resources. Indeed, redistribution should operate globally, with the developed world compensating the undeveloped world for their consumption of resources to which the undeveloped world is equally entitled.

Perhaps, then, a person may have an absolute right to his labour and to the value that his labour has added to an object, but not an absolute right to the whole object. This is because natural resources are not brought into existence by anyone, and there is no reason why any person should have a greater right to them than another person. But if this argument applies to natural resources, would it not also apply to natural talents and abilities? They are not possessed by an individual as a result of any labour on his part, but are the result of a natural distribution which is arbitrary from a moral point of view. And is this not Rawls' point in arguing that natural talents and abilities should be regarded as resources to be exploited for the benefit of people generally, and not just for the benefit of the person who possesses the talent or ability?

One response to this argument might be that our basic premise is the distinctness of persons, and the idea that personal abilities are common resources directly contradicts that premise. We might feel that it is possible to draw a distinction between those things which are part of or an aspect of the person, and those things that the person possesses "externally": things that he uses but which are not part of him. Natural resources would fall into the latter category and natural abilities into the former. The basic idea of an exclusive right in oneself and in one's labour is itself a right in something that one has not brought into existence. An exclusive right in one's labour must necessarily entail an exclusive right in one's own ability; but, as we have seen, it does not entail an unrestricted right to appropriate the whole value of natural resources.

PALE SELF-OWNERSHIP

We noted above that natural resources are not themselves brought into existence by the expenditure of labour, but pre-exist the acquisition of individual property rights. Is Nozick right to treat such resources as unowned prior to their private acquisition? Or should they rather be treated as jointly-owned by everyone, so that they could be legitimately exploited only with everyone's consent?

G.A. Cohen has developed a large number of challenging criticisms of Nozick in his book *Self-Ownership, Freedom and Equality*.[4] One of his most interesting criticisms builds upon the idea that natural resources might be owned jointly, rather than

---

[4]   G.A. Cohen, *Self-Ownership, Freedom and Equality* (Cambridge, 1995).

being unowned, and it is therefore convenient to examine the argument here. If we were joint-owners of the world's natural resources, we might prohibit the appropriation of individual chunks of those resources, thereby preventing individual ownership from legitimately arising in the first place. So what justification has Nozick for his assumption that natural resources, prior to such acts of appropriation, are unowned?

Somewhat surprisingly, Nozick does not himself address this problem. However, Cohen suggests that, in reply, Nozick would point out that the utilisation of any resource would be impossible if one were to require the consent of every other human being before the resource could be legitimately used. Hence, joint ownership of natural resources would render individual self-ownership empty and formal: since all exercises of freedom demand the use of some objects or spaces, joint ownership of natural resources would mean that freedom could not be exercised without the consent of everyone else. If self-ownership is to be a substantial reality, therefore, natural resources (prior to individual acquisition) must be unowned.

Having provided Nozick with this seemingly effective response, Cohen goes on to criticise it. He argues that such a reply would contradict other claims that Nozick needs to make if he is to defend the night-watchman state and the free market. To see this point, we should reflect that the empty and formal type of self-ownership that exists in the world of jointly owned natural resources closely resembles the self-ownership of propertyless proletarians in the capitalist society of the Nozickean night-watchman state.

It would be perfectly possible for some people to wind-up, in Nozick's state, owning nothing except their own bodies (and their own labour). Whether or not such a situation was just would depend, for Nozick, on how it had come about: and it might well be the result of a series of freely consented to market transactions. Proletarians who own nothing but their labour are (Cohen argues) in effectively the same situation as individuals in the world of jointly owned natural resources: they would need to obtain the consent of other people (the owners of resources) before they could do anything.

In relation to the propertyless proletarians, Nozick would presumably wish to claim that the existence of such a state of affairs would not show that the rights to self-ownership of the proletarians had been violated or rendered unreal. Thus, he might point out that, while proletarians who own no external resources are in an unfortunate position, they still possess rights (to their own bodies and labour), and those rights have not been violated.

Cohen argues that Nozick cannot have it both ways. If the ownership of resources by the capitalist class is not incompatible with the proletarian's basic right of self-ownership, then that same basic right cannot rule out the joint ownership of natural resources. Nozick must either concede that there is no ground for treating natural resources as unowned (rather than jointly owned) or he must concede that capitalism is incompatible with the rights of self-ownership of proletarians.

Two problems can be identified in Cohen's argument. In the first place, the propertyless proletarian is not quite as badly placed as persons in a state of nature where natural resources are jointly owned. In the latter situation, one would have to get the consent of everyone else in the world before one could use anything at all; since this would obviously be impossible, one could never do anything without encroaching upon the joint rights of all others. The propertyless proletarian, however, only needs the consent of some individual owner of property: this need not be difficult to obtain, but will in any case not be in principle impossible to obtain.

Secondly, even if the rights of self-ownership of the proletarian are, in some sense, rendered empty and formal by the property rights of others, there still seems to be a difference between this situation and the envisaged state of nature with equal ownership of natural resources. We need to distinguish between rights that are, in essence and in origin, devoid of real content (empty and formal) and rights that are rendered empty and formal by possible future develoments. The circumstances of the proper-tyless proletarian are such that his rights have been rendered empty and formal by the contingent outcome of the market; but it does not follow from this that his rights have been *violated*. To treat natural resources as jointly owned, on the other hand, would build emptiness and formality into the very foundations of the theory. Rights that have, in principle, a genuine content can be robbed of that content without the rights being violated; rights that are defined from the outset in such a way that they lack content are not genuine rights. Hence, Nozick might well be able to reject the joint ownership of natural resources (by claiming that it would rob self-ownership of content) while nevertheless denying that the proletarian's rights have been infringed.

We must also remember the "proviso" that Nozick views as limiting the legitimacy of acquisitions of ownership in formerly unowned resources. If the proletarian's rights of self-ownership are rendered empty and formal by the acquisition of private property, has the proletarian not been made worse-off than he would have been in a state of nature where no private property existed?

PATTERNED DISTRIBUTION AND HISTORICAL ENTITLEMENT

Popular political discussions very often assume that it is possible and desirable for the law to foster both liberty and equality. It is assumed that we can be made more free and that, at the same time, a more equal distribution of resources can be achieved. In fact one of the long-running disputes of modern political theory concerns the relationship between liberty and equality and the question of whether they are indeed compatible.

Nozick argues that any attempt to maintain an equal or near equal distribution of resources will demand constant interference with liberty. He asks us to imagine that we have, at long last, been able to achieve an equal distribution of wealth and resources in our society. What will be the result? Inevitably people will begin trading and making contracts with each other. Very soon, their transactions will upset the originally equal distribution of wealth. If, for example, a very large number of people like to hear X sing, they may be prepared to pay a small sum to attend her concerts, or to purchase her records. The result will be that X soon has a lot more money than many other people who do not have such a fine singing voice, or other marketable talents. The transactions through which X makes this money are individually fair and freely entered into, but they have the effect of bringing about an unequal distribution of wealth. If we wish to maintain an equal distribution, we will have to interfere with such free and fair transactions.

It is not only the strict egalitarian who, in Nozick's view, will have to embark on such constant interference with liberty: the same applies to anyone who holds what Nozick calls a "patterned" conception of justice. A "patterned" conception of justice views justice as a matter of the pattern of distribution which *results* from transactions, rather than being a matter of the voluntary nature of the transactions themselves. Thus "distribution according to need", "distribution according to intelligence", and "equal distribution", would all be patterned conceptions of justice: they judge the justice of a situation by where the resources end up. Against such conceptions of justice, Nozick presents a "historical entitlement" view of justice. According to this view, the justice of a distribution of goods should be assessed not by where the goods end up, but by how the distribution came about. If it came about entirely as a result of transactions which were freely entered into, and without the use of force or fraud, then it is a fair distribution.

Nozick does not present a fully developed version of the historical entitlement theory of justice. Rather, he tells us what the general features of such a theory would be. The theory would consist of three sets of principles: principles of acquisition, of transfer, and of rectification. Principles of acquisition determine the circumstances in which someone can acquire ownership of formerly unowned resources. Principles of transfer determine the way in which the ownership of resources may be transferred from one person to another. Principles of rectification determine what should be done to rectify a distribution that is unjust in terms of the first two principles, *e.g.* what should be done when property has been acquired by fraud.

The argument that patterned conceptions of justice conflict with liberty is somewhat less convincing than it might seem at first glance. It leaves out of account the fact that enforcing a system of property rights *also* encroaches upon liberty: in this case, the liberty of the non-owners who are now prohibited from occupying and using objects and spaces that might, in the absence of property rights, have been available to them. It may therefore be wrong to conceive of the debate concerning the redistribution of wealth as a debate between the competing values of liberty and equality. Liberty figures on both sides of the argument because, by ensuring that property is distributed more equally, one ensures that the freedom to use objects and spaces (together with the corresponding prohibitions) is itself distributed more equally: one restricts the freedom of some in order to increase that of others.

Nozick might respond by saying that liberty is to be *defined* by reference to one's rights. Hence, when we enforce the rights of an owner, we encroach on no one's liberty; whereas, when we prohibit the owner from tranferring his property, we restrict the liberty of the owner. The trouble with this argument is that it simply assumes the accuracy of Nozick's account of "rights". Certainly, if people have just those rights that Nozick ascribes to them, the attempt to maintain a patterned distribution will encroach upon liberty (in that it will encroach upon rights): but this is surely obvious. If, on the other hand, Nozick is wrong about the content of people's rights, it may be that owners do not have an unrestricted entitlement to transfer property, and in prohibiting them from doing so we will not (if "liberty" is defined by reference to "rights") be restricting their liberty.

Fortunately for Nozick, his claim that interference with liberty is inherent in patterned theories may be abandoned without serious loss. The real nub of his argument at this point lies in the exposure of an apparent anomaly in the patterned view of justice.

Suppose that we believe in equal distribution. We will then consider Distribution 1 to be just, and Distribution 2 to be unjust:

(Persons)	A	B	C	D	E	F
Distribution 1:	100	100	100	100	100	100
Distribution 2:	98	98	98	98	98	110

But Distribution 2 may have come about as the result of voluntary exchanges from the starting point of Distribution 1. If Distribution 1 was just, how can Distribution 2 be unjust? What acts of injustice are involved in the transition from 1 to 2? The defenders of patterned theories have a limited number of options available at this point. They can (i) deny that Distribution 2 is unjust; or (ii) identify some unjust steps leading from Distribution 1 to Distribution 2; or (iii) claim that unjust distributions can arise from just ones without any unjust steps. Which option would you plump for?

MARKETS AND EQUALITY

Is Nozick correct when he claims that market transactions will inevitably upset any patterned distribution, such as an equal distribution? So long as we focus our attention on money, and physical resources, Nozick's claim would seem to be obviously true. But there is no reason why an egalitarian should disregard other resources such as spare time, entertainment and travel. Once we do take account of this wider range of "goods", transactions on the free market may very often be regarded as preserving rather than upsetting equality. Suppose that, in a certain community, individuals all have an equal amount of money on January 1. On January 2 many of them attend pop concerts, theatres and football matches, paying a small admission price in order to do so. The result is that the pop stars, theatre companies and football clubs have more money and the audiences have less money than they had on January 1. An inequality of monetary wealth has been produced. Should an egalitarian set about rectifying this inequality by redistributing the money? Before he does so, he should reflect that the people who attended the concerts, shows and football matches must have considered the opportunity of attending to be worth the admission price: otherwise they would not have gone. So, in terms of their own evaluations, they were no worse-off (except in purely monetary terms) as a result of attending. If we make the highly artificial assumption of perfect competition in the market, we can also say that the admission price for each is based on the lowest margin of profit for which the performers will be prepared to perform: if the price was any lower, fewer shows and matches would take place. On these assumptions it can be seen that any redistribution of money would not rectify an inequality but produce one. The audiences would have had the benefit of the entertainment, and would get their money (which they were happy to spend) returned. The performers, who were prepared to work only for a financial return of a certain size, will have laboured without reward.

The example proceeds on the basis of very simplistic and unrealistic assumptions. Nevertheless, it should demonstrate the point that mere differences in monetary wealth do not always represent an inequality in resources: to rectify a monetary inequality can be to produce an inequality at the more fundamental level of resources. If, for example, I like fast cars and lots of cash and am prepared to work for them, and you like lots of spare time and are prepared to make do with less money, the difference in our incomes is likely to reflect differing tastes, rather than anything else. We may both be getting what we want out of life; we may both have an equally high level of welfare, if that is judged in terms of how far we are getting what we want; and, if leisure time may be regarded as a resource, we may have equal resources, since my greater income will be matched by your greater leisure. An egalitarian who focuses solely on money and sets about taxing me and benefiting you, is making us unequal. You are now getting the spare time and the money, while I am having to work hard to get the cash that I want, whilst also having to get the cash that benefits you.

Notice also that this crude monetary egalitarianism discriminates unfairly between different conceptions of a good life. The chap who likes leisure time and little money does very nicely thank you: the chap who likes money and fast cars has to work much harder than would otherwise be necessary.

Nevertheless, it is only within very narrow constraints and on rather artificial assumptions that the market can be regarded as equality-preserving. Differences in monetary income do not always (or even largely) reflect differing preferences between, for example, leisure and cash: to a considerable extent they reflect the accident of social circumstance and differences in ability. Both of these factors, as Rawls emphasises, are arbitrary from a moral point of view. So there is little doubt that a concern with equality (of resources or of welfare) will demand extensive interference with market transactions (in the sense that taxation will be necessary) and to that extent Nozick's objections to such "patterned" theories of justice are relevant.

We should be careful to note (on the other side of the coin) that the egalitarian has good reasons for being concerned to preserve the operation of the market, within limits. Only through the market can differing wants and preferences be co-ordinated, so that equal concern and respect for such differing wants demands preservation of free market transactions. The market in commodities and in labour enables us to choose between different packages of resources and different lifestyles, and if we could not make those choices we would be treated as equals only in a Procrustean sense.

It should be noted that Rawls' own theory carefully provides for the operation, within limits, of market transactions. His two principles of justice are intended to apply only to what he calls the "basic structure" of society. By this he means the major institutions such as property rights, the constitution, the market and the family. Within the framework of the basic structure, particular distributions of wealth are not to be judged by reference to the two principles of justice, but by reference to criteria of procedural justice. The basic structure is to be judged by (*inter alia*) its tendency to produce, over the long-run, distributions satisfying the difference principle. Particular distributions are to be judged by their compliance with the laws and practices resulting from a just basic structure. This seems to represent an acknowledgment, by Rawls, that even a patterned theory of justice must respect within limits the moral importance of market transactions.

GIVING CONTENT TO RIGHTS

Theories that give priority to "the right" over "the good" (such as those of Rawls and Nozick) seek to establish principles of justice without reliance upon particular conceptions of excellence. This is a difficult trick to pull off. We saw in discussing Rawls, for example, that his first principle of justice protects, not liberty in general, but certain specific liberties. Yet how does he select some liberties rather than others for protection under the first principle? It is hard to see how this can be done without assuming that some liberties are more *important* than others: that the exercise of some liberties forms a central element in excellent or admirable ways of life.

Similarly, Kant placed the notion of "equal freedom" at the centre of his account of justice, hoping in this way to secure the priority of "the right" over "the good". Rather than taking justice to concern the virtue or worthiness of conduct, he took it to concern the impact that one person's conduct may have upon the freedom of others: one might be justly entitled to perform acts that are demeaning or unworthy, if those acts do not impact significantly upon others; and one might be prohibited from performing otherwise valuable actions if those actions encroach unreasonably upon the freedom of others. Freedom for Kant could justly be restricted only to maintain equal freedom. Yet how can freedom be measured? How can we say whether my trumpet playing interferes with your freedom to study more or less than a prohibition upon such noise would interfere with my freedom? There is no way of measuring the extent of freedom independently of its importance; and the importance of different freedoms can be compared only by judging their significance for different ways of life: important freedoms are those that would figure in what we consider to be valuable or excellent ways of life. When confronted by the clash between freedom to play the trumpet and freedom to study, jazz musicians and studious scholars are likely to reach different conclusions about which set of arrangements will best maintain equal freedom.

Does Nozick overcome some of these problems of indeterminacy by focusing upon *property* rights? Within his theory, rights are basically rights to control the use of certain objects and spaces. I have a right to use my own body, and to use other objects and spaces that I have come to own; and I have no right to use your body, or objects and spaces that you own. At least if we overlook the difficulties in defining the extent of the property that I acquire by the "mixing of labour" (the whole meadow, or just the part I have worked upon?), it might seem that the physical bounds of the relevant objects and spaces therefore help to determine the scope of the relevant rights.

The appearance is, however, misleading. A host of issues remain undetermined by the general idea of a property right. For what, we may ask, is to count as an encroachment upon your property? Physical invasion? Transmission of noise? Of offensive smells? To give precision to the requirements of Nozick's general theory, one would need to resolve a great many such questions, and it is far from clear that the theory provides any intellectual resources by reference to which the issues could be settled. We are left wondering whether, in attempting to determine the precise bounds of his rights, Nozick would not be forced to fall back upon considerations of the general welfare, or the distributive effects of alternative rules. When smoke from X's factory drifts across Y's garden, should we not weigh, against the discomfort caused to Y, all the benefits flowing to the community from X's factory? Or would it be better to compel X to compensate Y, so that the cost of such pollution is "internalised" by the polluter, and duly passed on to those who purchase the products of X's factory? To consider such questions would be to step outside of the framework of historical entitlement theory, and seek to determine the requirements of justice by reference to distributive or aggregative considerations. Yet, if Nozick is to avoid resolving such questions by mere arbitrary fiat, it is hard to see how he can avoid some approach along these lines.

A similar problem of indeterminacy infects Nozick's assumption that property rights are freely transferable. He believes that, if I acquire ownership of a resource, I can transfer the ownership to someone else. But what justifies this assumption? The right of ownership is usually thought of as a complicated bundle of logically separable elements which would normally include a power of transfer. Yet, precisely because the various elements in the bundle are logically separable, ownership does not *entail* the existence of such a power. In any case, the right of exclusive self-ownership is justified (as we saw above) by a set of claims about our non-availability for utilisation in the projects of others. How do we get from that idea to the idea of transferability? Nozick seems to think that the step is easy and inevitable, but the assumption seems to be too glib.

Nozick does not claim to offer a fully developed theory, so it would be foolish to point out the large number of issues that he does not resolve. Indeed, even a very rich and fully articulated theory will generate a host of interpretative problems in the course of its application and implementation. The present objections, however, are rather different. The point is not that Nozick does not provide answers to these questions, but that it is difficult even to imagine answers that would not necessitate a step outside the bounds of Nozick's right-based reasoning. Like the notion of "equal freedom", Nozick's "self-ownership" seems incapable of providing a response to such questions; and conceivable responses seem to require reference to "the good", in the form of issues about welfare or well-being, rather than to "the right", understood as a realm independent of such considerations.

Selected reading

R. Nozick, *Anarchy, State and Utopia* (1974).
J. Paul, *Reading Nozick* (1981): a very useful collection of essays.
G.A. Cohen, *Self-Ownership, Freedom and Equality* (1995).
J. Wolff, *Robert Nozick: Property, Justice and the Minimal State* (1991).
A very different libertarian theory that merits comparison with Nozick's is offered by Hillel Steiner, *An Essay on Rights* (1994).

Chapter 4

FINNIS ON OBJECTIVE GOODS

The various theories that we have examined so far all seek to offer an account of justice that is neutral between different conceptions of a valuable and worthwhile life. The classical political theories offered by the Greeks had treated the nature of the good life as a central and fundamental problem for politics; but modern liberal theories have tended to view justice, the law and the state as ideally constituting a framework within which individuals can pursue their own ideas of a good and worthwhile existence. This is even true of utilitarianism, for, although that theory defines the right in terms of the good, the central value of happiness or welfare is thought of as a catch-all value, sufficiently broad to cover virtually any goal or project that the individual might choose.

Political and jurisprudential theories frequently rest upon deeper philosophical views concerning the nature of reasons for action. We invoke reasons for action when we are trying to decide what to do, when we prescribe the conduct of others, and when we try to explain the conduct of others. Thus a theory of "practical reason" (the term "practical reason" refers to reasons for action, as opposed to reasons for belief) will occupy an unusually fundamental place in the philosophy of human affairs. Much contemporary liberal theory tacitly takes for granted a particular conception of practical reason. In turning to the jurisprudential theories of John Finnis, we will be studying the work of someone who seeks to restore an old and well-established, but somewhat unfashionable, conception of practical reason drawn ultimately from Aristotle and Aquinas. That broadly Aristotelian conception is fundamental to the whole of Finnis's thinking.

One influential way of thinking about practical reason holds that rationality is almost entirely a matter of fitting means to ends in an instrumental manner. This conception of reason is historically associated with the name of David Hume, the eighteenth-century Scottish philosopher. In fact Hume's position is both more radical and more complex than is usually assumed, but there is some truth in the conventional understanding of his theory, and it is that conventional picture that I shall describe as "the Humean conception of reason".

Hume argued that reason cannot tell us what we ought to pursue, but only how to attain ends we have already chosen. Thus reason can tell me that, if I want to keep dry on a rainy day, I ought to carry an umbrella. Reason can also tell me that, if I want to stay fit and healthy, I should avoid getting wet (and so should carry an umbrella, etc). But reason cannot tell me whether fitness and health are things worth pursuing. I simply have to decide for myself what I want: do I want to be healthy, happy, etc? If I should decide that I do not want to be healthy, happy, or even alive, no one can accuse me of being irrational, provided that I am fully informed of the relevant facts and have not based my preferences on false factual beliefs.

Some eighteenth-century writers had argued that reason could demonstrate certain basic moral propositions (such as "promises ought to be kept") to be true. Hume rejected such theories since they relied upon a wildly exaggerated idea of what human reason could achieve. Ultimately, Hume argued, our moral beliefs must be based on preferences, such as the preference for an orderly society where promises are kept and therefore commercial life and material prosperity is possible. Such preferences are themselves neither reasonable nor unreasonable: they are merely given facts of individual psychology or of human nature.

Aristotelians such as Finnis reject the Humean conception of practical reason. Our first task, therefore, is to gain an understanding of their reasons for doing so, and the nature of their own alternative.

GOODS AND DESIRES

The Humean conception of reason holds that every reason for action is related to a desire that the actor has. Reason can only tell us how best to attain the object of our desires. Reason cannot tell us that we ought to desire this or that: from the point of view of reason, one desire is as good as another.

A desire, however, is not a simple psychological fact. There are limits to what will count as an intelligible desire. Once we begin to appreciate those limits, we see the weaknesses of the Humean approach.

Suppose that we met a man who announced that he wanted a saucer of mud. We would be puzzled by such a curious desire, and would no doubt want to know why he wanted a saucer of mud. "Oh, no reason", he might reply, "I just want a saucer of mud." "Well", we could ask, "are you studying mud? Do you want to carry out tests of some sort on the mud?" "No, I'm not interested in mud at all. In fact I find it rather boring." "Do you want to use the mud for something? To make mud-pies, or to fill a hole in the wall?" "No, I've no use for it at all." "Do you find mud pleasing? Do you like the way the light gleams over its surface? Does its smell remind you of seaside holidays?" "No. I've already told you, I just want a saucer of mud. As David Hume has demonstrated, one desire is as good as another from the point of view of reason. No desire can be said to be irrational unless it depends on false factual beliefs, which mine does not. I just want a saucer of mud and that's all there is to it!"

Hume would have to argue here that a desire for a saucer of mud strikes us as odd simply because it is unusual. But we tend to feel that such a desire is not simply unusual: it is unintelligible. The questions that we ask about this strange desire are attempts to understand it; and the questions are in effect trying to discover what it is about mud that makes it desirable. What makes mud a good thing to have? The insistence that one just wants a saucer of mud for no particular reason is an attempt to detach the notion of desire from the ideas of being good and being desirable. For anyone sympathetic to the Humean account, things count as good in so far as they are desired. But the example of the saucer of mud suggests that a desire is unintelligible unless it is related to some objectively good characteristics of the thing desired. The Humean account treats the notion of "desire" as fundamental and as in need of no further explanation. But we can now begin to see that desires may perhaps only make sense by reference to a deeper and more fundamental notion: the idea of objective goods.

The Humean account of practical reason also has difficulty in explaining how we can rationally deliberate on what to do in those very common circumstances where our desires conflict. Suppose, for example, that you would like to have a walk on the beach while the tide is out, but would also like to watch the cricket on T.V.; since going for the walk involves missing the cricket, you are forced to choose. A Humean will probably say that you must reflect upon the *intensity* of your desires, and pursue whichever option you *most* desire to do. The trouble is that, as Hegel points out, a desire has no "measuring rod" in itself, by reference to which intensity can be judged; the Humean account therefore makes our deliberation look like an arbitrary exercise.[1] In reality, when we do try to reflect on what we would most like to do, we do not usually turn our gaze inward to consider our own feelings: rather, we reflect upon circumstances such as the beauty of the afternoon and the emptiness of the beach, the importance of the cricket match and the finely poised state of play. In other words, we find ourselves thinking about the various good properties of the objects desired.

Finnis does not use these particular arguments (though they have a well established place in the literature[2]) but they represent the general strategy of his attack on the Humean conception. An account of practical reason must start, not from desires, but from goods; and, being good independently of desire, such goods will be objective goods.

OBJECTIVE GOODS

It is most important to realise, at this stage, that when we talk about "goods" we do not mean "morally good". Objective goods are not moral values, but things which make life worthwhile; qualities which render activities and forms of life desirable; they are, in Finnis's words, "forms of human flourishing".

It is also important to realise that "objective" here means something like "good independently of desire". An objective good is not an object that you might trip over: it is something that is good, whether or not you desire it. Thus we might say that education is good, and the fact that it is good gives one a reason for desiring it. "Subjective" goods, by contrast, are things that are good only because and in so far as you happen to desire them.

Finnis lists seven basic objective goods: these are life, knowledge, play, aesthetic experience, friendship (or sociability), practical reasonableness and religion. These goods do not form a hierarchy and are all equally fundamental.

How do we know that there are indeed these various objective

---

[1] Hegel, *Philosophy of Right* para. 17.
[2] The "saucer of mud" argument is borrowed from G. E. M. Anscombe, *Intention* (Blackwell Oxford, 1976) pp.70–71. See also Joseph Raz, *Engaging Reason* (Oxford 1999) pp.51–52; Kurt Baier, *The Rational and the Moral Order* (Illinois, 1995) pp.9–13.

goods? Finnis believes that there is no way of deducing the goods from something more fundamental, because they themselves occupy an axiomatic position within our practical reason. Instead, we must reflect carefully upon our own engagements in practical reason, and consider if those engagements are not in fact rendered intelligible by their relatedness to the various objective goods. We must reflect upon our own decisions to do this or that, upon the reasons for action that we offer to other people (*e.g.* "You ought to give up smoking"), and the way in which we explain the actions of other people ("He gave up smoking out of a concern for his health"). We will then see that these invocations of reasons for action are all ultimately related, in one way or another, not to desires, but to the various objective goods.

Finnis claims that the objective goods are self-evident. It is self-evidently true that, for example, knowledge is better than ignorance. This does not mean that it is obvious, or that everyone agrees on the good of knowledge. Rather the objective goods are presupposed by anything that could count as an argument of practical reason. The theoretical inquiries of science presuppose certain principles of theoretical rationality; those principles cannot be demonstrated or proved, for they would be presupposed by anything that could count as a proof. In just the same way one cannot demonstrate that friendship ought to be pursued: for goods such as friendship would be presupposed by any argument that sought to offer reasons for action. To offer someone a reason for action is always to show how the action is related to an objective good. It follows that one cannot offer reasons for pursuing the objective goods: anyone who genuinely cannot grasp the importance that such goods must have for his conduct is simply unreasonable.

In relation to the basic good of knowledge, Finnis offers an additional argument. He claims that the denial that knowledge is a basic good is self-refuting. If I deny that knowledge is good, I must nevertheless believe that my denial is worthwhile. In telling you that knowledge is not good, I must believe that that item of information (*i.e.* that knowledge is not good) is worth having. Thus, in denying that knowledge is good I am also assuming that knowledge is good: my denial is therefore self-refuting.

It is doubtful if this latter argument (on knowledge) is successful. In giving you this or that information I may be committed to the judgment that the information is worth having.

But I am not committed to the judgment that knowledge is an objective good. I may hold that knowledge is valuable only instrumentally, when it helps us attain our other goals without wasted effort. I may consider it worth knowing that knowledge is not in itself an objective good because this will save wasted effort in the acquisition of useless knowledge. In assuming that this item of knowledge is (instrumentally) good I am not committed to the view that all knowledge is in itself good.

Suppose, for example, that I find you memorising car number plates in the street, and getting very anxious because you keep forgetting them. When I ask you why you are doing this, you say it is because knowledge is good in itself, and the knowledge of car number plates is an instance of knowledge. I tell you that knowledge is not good in itself, but only good instrumentally; and that you are wasting your time and suffering much anguish in pursuit of valueless knowledge. In telling you this, I am certainly committed to regarding the information I have given you (namely, that knowledge is not good in itself) as valuable. But I regard it as valuable instrumentally (it saves you from wasting your time): I am not committed to the view that it is good in itself.

GOODS AND HUMAN NATURE

By reflecting upon our own grasp of practical reason, we can arrive at a set of objective goods. Since these goods represent "forms of human flourishing", they could be said to amount to a conception of human nature. One traditional image of natural law theory sees it as attempting to deduce prescriptive conclusions (about what we ought to do) from factual premises about human nature. Such an argument would fall foul of the is/ought distinction which is forever associated with David Hume. According to the is/ought argument, one cannot validly pass from purely descriptive premises to a prescriptive conclusion. Thus, from the premise "all men are sociable" one cannot conclude "you ought to seek society". No description of observable facts about human nature will in itself justify conclusions about right and wrong, good and bad, or what one ought to do.

Finnis maintains that his own argument does not violate the is/ought distinction. He does not deduce his objective goods from any descriptive account of human nature. His argument is quite different, and an altogether more subtle one. We already engage in the practice of practical reason: that is, the business of guiding and explaining action by reference to reasons. By reflecting upon our intuitive grasp of such reasons, we can see that certain "forms of human flourishing" occupy a fundamental position within our appeals to practical reason. Thus, the prescriptive conclusions are not deduced from factual propositions, but are a matter of bringing into full reflective awareness something that we already, in some sense, understand.

Finnis's theory certainly implies or imports an understanding of human nature. But his prescriptive conclusions are not *deduced* from factual generalisations about characteristic patterns of human behaviour or the like. Rather, we arrive at prescriptive conclusions about the goods that we ought to pursue, and at an understanding of our shared human nature, by reflecting upon our own engagements in practical reason.

PRUDENCE AND MORALITY

"Good" in Finnis's theory does not mean "morally good", but something like "well-being" or "flourishing". Neverthless, Finnis hopes to show that morality is ultimately grounded in a concern for the objective goods. How is this transition from "good" to morality to be made?

Even if we accept Finnis's claim that some list of objective goods must form the basis of our conceptions of practical reason, we may still refuse to regard the objective goods as the basis of morality. Suppose that knowledge, play and aesthetic experience are indeed good things that ought to be pursued or participated in. Nevertheless, we may argue, there is no reason why I should be concerned with the enjoyment of these goods by other people: we have reason to pursue these goods for ourselves, but not for others. Yet morality is distinguished from mere prudence by the fact that it is not limited to a concern for self-interest, but is based on generalised concern for others. So how can Finnis's objective goods provide the basis for a theory of morality?

One argument offered by Finnis relies on the notion that friendship is itself an objective good. It is good to have friends and one's life is impoverished if one has no friends. But having a friend is not simply a matter of enjoying someone's company or finding someone amusing. Friendship involves caring about the welfare of the other person for his or her own sake. Thus friendship is an objective good which leads us beyond an exclusive concern with ourselves. The complete egoist who regards all other persons as resources or means to his own satisfaction will lead an impoverished life because he will be incapable of friendship.

The political community is not a relationship between friends, but it is nevertheless analogous in some respects to friendship: both friendship and community are forms of the objective good of sociability. The realisation of this objective good therefore leads us beyond exclusive concern with ourselves and into a concern with community, or the "common good". Life in a community is itself a constituent of the good life (not merely a means to that end) which can be attained only by our concern for the common good.

This line of argument is an attractive and plausible one. Instead of dramatically contrasting moral concern with a concern for one's own well-being, it suggests that a flourishing life requires some degree of concern for others. Some philosophers (such as Kant) would *contrast* prudential concern for one's own well-being with moral concern for others; but they then face the difficulty of explaining why we should be moral: why not simply act selfishly? The classical tradition of Plato and Aristotle, on the other hand, grounds our moral concern for others within our concern for the flourishing of our own life: the immoral person, on this view, leads an impoverished life and fails to secure the goal of a flourishing life. Thus the contrast between prudence and morality is regarded as ultimately insubstantial, in so far as a fully informed prudential concern for one's own flourishing will encompass due concern for the well-being of others.

But does the classical argument go far enough? Could it ever explain why we should feel moral concern for anonymous needy people on a distant continent, for example? Some people (Kantians and some utilitarians) would identify morality with an impartial concern for the whole of humanity (or for all sentient beings). Finnis's argument based on notions of "friendship" and "community" seems to operate by distinguishing between "friends" and "non-friends", members of one's own community, and non-members. This does not seem to get us all the way to impartial moral concern. Is that a defect in the argument?

Finnis does not adhere firmly to the classical view. In an effort to accommodate some element of the notion of moral impartiality, he invokes the good of practical reasonableness. Practical reasonableness structures our pursuit of the other basic goods, requiring us (for example) to formulate a coherent plan of life which intelligently pursues the basic goods, or some range of them. One of the requirements of practical reasonableness (Finnis tells us) is that there should be "no arbitrary preferences amongst persons". This involves accepting that the basic goods are capable of being pursued and enjoyed by any human being and that they are just as good when enjoyed by some other person as when enjoyed by myself.

Finnis here faces a problem that confronts a number of other moral theories, such as utilitarianism. If the welfare of others matters just as much as my own welfare, should I not be ridden with moral concern for others? Should I not be constantly slaving away to improve the position of the poor, the sick, the starving, the underprivileged? But can the prescriptions of morality really be that demanding? One reply is "Yes, of course morality is that demanding. We really should live like that. Of course we all fall short of that ideal standard, but it nevertheless represents what we ought to do." Underneath its appearance of moral stringency, however, this response actually embodies a slack and potentially vicious attitude to morality. For the response accepts too easily and too comfortably the idea of falling short of what morality requires. By happily conceding that morality says we ought to do all sorts of things that we never have done or will do, the response actually undermines the seriousness of morality itself.

Another reply is sometimes offered by utilitarians. Although the welfare of others matters just as much as your own welfare, you may still have reasonable grounds for being mainly concerned with your own welfare. This is because looking after your own welfare may be the most effective way of looking after welfare generally (I know more about myself than about others; I am able to affect the circumstances of my own life more easily than the lives of others; etc). Similarly, the utilitarian may seek to justify the special priority that we tend to give to the interests of friends and family over others: utility will be maximised (it is argued) if the institutions of friendship and family exist; but such institutions can only exist if we exhibit special concern for some above others, since the mainfestation of such special concern is an integral part of the relevant institutions.

As we will see in due course, Finnis rules out the type of "consequentialist" reasoning that the utilitarian here invokes: goods are incommensurable, Finnis claims, and therefore cannot be balanced or maximised. He nevertheless claims that my own well-being is the first claim on my conduct and reasonably so: we have reasonable grounds for self-preference.

How is this possible? How is it possible for everyone's good to count as much as my own, and yet for me to have reasonable grounds for concentrating on my own good? A part of the answer seems to be found in the notion of incommensurability that (in Finnis's opinion) excludes consequentialist reasoning: if goods are wholly incommensurable, perhaps it makes no sense to say that (for example) I could do "more good" helping in the Third World instead of studying jurisprudence in Cambridge. Unqualified reliance on this argument, however, would seem to undercut any basis for impartial concern. Finnis wants to argue that there are limits to reasonable self-preference: a degree of impartiality is required of us. It is fair to say that the pages of Finnis's *Natural Law and Natural Rights* dealing with this topic (pp.107–109; see also p.177, pp.304–305, and p.406) are amongst the most tortured (and also, perhaps, the most suggestive) in the whole book. This is, no doubt, because Finnis is trying to steer something of a middle course between classical and Kantian views concerning the relationship between prudence and morality.

INCOMMENSURABILITY OF GOODS

As we have already mentioned, "practical reasonableness" is itself (according to Finnis) one of the objective goods. Practical reasonableness includes many different aspects and requirements, but one of these is the requirement that we should adopt a coherent plan of life: each of us must lead his or her own life, and this implies a positive role in giving shape or coherence to that life judged as a whole. This requirement of practical reasonableness is one of a number of elements that lends to Finnis's theory a liberal character, in spite of the fact that he does not espouse "neutrality between conceptions of the good". To live fully reasonable lives, we must *lead* our own lives, and not have those lives imposed upon us by authority.

A further dimension is added to this liberal aspect by the claim that the various objective goods are "incommensurable", in the sense that there is no common scale against which they could be measured. We cannot say that a certain incremental gain in friendship compensates (or does not compensate) for a certain loss of aesthetic experience (for example), because there is no scale against which both friendship and aesthetic experience can be measured. It follows from this that there is no single ideal way of life that we should all aim to live, or that the state might aim to impose or encourage. Many quite different lives may all be equally reasonable, for they may combine the various objective goods in diverse ways. At the same time, it does not follow that *any* conceivable life will count as reasonable: if one fails to pursue the objective goods at all (for example) one does not lead a practically reasonable life.

We may agree with Finnis that, if goods are incommensurable, there will be many different equally reasonable lives. He goes on, however, to extract a more questionable conclusion from the premise of incommensurability: he claims that the incommensurability of goods should lead us to reject consequentialism. (For present purposes, "consequentialism" can be treated as an alternative name for "utilitarianism". See Chapter 1).

One might well have expected that a moral philosophy grounded in the notion of "good" would propose that we should seek to maximise "good" consequences. Finnis claims, however, that the injunction to maximise good is meaningless. Goods are incommensurable. There is therefore no common scale on which they can be measured. Because the various goods are incommensurable in this way, the injunction to maximise them simply makes no sense, just as it would make no sense "to try to sum up the quantity of the size of this page, the quantity of the number six, and the quantity of the mass of this book" (p. 115).

Finnis's argument here is not beyond challenge. If the goods are incommensurable, then one clearly cannot add them up to an overall total. Yet the consequentialist injunction to maximise good consequences overall may not be empty or meaningless: it may simply exhibit an acceptable (or even commendable) degree of indeterminacy.

Suppose that we have three "incommensurable" entities: a line, a weight and a two-dimensional figure (let's say, a circle). We are concerned with the length of the line, the weight of the weight, and the area of the circle. These three things are incommensurable: but an injunction to maximise them overall would seem to make good sense. Incommensurability entails, not the emptiness of the maximising injunction, but the fact that a number of different outcomes would all count as complying with the injunction. Thus, in some conceivable situations, I might only be able to increase the length of the line by decreasing the area of the circle; or I might only be able to increase the weight by shortening the line. Since we cannot say (given incommensurability) that any particular gain in one value (length, weight or area) does or does not compensate for a loss in some other value, all outcomes where one value can be increased only by a diminution in another would count as maximising outcomes.

At the same time, not every conceivable situation would count as complying with the injunction to maximise (if this *were* the case, the injunction really would be empty). There might be situations where I could increase the length of the line without any resulting diminution in the weight or the area. If, in such a circumstance, I failed to increase the length of the line, I would be failing to comply with the injunction to maximise.

What follows from this is that the incommensurability of goods does not show consequentialism to be empty or meaningless. Indeed, if we are still inclined to be persuaded by consequentialism, we will be led to the not unattractive conclusion that there are many different sets of social arrangements that count as equally acceptable from a moral perspective, but still some others that count as unacceptable.

Finnis might say that I have begged the question by assuming that we can measure the amount of each individual good as we can measure length, weight and area: but friendship and aesthetic experience (and the other goods) are not even measurable in themselves. Hence the incommensurability of different goods as against each other does not tell the whole story.

This response will not work, however. For the example of line, weight and circle to make sense, we only have to be able to make "ordinal" judgments, not "cardinal" judgments. That is, we need to be able to say whether one line is longer or shorter than another: but we do not need to say *by how much* it is longer. If Finnis is to deny our capacity to make even ordinal judgments within the same good, his entire theory would be problematised. For example, he wishes to claim that one should not perform acts that simply damage or impede the realisation of any of the basic goods: but if we can't say whether the end result of an act is "more" or "less" of any of the goods, it is hard to see how such notions as "damage" and "impede" could have any application.

THE COMMON GOOD

Practical reasonableness allows some degree of self-preference, but also requires that we should be concerned for the common good. But what is "the common good"? Given Finnis's argument on incommensurability and his rejection of consequentialism, he cannot say that "the common good" is the sum total of individual goods. So how should we think of the common good?

Finnis's answer to this question is essentially that the common good consists in the set of conditions which enables the members of a community to exercise practical reasonableness and lead flourishing lives. It is only given certain conditions of co-ordination in human affairs (thereby yielding stability and order) that people can formulate and pursue their personal plans of life in accordance with the requirements of practical reasonableness. The common good (which for Finnis represents the central concern of law and justice) is the total set of conditions which makes such personal plans and projects a possibility. At the same time, the common good is not simply a pre-condition for the pursuit of individual goods. The political community is itself a manifestation of the good of sociability, analogous to friendship: to the extent that one does not live in a community marked by some degree of mutual concern, one's life is impoverished. Consequently, the common good realised in the political community is itself an aspect of human flourishing, and not simply a means to such flourishing.

This conception of the common good has a number of implications. First of all, it entails what Finnis calls the "principle of subsidiarity". This principle affirms that it is the proper function of a community to help individuals to help themselves, and to assist individuals in the pursuit of their projects. The purpose of the political community is to provide the essential pre-conditions for the exercise of reasonable choice by its citizens: its purpose is not to make the basic choices for citizens. Furthermore, Finnis's account of the common good helps to underpin the conclusion that our moral concern for the common good need not be an obsessive concern with how well other people's lives are going, but is primarily a matter of fulfilling one's particular obligations in justice, performing contracts, and so on (p. 305).

LAW

Finnis's notion of the common good also provides the basis for his theory of law's nature. For, if the common good consists primarily in a set of conditions that will enable us to pursue diverse forms of human flourishing, it can be secured only by the institutions of law. To flourish, we must choose and pursue projects, and this requires that we should live in an orderly world where we can form reliable expectations about the conduct of others. Human conduct must therefore be ordered (co-ordinated). Since different forms of ordering might be equally reasonable (the principles of practical reasonableness afford only very general guidance), communities need to establish authoritative mechanisms such as legislatures and courts for deciding upon specific laws to govern conduct. The resulting laws should in general be ascertainable by their source of enactment, so that we can identify the law's content without being forced back into less determinate reflections upon the requirements of morality. We understand the nature of law by understanding how it is the solution to this general problem: law's nature is to be understood by seeing how, in providing such a form of ordering, law serves the common good.

Finnis is, of course, well aware that law can be used as an instrument of oppression, as well as to serve the common good. He claims, however, that law's nature (as a body of authoritative standards) is understood by seeing how, in what he calls its "focal" instances, law does indeed serve the common good. Instances where law is used as an instrument of oppression and injustice are to be understood as degenerate instances of law: we understand them precisely by seeing how they diverge from (while in some respects resembling) the "focal" instances.

HUME'S RETURN?

Not all lives will count as "practically reasonable" for Finnis: one might fail to lead a flourishing life by simply allowing one's capacities to wither, or by spending one's days in a drug-induced stupor. Nevertheless, Finnis may seem to have offered a theory, grounded in an account of the "good", which leads to broadly liberal conclusions while avoiding the problems of emptiness and arbitrariness that could stem from the notion of "neutrality between conceptions of the good". His conception of the common good, with its liberal implications, depends for its coherence on the idea that widely differing plans of life may be equally reasonable. If there was just one correct way of pursuing the various objective goods, then moral concern might well require the enforcement of that one correct way as being "the common good".

The liberal aspect of the theory depends in part upon Finnis's insistence that the capacity of individuals to choose for themselves is itself (under the heading of "practical reason-ableness") an objective good. On its own, however, this claim is not decisive. It is true that people who were simply coerced into conformity would not themselves be leading flourishing lives: for, in being the outcome of coercion, their lives would not be manifestations of the capacities for deliberation and choice that constitute the good of "practical reasonableness". The coercion might nevertheless be justified, however, for it might be said to remove corrupting examples from the visible array of available lifestyles, making it more likely that others will find it natural to choose good and valuable lives.

Finnis therefore needs to reinforce the liberal aspect of his theory by emphasising the great diversity of different lives that may count as equally reasonable.

Some problems emerge, however, when we ask how the choice between different possible lives is to be made. Suppose that I am choosing between various careers. Should I be a lawyer or a scholar? A doctor or an artist? Since the various goods are incommensurable, we cannot say that one or another way of life is "best". But the notion of incommensurability might also suggest that the choice between different projected lives is an arbitrary one that might appropriately be settled by the tossing of a coin. Since we are all confronted by the same range of objective goods, it is hard to see how (given equal opportunity) it might be more reasonable for me to choose one option while you ought to choose another.

Once again we see Finnis trying to steer a difficult middle course here. He does not want to say that, because all the available options are equally reasonable, the choice between them is, for each of us, an arbitrary one: he wishes to preserve the sense that it is a serious choice to be made reflectively and responsibly. On the other hand, he does want to say that you and I may choose quite different things and yet choose fully reasonably.

Finnis's solution to this problem is to say that one must choose a coherent plan of life on the basis of one's capacities, circumstances and tastes. Such a plan of life will involve concentration on some objective goods at the expense of others. Thus (to use Finnis's example) a scholar may have little taste for friendship, and may be completely committed to the search for knowledge: but it would be unreasonable for him to deny that friendship is a good in itself. It is one thing to have no taste for friendship, but it is "another thing, and stupid or arbitrary, to think or speak or act as if these were not real forms of good" (p. 105).

We may agree with Finnis that my capacities are inevitably relevant here. The life of a mathematician may be just as good as the life of a jurisprudential scholar: but there would have been little point in my choosing to be a mathematician, since I do not have the relevant capacities. Surely we do not want to conclude, however, that I must always choose the life for which I have the most appropriate capacities. Does my light bone-structure and slow heartbeat mean that, if I am to be fully practically reasonable, I must become a marathon runner even though I would prefer to be a scholar? May I not choose to be a mediocre scholar instead of a superb marathon runner, and make that choice simply because it reflects my desires?

To concede this point might come close to reintroducing elements of the Humean conception of practical reason within Finnis's theory. Hume holds that we have reason to pursue something (*e.g.* knowledge) only if we desire that thing, or if that thing will assist us in attaining our other desires. The broadly Aristotelian view on which Finnis relies claims that knowledge (for example) is in itself good, and that that in itself gives us a reason to pursue knowledge. We should pursue knowledge because it is good, and not merely because, and in so far as, we desire it.

How then do desires fit into the Aristotelian picture? In some (pathological) cases, they may be simply brute psychological phenomena that provide us with no genuine reason to pursue the desired object: if I find myself suddenly filled with an intense desire to split your head open, I may have reason to see a psychiatrist, but I have no reason to purchase an axe. In other cases, desires may be the manifestation of some simple bodily need: I happen to desire a drink of water. In yet other cases, my desire arises in consequence of recognising the goodness of the object (when you see how interesting jurisprudence is, you will want to know more about it!). The trouble with Finnis's employment of "desire" is that it does not seem to fit comfortably into any of these categories. This complaint, however, perhaps amounts to no more than saying that Finnis has not offered us a fully developed account of practical reason.

JUSTICE

According to Finnis, principles of justice are simply the concrete implications of the general requirement that one should foster the common good in one's community. The common good requires some degree of collaboration and co-ordination of conduct. This means that questions will arise about how the benefits and burdens of communal enterprises should be distributed. Should they be shared out equally, or according to needs and abilities, or according to "merit"? Also, there will be natural resources that are not the exclusive entitlement of any individual: a society must adopt principles governing the distribution of such natural resources, and governing access to, and rights in, communally-owned property.

In addition to such problems of "distributive" justice, there will be problems of justice in the dealings between specific persons, *e.g.* the justice of keeping promises, or of compensating for injuries. These are often called questions of "corrective justice", but Finnis prefers the wider term used by Aquinas: "commutative justice". Because Finnis sees the requirements of justice as simply a matter of fostering the common good, his account of justice is a flexible and pluralistic one. For example, he is not attracted by theories which offer a single principle to regulate all questions of distributive justice: distribute "according to need", or "distribute equally". Considerations of need have, according to Finnis, a certain priority, but other considerations are also very important. Considerations of desert, the functional requirements of one's role, and capacities (*e.g.* higher education for those capable of benefiting from it) are all relevant.

Some theorists draw a very fundamental contrast between distributive justice and commutative (or corrective) justice. On the one hand are theorists who give the central role to commutative justice. Justice for them is primarily a matter of property rights, the keeping of contracts, and the correcting (by punishment or by compensation) of injuries. Questions of distributive justice arise (on this view) only when the owner of some property wishes to distribute it, *e.g.* if I am considering how I should distribute my property amongst my children in making my will. Should I share it out equally, or according to need?

Another approach gives the upper-hand to distributive justice. Here the basic questions of justice concern how the benefits and burdens of social life should be distributed. Once a just distribution is achieved, any upset in the status quo (by theft, or injury, or breach of contract) must be rectified in order to restore the distributively just situation: this is the role of corrective (commutative) justice.

These rival approaches are well represented in different ways of thinking about questions of contract and tort, for example. On the theory which gives the principal role to commutative justice the main point about contract and tort must be that torts and breaches of contract are wrong. As wrongs they should be rectified, by the payment of compensation. The impact that such compensation will have on the way in which wealth is distributed generally is irrelevant. But an increasingly influential way of thinking presents the basic question as one of distributive justice. In tort, for example, the main question is no longer thought to be one of who has wronged whom, but rather it is thought to be a question of who should bear certain risks and responsibilities. The mass production of consumer goods is an enterprise that benefits everyone but which, in various ways, is liable to harm unfortunate individuals. Who should bear the risk of such harm: the producer? the injured parties? everyone (*i.e.* should compensation to injured persons be paid from public revenues, financed out of taxation)? Instead of posing a question of how wrongs should be rectified (commutative justice) we can pose a question of how burdens should be distributed (distributive justice).

Finnis invites us to understand the nature of these debates by viewing the notions of distributive and commutative justice as labels adopted for convenience rather than as fundamentally different conceptions. They simply represent two different aspects of the general problem of fostering the common good.

The basic question is always that of how the common good can best be served. When it is appropriate to think of people as engaged in a common enterprise, it may be appropriate to adopt the perspective of distributive justice. When people are not engaged in any common enterprise, their relationships are a matter of commutative justice. In the law of contract, for example, we may treat the parties as dealing with each other at arm's length, and this approach may encourage us to hold each contracting party strictly to the letter of his promises. But, from another point of view, a commercial contract can be seen as a kind of limited partnership, where the parties undertake shared risks. On the latter approach, when unforeseen circumstances occur which frustrate the common intentions of the parties, the resulting losses should be shared, rather than being borne by one party alone.

BASIC RIGHTS

Finnis regards "the modern language of rights" as "a supple and potentially precise instrument for sorting out and expressing the demands of justice". But he also sees that language as "a hindrance to clear thought" when we are trying to work out what justice requires (p.210). Finnis's theory is centred on notions of the common good, not on individual rights: but because the requirements of the common good are complex, it is useful to be able to report the implications (for specific individuals in specific circumstances) of those requirements in the terminology of rights.

In one important respect, however, Finnis's theory does offer a more direct grounding for fundamental and inviolable rights. This arises from one of the aspects of the requirement of practical reasonableness: the requirement that one must never perform an act that in itself simply harms or impedes the attainment of any one of the basic goods. This prohibition applies even if the act in question will certainly have more remote consequences that will promote or realise the objective goods. Suppose that a madman tells me that, unless I shoot an innocent person, he will shoot 100 innocent persons. Even if I believe him and have good reason to think that, by shooting one person, I could save 100, I should not do the shooting. My act will merely be an act of killing, according to Finnis. Any good consequences that later follow will be realised as the result of other acts subsequent to mine.

This argument is a puzzling one. It presupposes that we have some way of individuating and describing actions independently of our moral judgments. But this is doubtful. If I shoot the innocent man, am I killing one person, or saving 100 ? There seems no reason why I should not say that I both killed one man and saved 100. Someone might emphasise the point that the lives saved are saved by the madman's restraint, not by my intervention. There is some slender basis for this argument in the idea that human interventions are frequently treated by the law as breaking the chain of causal connection (think of the doctrine of *novus actus interveniens* in tort law).

The remote but foreseeable consequences of many of our actions harm basic goods. For example, when we decide to construct a major tunnel or a high-speed railway it may be statistically predictable with a probability approaching one that a certain number of people will die in the course of the new project. Finnis therefore accepts that we may reasonably perform actions and make choices that *indirectly* damage a basic good; what we may *not* do, according to him, is *directly* damage a basic good (p.120). We will see in a moment that the distinction between direct and indirect harms is a problematic one that leads us to a host of difficulties.

Finnis is inclined to invoke his "incommensurability" argument in this context. Thus, he says that the only reason one might offer for performing an act that harms a basic good would consist in the claim that the good consequences of the action outweigh the damage done "in and through the act itself"; but the incommensurability of the goods means that such consequentialist "weighing" of one good against another is senseless (p.118–119).

Here as elsewhere in Finnis's work, one wonders whether his version of the "incommensurability" argument does not threaten rational decision-making as a whole. For, when we are considering building a tunnel, we must surely ask ourselves whether the (almost inevitable) deaths and injuries that will result are really justified by the benefits that the tunnel will yield. If judgments of this sort require a "senseless" form of consequentialist weighing, they must be as unacceptable in the context of indirect harm as they are in the context of direct harm: one cannot use the "senselessness" argument in one context without being committed to its use in the other context also. If incommensurability grounds the prohibition on direct harm, it seems to do so only by ruling out all forms of rational deliberation.

We therefore seem to be led to a dispiriting conclusion about Finnis's argument at this point. In some contexts (where the harm to a basic good is "direct") Finnis seems to want to treat incommensurability as ruling out any comparison of and reasoned choice between consequences; in other contexts (where one is choosing a plan of life; or where the harm to a basic good is indirect) incommensurability does not entail the impossibility of reasoned deliberation, or reduce choice to an arbitrary "plumping" for options. One simply cannot have it both ways, however.

The absence of a common scale by reference to which we can measure distinct values may be conceded. That almost certainly rules out those theories that would propose a more or less mechanical decision procedure for ethics. What is not clear is whether it also rules out all bases for judging between different values. If it does, then rational decision-making seems impossible; if it does not, then some forms of judgment between competing values continue to be perfectly reasonable. What is hard to see is how any of this could turn upon the distinction between "direct" and "indirect" harms.

The theoretical burden borne by the direct/indirect distinction seems to be huge, yet Finnis says remarkably little about it (note, however, the modesty of aim articulated in his Preface to *Natural Law and Natural Rights*). If fully developed, Finnis's argument would probably need to rely upon a distinction between the intended effects of an action, and unintended but foreseen side-effects (p.122). The claim would then be that, where harm to a basic good is a directly intended effect of an action, the action is absolutely prohibited; but where the harm is a foreseen but unintended side-effect, the permissibility of the action depends upon all the circumstances (it is not absolutely prohibited in all circumstances). The doctrine relies upon a very narrow account of "intention": only those consequences that one *desires* (either as an end, or as a means to one's end) count as intended; consequences may be foreseen as certain and yet not be intended if it is not part of the point of my action to bring those consequences about.

Thus, an attack in wartime upon a military target may (in appropriate circumstances) be permissible, even though it is foreseeable that a certain number of innocent civilians will be killed in the course of the attack: here the deaths of the civilians are unintended (although foreseen) side-effects. On the other hand, an attack upon a civilian population would be absolutely prohibited, even if the attack might lead to the surrender of the enemy, thereby shortening the length of the war, reducing the total number of casualties of the war, and defeating an evil enemy. This is because the whole point of an attack upon a civilian population is to kill civilians: if we do not succeed in killing them the attack will have failed in its purpose.

Doctrines of this sort tend to lead to a host of bewilderingly arbitrary distinctions. Thus it is sometimes argued that abortion is absolutely prohibited, even to save the life of the mother, if it can only be performed by killing the foetus: here the death of the foetus is a means to our end (saving the mother's life) and is therefore desired, and so prohibited. Yet if we could save the mother by removing the foetus from her womb, or by removing the entire womb including the foetus, this might be permissible, even if the foetus will inevitably die as a result. For here the death is not intended, but merely foreseen: if by a miracle the foetus were to survive, we would not feel that our project had failed. Pursued to its logical conclusion, this argument may even make the permissibility of abortion depend upon the type of medical technology that is available (much may turn on precisely *how* the foetus is to be removed from the womb). Such a result seems puzzling: surely, we tend to feel, the important issue is the fact that the foetus (or the mother) will in fact die as a result of our performance of (or our failure to perform) the operation. Why should the precise way in which the operation is carried out bear such moral weight?

If you are amongst those who found the last paragraph convincing as an argument against Finnis, ask yourself this question: "If I am not prepared to accept something like the doctrine that Simmonds is attacking, am I saying that any act of any sort may be permissible in certain circumstances? Are there no acts that are absolutely prohibited? Does it follow from that that there are no such things as inviolable human rights?" Whilst we have been very critical of Finnis's position, we should not underestimate the difficulty of the problem. Nor should we fail to applaud Finnis's courage in addressing these critically important issues.

Selected reading

J. Finnis, *Natural Law and Natural Rights* (1980).
J. Finnis, *Fundamentals of Ethics* (1983).
J. Finnis, *Aquinas* (1998).
R. George, *In Defense of Natural Law* (1999).
R. George, *Making Men Moral* (1993).

INTRODUCTION TO PART 2

LAW

We now turn from thinking about the nature of justice to thinking about the nature of law; and in doing so we immediately encounter a difficulty. All educated people are familiar with the idea that disciplined reflection upon justice falls within the province of philosophy; but why should philosophical debate have anything to contribute to a discussion of the nature of law? Is not law a social institution that lies open to inspection? Law is studied by social scientists, historians, and (of course) by doctrinal scholars. Surely, we may think, what can be learnt about law can be learnt from these disciplines: why should the armchair reflections of the philosopher have anything to contribute? How can there be questions about law's nature that are not addressed by the conventional doctrinal study of law, or perhaps by the sociology or history of law?

Needless to say, there are numerous moral issues that arise in the context of law. When these questions are addressed at a certain level of abstraction, they form accepted philosophical topics: Is there an obligation to obey the law? Can punishment be justified? Such questions as these, however, seem to take the *nature* of law for granted: they are questions of applied ethics, rather than questions concerning the nature of law. We are therefore returned to our starting point: how can the philosopher hope to contribute to our understanding of the nature of law something that is not contributed by more familiar forms of legal study?

One part of the answer might be found in the fact that some familiar forms of legal study employ concepts that are taken for granted but never explained. When we do try to explain their significance, we hit problems. Take, for example, the concept of "legal validity". A textbook of tort law tries to state the currently "valid" rules and doctrines of tort law in a particular jurisdiction: but what does "valid" mean here? One might at first think it means something like "applied by the courts", but this would be a mistake: it is conceivable that a rule might be legally valid, and yet be regularly overlooked by the courts (*e.g.* imagine a textbook writer pointing out a statutory provision, the relevance of which has been overlooked by the courts). Could it be that, in describing a rule as "legally valid", we are saying that it *ought* to be applied by the courts? Perhaps; but is the "ought" here a moral "ought"? Many legal theorists would say that there can be valid legal rules that morally *ought not* to be applied, because they are so unjust. We might say that the "ought" means "legally ought", so that a "legally valid" rule is one that the courts "legally ought" to apply. This is rather uninformative, however. To say that I "legally ought" to do something is to say that the act is required by a "valid" legal rule. If we must explain the nature of the "legal ought" by reference to "legal validity", we cannot helpfully explain the nature of "legal validity" by reference to the "legal ought".

It seems, therefore, that familiar forms of legal study may rest upon concepts that they employ but do not explain; when we try to explain those concepts, the task proves to be difficult, and our attempts develop into complex theories of law's nature. We will see in the next chapter, for example, that an adequate explanation of the nature of "legal validity" requires subtle and complex theoretical arguments.

Consider the way in which we speak of law as imposing duties and conferring rights. Does this way of speaking assume that the law is morally binding upon us? Are legal rights a type of moral right (a moral right that we enjoy in consequence of the existence of certain legal rules, for example)? Can a law confer rights and impose duties even if it is unjust? Here is a set of questions that appear to be interesting and important: but one will not find answers to them by consulting your textbook on property or tort law, still less by asking a sociologist or a historian. They are questions concerned with the significance of our concepts and practices. What are we really saying when we speak of someone as possessed of a legal right? What do our practices of ascribing rights and duties really amount to? These are reflective intellectual questions for the philosopher, and they seem to go to the heart of a proper understanding of law's nature.

Let us take yet another exmple. If you have been studying law for some time you will be aware that much of the law is the product of judicial decisions. You will also be aware that the law constantly evolves and changes (slowly in some areas of law, and more swiftly in others). Yet we take it for granted that judges are bound by the law, and must decide cases by applying pre-existing law: they cannot simply ignore the law and do whatever they think is just. When we put these familiar facts together, however, we have a problem: how can the judges constantly be making and changing the law if they are bound to apply pre-existing law?

You may at first think that this question has a straightforward answer. Further reflection is likely to show you that the answer is not so easy as you might think. Consider, for example, this response:

"No set of rules can cover every situation. Sometimes new situations come up. When a new situation arises in a 'gap' not covered by any existing rule, the judge has to give a decision that is not simply an application of existing law. That decision creates new law. This is how the law evolves. But most of the time the case falls under some established rule, and there the judge is bound to apply the settled law."

Seems convincing? Now consider this reply:

"If you sue me, accusing me of a legal wrong, you must show that I have violated some existing legal principle. If you cannot point to any such principle, I ought to win. The idea that there are 'gaps' not covered by existing law ignores this fact (legal theorists sometimes speak of legal systems as having 'closure rules', such as 'everything that is not prohibited is permitted'). In any case, we know that advocates in innovative cases do not say 'there is no law on this point, so the court ought to make some new law'. They argue that their client's case is already supported by existing law: they argue that their client is, by law, *entitled* to win. We also know that the development of the law is not just a matter of new rules being added in 'gaps'. Old rules get altered or abandoned. Rules get increasingly qualified, complex and refined."

You need not try to decide at this point who is right! (Both of the above responses are misguided, partly because they both rely upon an unduly simplistic notion of what would amount to a "gap" in the law). There is a difficult question here, but not one addressed by your books on contract, tort or property. While difficult to answer, the question is also (one might have thought) an obvious one to ask. One could imagine a law student asking such a question in his or her first couple of weeks studying law (if they did ask it, their teacher might well dismiss the question in a manner that suggested it was a stupid question with an easy, but undisclosed, answer). How then is it possible for such obvious questions to remain unasked for so long? How is it possible for people to pass through three years (perhaps even a lifetime) of studying law without ever being exposed to such questions?

Like most people, legal scholars choose to concentrate on questions that they feel they might be able to answer. Therefore they do not ask tough questions. Sadly, much university education (in all subjects) is aimed at subtly encouraging you *not* to ask difficult questions. That is where jurisprudence is different. Jurisprudence is aimed at remembering the obvious and difficult questions that the other courses encourage you to forget. By remembering those questions, we can ultimately be led to connect our legal studies with matters of real intellectual and moral significance.

In studying theories of law, it is often best to begin with fairly narrow questions that arise directly out of the lawyer's experience: "how can judges be bound by the law when they constantly change the law?" is one example. What we tend to find, however, is that the attempt to answer such questions forces us to reflect more broadly upon law: we find ourselves thinking about the forest as a whole, rather than letting our vision be obstructed by the trees around us.

Here are some black-robed lawyers in court. They offer arguments which appeal to the published text of rules, and they make rival claims about the proper interpretation of those texts. They also appeal to earlier judicial decisions, and here their disagreements focus less upon what earlier judges *said*, and more upon the factual differences between earlier cases and the present case. Some of the lawyers say that those differences entail that a different outcome would be justified in this case; other lawyers deny that. All of these arguments are permeated with claims about what is "reasonable" or "fair"; about who should bear "responsibility" for this or that; and about what the consequences of alternative decisions would be for various desirable social goals.

But what do these facts amount to? Is the lawyers' concern with published rules and consistency grounded upon values of order and predictability, for example? Is legal reasoning a technical matter of reconciling conflicts and contradictions between authoritatively formulated rules? Or is it an exercise in moral reasoning, guided at every point by the desire to do justice all things considered? (In this way, reflection upon the nature of law may lead us back to the debates of Part 1, concerning the nature of justice).

It is clear from the history of philosophy that there is a long tradition of philosophical thought concerning law's nature; but the tradition contains quite diverse conceptions of the enterprise of offering a theory of law. In this respect, legal theory is really no different from other areas of philosophical inquiry: philosophy as a discipline is always concerned to reflect upon its own status, and views about the nature of philosophical inquiry cannot be separated from other questions that are addressed in the course of that inquiry. Fundamentally, this is just as true of debates about justice as it is of debates about law, but the disagreements become particularly obvious and striking in the latter debates. Sceptics sometimes conclude that legal theorists are not really engaging in genuine disagreements: their apparent disagreements are, on this view, phoney and trumped up. But a better conclusion is that legal theorists disagree with each other on many different levels. It is important (but often difficult) to keep these different levels of disagreement separate. In particular, we must keep in mind that legal theorists are often disagreeing about the nature of legal theory just as much as they disagree about the nature of law (or justice); this will considerably complicate our account of their views.

NATURAL LAW AND LEGAL POSITIVISM

Jurisprudential debate concerning the nature of law is often thought of as a long-running battle between two schools of thought: the rival camps of "natural law" and "legal positivism". The natural law tradition has always emphasised law's groundedness in justice and the common good, while legal positivism has tended to emphasise law's basis in authority. Each tradition contains a great deal of complexity, however, and the idea of some simple single issue that divides the two camps is deeply misleading. To begin sorting out some of the complexity, a certain historical perspective is necessary.

The main (classical) tradition of natural law theory stems from Aristotle and Aquinas, and its principal modern exponent is

Finnis. Indeed, one of the central claims of this tradition is succinctly explained by the opening passage of Finnis's book, *Natural Law and Natural Rights*:

"There are human goods that can be secured only through the institutions of human law, and requirements of practical reasonableness that only those institutions can satisfy."

This type of natural law theory begins by seeking to understand what is good for human beings (what counts as human flourishing); such inquiry establishes that human goods can be realised only in community, but the existence of community requires the co-ordination of human conduct. To order human conduct in appropriate ways it is necessary to have laws that are established and enforced by authority. Human communities will require conventions that establish certain authoritative sources of law. We cannot, however, understand the real nature of law by simply describing the existence of such institutions of enactment and enforcement. To understand law's nature we must understand how law is the answer to a problem set by "practical reasonableness": we must understand how certain human goods "can be secured only through the institutions of human law". When we have understood the problem, and seen how law is the solution, we have understood law's nature.

This approach suggests that law's nature is to be understood by reference to what Finnis sees as its "focal" instances, where law serves the common good. Situations where the institutions of law are employed as instruments of oppression and injustice are real enough: but they are to be understood by the way in which they diverge from (and resemble) the "focal" cases where law serves the common good. They are degenerate instances of law, and will be inherently misleading if taken as a guide to the general nature of law.

The "classical" tradition of natural law stemming from Aristotle and Aquinas began to meet stiff opposition in the seventeenth century, for reasons that played a large part in our discussions earlier in this book. Aristotelian political and jurisprudential thought centred upon notions of excellence and "the good": political and legal institutions were to be compre-hended and evaluated by their capacity to foster human flourishing. Post-Reformation Europe, however, appeared to lack the shared notions of the good that such an approach might seem to presuppose. Forms of political thinking began to emerge that sought to entrench a distinction between the juridical realm of justice and rights (on the one hand) and the ethical realm of virtue, excellence and the good (on the other).

Two of the most important figures in this development were Grotius and Hobbes. Both of them rejected (wholly or in part) Aristotelian approaches, while both of them invoked notions of natural law that avoided reliance upon a shared notion of excellence or the good. Yet, in spite of these similarities, Grotius is thought of as one of the major figures in the natural law tradition, while Hobbes is often thought of as an originator of legal positivism.

Grotius regards law as the set of principles defining individual rights. Such rights are not derived from some notion of the common good, but are (in effect) domains of self-ownership, within which one may order one's own actions.[1] One has a right to advance one's own interests, but only provided that the rights of others are not infringed.[2] Actions that encroach upon the legitimate domain of another are violations of right. The picture presented by Grotius is therefore one of a realm of non-overlapping rights: when one acts within the scope of one's rights, one cannot, in doing so, be violating the rights of others.

The position of Hobbes is quite different. Hobbes *contrasts* "right" and "law", saying that they differ as much as do "obligation" and "liberty': for "Right consisteth in liberty to do or forebear; Whereas Law determineth, and bindeth to one of them."[3] For Hobbes, rights are inherently conflicting: each person in the state of nature has a right to everything, "even to one another's body."[4] Law for Hobbes is necessary to make social order possible, but in doing so it does not fulfill the requirements of any underlying structure of rights: it simply restricts or abrogates rights. For Grotius, on the other hand, rights indicate the possibility of a non-conflictual social order; positive law should trace out the content of non-conflicting rights, and it presents a systematic structure in so far as it reflects that order.

When Hobbes is thought of as a legal positivist it is because and in so far as he emphasises the need for authority to establish rules that create boundaries between otherwise conflicting

---

[1] *De Iure Belli ac Pacis* 1.1.5.
[2] Grotius, *op. cit.*, 1.2.1.6.
[3] Hobbes, *Leviathan* Chap.14.
[4] *loc. cit.*

interests. For Hobbes it is the authority of the legislator that makes a rule a law, and not the justice or reasonableness of the rule. Grotius does not deny the need for law-making authority, but he thinks that law should properly embody and reflect an ordering of rights (as non-overlapping domains of liberty) that is prior to and independent of legislative authority. Thus, for Grotius, law embodies principles of moral reason, and is not a product of authority alone.

Like the exponents of the classical, Aristotelian, tradition, both Grotius and Hobbes are offering prescriptive arguments. That is to say, their arguments are meant to have a bearing upon what we ought to do. The point is to demonstrate that law has a certain moral authority (in virtue of its connections with human flourishing, or with our pre-existing rights, or in virtue of the need to discipline the clash between conflicting interests).

Modern legal positivism, of the kind we will examine in the next chapter (on Hart), is somewhat different. Modern legal positivists do not see themselves as offering a prescriptive argument about law's moral authority. They are trying to offer a way of understanding law's nature that sets on one side all moral issues. In effect they are saying that to understand law's nature is one thing, to evaluate it as morally good or bad is another. Once we have (under positivist guidance) "clarified" our "concept" of law, we will be better placed to think clearly about such issues as the moral authority of law and our obligation (if any) to obey: but legal positivism of Hart's type is not itself intended to propose answers to such questions.

This suggests a very fundamental contrast between the long tradition of philosophical reflection upon law (Aristotle, Hobbes, etc) and the narrower and more antiseptic approach of modern positivists. The great classics of the philosophy of law viewed law as an expression of human nature and the human condition; an understanding of law's nature formed for them but one element in a broader moral and political philosophy. Many modern legal theorists, by contrast, have seen their enterprise as one of "conceptual clarification" the object of which is to provide us with a more transparent, systematic, and univocal set of concepts in terms of which substantive moral and empirical questions can be better formulated and addressed. If legal theory is conceived in this way, there is room for scepticism about its value, and (as we shall see) theorists such as Dworkin have voiced such scepticism.

Chapter 5

HART

LEGAL POSITIVISM

H.L.A. Hart was, without question, one of the two greatest twentieth-century exponents of the position known as "legal positivism" (the other great legal positivist was Hans Kelsen). As explained in the last few pages, the tradition of "legal positivism" is usually contrasted with the tradition of "natural law". Both traditions of legal theory are complex, however, and we must try to avoid oversimplifying Hart's position, or that of his critics.

Legal positivism emerged in its modern dress in the work of Jeremy Bentham and his disciple John Austin. Bentham mounted an assault on the forms of legal writing and reflection characteristic of the eighteenth century and epitomised by the writings of Sir William Blackstone. Legal writers such as Blackstone represented the law as enforcing natural rights. The systematic classifications they employed, and the principles they extracted, were based on a theory of natural rights. In this way, their expositions of the law were intimately bound up with attempted moral justifications of the law. According to Bentham this approach confused two quite different enterprises. On the one hand, the task of "expository jurisprudence" was to set out the existing law as it stood. On the other hand, the task of "censorial jurisprudence" was to subject the law to moral scrutiny, to expose its defects, and to propose reform. To expound the law as the expression and embodiment of natural rights was a dangerous conflation of different issues. It was particularly objectionable, in Bentham's view, because the law should be criticised and evaluated by reference to the principle of utility and not by reference to a misguided belief in the existence of natural law or natural rights.

Another feature of traditional approaches to the law that Bentham considered objectionable was the tendency to treat law-making authority as a matter of moral or political legitimacy, appealing (in many cases) to a version of social contract theory as an explanation of the authority of the legislator to enact laws. Once again this confused factual issues about what the law is with moral issues about whether it ought to be obeyed. Law-making authority, like law itself, should be treated (Bentham thought) as a matter of social fact quite separate from questions of morality.

Bentham and Austin endeavoured to provide a firm foundation for the separation of expository and censorial jurisprudence by their general theories of law. Both Bentham and Austin treated law as a body of commands laid down by a supreme legislative body (called "the sovereign") in each legal system. Sovereignty was treated as a matter of social fact, consisting in the regular tendency of the bulk of the population to obey the commands of the sovereign.

Although profoundly critical of the legal theories offered by Bentham and Austin (indeed, Hart develops his own theory by exposing the flaws in Austin's), Hart shares with them the general aspiration to construct a positivist theory of law that distinguishes clearly between law and morals.

WHAT POSITIVISTS DO AND DO NOT CLAIM

Hart's principal book, *The Concept of Law*,[1] offers a host of subtle insights into the nature of law, and (as he himself puts it) "the general framework of legal thought". It would be grossly unfair to reduce the rich contents of the book to the defence of a single thesis. A certain narrowness of attention is, however, inevitable in a brief and introductory chapter such as this, and we will follow the overwhelming bulk of Hart's commentators and critics in adopting as our focus the central thesis of legal positivism, described by Hart as "the simple contention that it is in no sense a necessary truth that laws reproduce or satisfy certain demands of morality, though in fact they have often done so."[2] Towards the end of the chapter we will express some scepticism about this focus.

The "simple contention" proves to be not so simple after all, and we must take some time to explain its significance. The central claim of legal positivism is that law is separate and distinct from morality. This really involves at least two distinguishable ideas:

[1]   Second Edition (Clarendon Press, Oxford 1994).
[2]   *op. cit.* pp.185–186.

1. Positivists claim that the legal validity of a rule is a matter of
    that rule's derivability from some basic conventional
    criterion of legal validity accepted in the particular legal
    system in question. In general, this will be a matter of the
    rule having been established in some recognised source,
    such as a statute or a binding precedent. The mere fact that a
    rule is just or reasonable will not make it a law; nor does the
    injustice of a rule demonstrate that it is *not* a law.

2. Positivists claim that propositions of law, in which we state
    the existence of legal rights and duties, are not moral
    judgments. Opponents of positivism might argue that we
    cannot speak of a law as imposing duties and conferring
    rights unless we regard the law as morally binding.
    Positivists such as Hart would reply that such an argument
    plays upon two different senses of the words "right" and
    "duty". Perhaps a law cannot confer moral rights and
    impose moral duties unless it is morally binding. But we can
    treat it as conferring legal rights and imposing legal duties
    whether or not we regard it as morally binding. Thus,
    positivists hold that legal rights and duties are not a variety
    of moral right or duty, but are quite different.

It is all too easy to confuse these two positivist claims with a
number of others, and we must note carefully at this point the
various positions that are sometimes erroneously attributed to
positivism:

3. Positivists do not deny the importance of morality; nor need
    they be moral sceptics of any sort. Rather, they see
    intellectual clarity as being served by separating the moral
    evaluation of law from an accurate understanding of its
    content and nature.

4. Positivists do not deny that moral views influence the
    content of law. Obviously, legislators often enact particular
    laws because of their moral convictions, and the law is
    influenced in its content by the moral views prevailing in
    society generally. But a rule does not become law (according
    to the positivists) until it has been established in some form
    recognised by the basic criteria of the legal system in
    question (*e.g.* laid down in a source such as a statute or a
    decided case).

5. Positivists do not deny that judges sometimes decide cases by reference to moral values, or considerations of social policy. What they do deny is that judges necessarily have to make moral judgments in working out what the existing law is. Having established what the relevant legal rules are, the judge may discover that these rules do not give an answer in the case he is dealing with. Since the pre-existing law does not give an answer, the judge must decide the case on the basis of extra-legal considerations. In doing so he will establish a new legal rule. But what makes the rule a legal rule is the fact that it has been laid down by a judge, not the fact that it was based on moral considerations.

6. Positivists do not necessarily deny that there may be a moral obligation to obey the law. They argue that the question of what the law is, and the question of whether it ought to be obeyed, are two separate questions. Indeed, positivists such as Hart argue that our moral reflections on the scope of the obligation to obey the law are clarified by adopting a positivist conception of law.

7. Equally (and to some extent this reiterates the preceding point) positivists such as Hart are not claiming that we should always obey the law, or that judges should always apply the legal rules . In defending the separation of law and morals, one neither asserts nor denies such claims. Particular positivists may adopt positions on this matter but they do not see these positions as entailed by their legal positivism.

8. The various claims made by legal positivism are claims about the *concept* of law, not about this or that particular instance of law. Thus, Hart allows for the fact that *some* legal systems may make moral values relevant to legal validity (some other positivists deny this); but, he would insist that, where this is so, it is in virtue of the particular conventional criteria accepted within that system. There is nothing in the *concept* of law itself that entails any such groundedness of legal validity in moral value. Partly to emphasise this point, some more recent theorists prefer to speak of the "separability" of law and morals, rather than their "separation". What they mean to emphasise is that, even if law and morals are closely bound up together in most systems, it is always *possible* that they may be separated in some conceivable legal system. If the connection between law and morals was a

conceptual one (rather than depending upon the specific conventions of particular systems), such a separation would be inconceivable (it would be like trying to separate the idea of being unmarried from the idea of being a bachelor).

NORMATIVITY AND REDUCTIONISM

Law claims to guide and to justify our conduct: it purports to impose obligations upon us, and to tell us what we "ought" to do; judges invoke legal rules as a justification for their decisions (decisions that may order the use of coercive measures such as punishment). We shall speak of this as law's "normative" character. It is tempting to equate law's normative character with moral bindingness: how can law impose obligations, or justify coercive sanctions, unless it is morally binding upon us? The normative character of law has always been seen as a major factor supporting theories that assert the existence of necessary connections between law and morality.

The same assumption (that law's normativity is a matter of moral bindingness) can encourage those who seek a morally neutral understanding of law to adopt perspectives on law that eliminate or deny the law's normativity: thus propositions of law might be treated as predictions of what judges and other officials are *likely* to do (in the application of sanctions, for example), rather than as propositions that *prescribe* conduct. Such theories can be described as "reductionist", because they try analytically to reduce apparently normative claims to non-normative descriptions of patterns of conduct.

The theory of law offered by the nineteenth-century jurist John Austin can be taken as illustrating one of these approaches. Austin analyses statements about legal obligations as being statements about the likelihood of suffering a sanction in certain circumstances. Thus, the statement that I have a legal obligation to pay you £100 means, according to Austin, that, if I do *not* pay you the money, I am likely to suffer a sanction. This analysis suffers from some rather obvious flaws: for example, I may in fact *not* be likely to suffer a sanction (because I am out of the jurisdiction and am not planning to return; or because £100 is too small a sum to make it worth your while suing me) yet I may nevertheless have a legal obligation to pay. Most importantly, it fails to capture the way in which my legal obligation might be cited by a judge as a *reason* for ordering a sanction against me:

this would fail to make sense if the obligation was, in itself, but a prediction of the likelihood of the judge's action.

Those amongst Austin's readers who saw the force of such criticisms not infrequently reacted by rejecting his claim that law was separate from morality. To explain the normative character of law, they concluded, we must accept that it is part of the concept of "valid law" that it is morally binding upon us. To conclude that a legislative decree is not morally binding is to conclude that it imposes no legal obligations and is not a valid law; conversely, to speak of legislation as imposing duties upon us is to assume that it is morally binding.

One of the central objectives of Hart's legal theory is best understood as an attempt to steer a middle course between these alternatives. Hart wishes to show that laws *prescribe* our conduct: they are not *descriptions* of what is likely to happen in this or that set of circumstances; propositions about legal validity, and legal rights and duties, are characteristically made in the context of practical claims about how people ought to behave, and from the viewpoint of those who invoke legal rules as standards that ought to be complied with. At the same time, the normativity of law (its status as a body of prescriptions) is not to be understood as a matter of moral bindingness. A legal obligation is not a kind of moral obligation; and, from the fact that I have a legal obligation to act in a certain way, nothing necessarily follows about what I morally ought to do. It is one thing to seek to determine the law's requirements, and another thing to judge those requirements to be morally binding. Hart's theory therefore seeks to preserve the normativity of law, and avoid reductionism, without abandoning the claim to separate law from morality. The middle course pursued by Hart is a difficult one to steer, but it is one that he traces with great skill and subtlety.

Although Hart says little about the philosophical ideas underpinning his approach, the general strategy that he adopts may depend upon a broader philosophical thesis (associated with the later philosophy of Wittgenstein) about the way in which we should elucidate the meaning of human utterances. In particular, the meaning of an utterance need not lie in some relationship whereby the utterance represents or describes the world; but nor need the utterance represent a "value-judgment" *upon* the world. To explain the meaning of an utterance, we must exhibit its point or rationale within its context.

Propositions of law are not, according to Hart, descriptions of the social facts of acceptance of rules, or predictions of the likely reactions of courts; but nor are they claims about what we "ought" to do, from a moral point of view. The significance of such propositions can only be clarified by reference to their role within a specific type of context, involving the existence of a basic practice, referred to by Hart as a "rule of recognition". Propositions of law can only be understood by grasping their role *within* such a social practice: they are not propositions *about* the practice.

Understanding a concept, on this approach, is not a matter of having a simple criterion for its applicability, or a set of necessary and sufficient conditions: it is a question of grasping the role of the concept within a wider practice, and the place of the practice within some wider way of life. Consequently, there can be no question of the explication of a concept terminating in the provision of an all-encompassing definition or criterion: what counts as conceptual clarification will always be relative to the puzzles that led us to the inquiry in the first place. A conceptual analysis will never be exhaustive, and its value will always be dependent upon the interest and importance of the problems that the analysis set out to solve.

RULES AND THE INTERNAL POINT OF VIEW

At one point, Hart observes that "the element of authority involved in law has always been one of the obstacles in the path of an easy explanation of what law is."[3] Legislatures, for example, possess a power to enact law that you and I do not possess: they are law-making authorities. But what is involved in such authority? Could one not argue that law-making authority is a matter of moral legitimacy? One who has the authority to make law (we might argue) is *entitled* to make law, and others are under an *obligation* to obey. Must not such authority be grounded in moral considerations? And (since the products of law-making authority are valid laws) does that not show law to be inextricably bound up with morality?

A positivist theory of law must offer an account of the nature of law-making authority. At the same time, positivists claim that the validity of a law does not entail an obligation to obey it. This means that their account of law-making authority must not be an

---

[3]   *Concept of Law* p.20.

account of moral legitimacy: it must be quite independent of any theory about the basis of a moral obligation to obey the law. Similarly, positivists must offer accounts of what it is to have a "legal obligation" or a "legal right". Their accounts must clearly distinguish these concepts from the notion of moral obligation or a moral right.

Bentham and Austin approached these problems by treating statements about sovereignty, rights, and obligations, as straightforward statements of observable social fact. For example, a body of persons constituted the "sovereign" (the supreme law-making authority) in Austin's theory when that body was habitually obeyed by the bulk of the population, and did not itself habitually obey any other person or body; and a person was under a legal obligation to do a certain act when, in the event of non-compliance with a sovereign command, he was likely to suffer a sanction at the sovereign's behest. In each case a legal concept is treated as referring to structures of human behaviour: "sovereignty" refers to regular patterns of obedience, and "obligation" refers to the likelihood of suffering a sanction.

Hart argues that this approach is inadequate. One cannot establish the separation of law and morals by simply reducing propositions of law to straightforward factual descriptions of regular patterns of behaviour. We can see this in relation to the concepts of "sovereignty", and "obligation". Suppose that the supreme law-maker in a certain legal system is an absolute monarch, Rex I. According to Austin, Rex I is the sovereign insofar as he is habitually obeyed by the bulk of the population. Now suppose that Rex I dies and is succeeded by his son, Rex II. Hart points out that we have, on Austin's theory, no reason for regarding Rex II as the new sovereign. Having only just taken over, he has not yet issued any orders and has not yet been obeyed. It follows that we cannot describe the bulk of the population as "habitually" obeying him. So, on Austin's definition of the sovereign, we cannot treat Rex II as the sovereign until he has issued some orders and been obeyed. What Austin lacks is the notion of a rule which entitles Rex II to succeed his father. His notion of a habit of obedience is a mere regularity of conduct, not a rule.

According to Austin, obligations exist insofar as the failure to obey the sovereign's orders is regularly followed by the application of sanctions. In stating that someone has a legal obligation we are saying that he is likely to suffer a sanction if he does not comply. In Hart's view, this simply will not do as an analysis of the concept of obligation. The likelihood of suffering a sanction might oblige me to act in a certain way, as I might be obliged to hand my money to a gunman who threatens me: but it would not impose an obligation on me. When we speak of someone as having a certain obligation, we are invoking a rule as a standard that ought to be complied with. When a judge refers to the defendant's obligations as a reason for ordering him to pay damages, the judge is invoking a rule as a justification for his decision, not predicting the likely application of a sanction.

By treating the legal order as a body of observable regularities of conduct, pure and simple, Austin was unable to accommodate such notions as right, entitlement, obligation, and justification. What Austin needed in place of the notion of a regular pattern of conduct, was the concept of an accepted rule. How, then, does an accepted rule differ from a mere regularity? Suppose that the great majority of people go to the cinema every Saturday night. This regular pattern of conduct does not demonstrate that they accept a rule that they ought to go to the cinema every Saturday. On the other hand, motorists regularly stop at red lights: here, there does seem to be an accepted rule that they ought to stop. So what is the difference?

Hart says that where an accepted rule exists, the regular pattern of conforming behaviour (which Hart calls "the external aspect") is accompanied by an "internal aspect". Where a rule exists people who do not conform to the regular pattern are criticised and the criticism is regarded as justified. The regular pattern of conduct is regarded as a standard that ought to be complied with. People regard the rule from an "internal point of view", treating it as a basis for the evaluation and criticism of action. This internal point of view carries along with it a certain vocabulary. People speak of what "ought" to be done; they treat the rule (in some cases) as imposing "obligations" or as conferring "rights". The rule is treated, not as a simple observable regularity, but as a prescription that guides conduct.

Hart uses these basic ideas to explain the nature of law-making authority, and to explicate the concepts of "legal obligation" and "legal right". The basis of law-making authority lies, not in habits of obedience as Austin would hold, but in the acceptance of a basic rule that authorises the enactment of new legal rules. Those who regard the laws from an internal point of view will speak of them as conferring rights and imposing duties.

POWERS AND SECONDARY RULES

Bentham and Austin treated all laws as duty-imposing. In Bentham's case this approach was linked to his view that every law is a restriction on liberty. Being a restriction on liberty, every law is, in itself, an evil which needs to be justified by reference to its utilitarian value.

In Hart's opinion, this tendency to reduce all law to a single pattern ignores the differing social functions of different laws. Not all laws restrict conduct by imposing duties: some laws are intended to provide facilities, to make available options that would not otherwise exist. For example, the law that confers the power to make a will is not a restriction on conduct: it does not compel us to do anything, but merely offers us a means of controlling the disposition of our property on death if we wish. Such power-conferring laws are, Hart argues, fundamentally different from duty-imposing laws.

Power-conferring laws confer the power to alter legal rights and legal relations, and to amend or enact legal rules. Examples of legal powers are the power to make a will, the power to make a binding contract, the power to enact by-laws, and so on. Rules which confer powers are an example of what Hart calls "secondary rules". "Primary rules" are rules about conduct, of the kind we are all familiar with: do not kill, do not steal, always stop at a red light, etc. "Secondary rules" are rules about other rules: about how to alter other rules, how to interpret them, how to enact them, and how to recognise them as valid rules. The most important type of secondary rule, in Hart's theory, is the type he calls a "rule of recognition". The nature of such a rule is best explained in the following way.

Suppose that we all lived in a society that lacked courts and legislatures, but where a number of straightforward primary rules were widely accepted. Everyone, or at least the great majority of people, accepted that you ought not to murder, or steal, or cheat, or tell lies. However firm the moral consensus was, such a society, possessing only primary rules, would face a number of serious problems. To begin with there would inevitably be arguments about exactly what the rules required in specific cases. For example, does the rule against murder extend to euthanasia? Or to abortion? Does the rule against fraud extend to non-disclosure of relevant facts in concluding an agreement? In a society without such a strong moral consensus, these disputes would extend beyond questions of how the rules are to be interpreted and would reach the issue of what rules should be observed in the first place (for instance, "What's wrong with stealing, if the existing distribution of property is unjust?"). Yet, even if people could not agree on what exactly the primary rules were, or what set of rules would be just, they would nevertheless require shared rules of some sort. So the answer would seem to be the acceptance of some basic "rule of recognition" which specifies (in Hart's words) "some feature or features possession of which by a suggested rule is taken as a conclusive affirmative indication that it is a rule of the group to be supported by the social pressure it exerts."[4]. The basic function of such a rule of recognition is to provide a body of publicly ascertainable[5] rules, so that we can regulate our conduct by shared rules even in the face of some degree of moral disagreement or uncertainty.

A simple rule of recognition might specify that only the rules carved on certain stone tablets were to be treated as binding. But a rule of recognition of this kind would render the primary rules immune from change. So the rule of recognition is likely to specify some sources of authority that are empowered to alter and enact new primary rules.

According to Hart, every legal system contains a basic rule of recognition by reference to which we can identify the fundamental sources of law. For example, in the United Kingdom the most important sources of law are statutes and precedents: we can establish that these are sources of law by reference to the basic rule of recognition. But how do we discover what the content of the rule of recognition is? Hart's answer is that the rule of recognition is a rule accepted by officials. If we examine the behaviour of officials deciding disputes we will discover a regular pattern of conduct (the external aspect of the rule) that consists in always deciding disputes by reference to the rules emanating from certain sources (statutes and precedents, in the case of the United Kingdom). The officials regard this way of deciding cases as the proper way; they regard the rule of recognition as a standard that ought to be complied with (*i.e.*

---

[4] *The Concept of Law*, p.94.
[5] The rules may be said to be publicly ascertainable in so far as we do not generally have to fall back upon our private moral judgment to discover the content of the laws. "Public ascertainability" in this sense should not be confused with the actual *publication* of laws, which Hart does not regard as a requirement of the concept of "law".

they take the internal point of view). These facts about official behaviour can be established by empirical observation. By reference to them, the content of the existing law can be determined.

This means that it is the existence of a basic rule of recognition that makes the legal order into a body of publicly ascertainable rules. In the absence of such a basic rule, we would have to regulate our conduct according to our own conceptions of justice and moral right. Where publicly ascertainable rules exist and are generally followed, our moral convictions may lead us to adopt those rules as a guide even where we consider them to be less than ideal.

It can now be seen how Hart's positivism (his claim that law is separate from morality) is directly linked to his idea of the rule of recognition. It is the whole point of the rule of recognition to provide a body of publicly ascertainable rules: the rules are publicly ascertainable in that their content can generally be established simply by reference to empirical facts, without making any moral judgments. Hence, the separation of law and morality is essential to law's basic function.

One point that will come to be of some importance later, however, concerns the nature of the criteria of legal validity established in the rule of recognition. Since the point of the rule of recognition is to facilitate greater certainty in our conclusions about the content of the rules governing conduct, it is likely to establish sources of law such that the content and validity of a law can be ascertained by the fact of its enactment or establishment by the relevant source. Hart expressly points out, however, that the criteria of legal validity for a particular system may include moral standards. Thus, some provisions of the U.S. Bill of Rights might be regarded as making certain moral standards relevant to the validity of law.[6] There is nothing inconsistent with legal positivism in such situations where moral value is relevant to legal validity, for the connection between law and morality is here a *contingent* one, dependent upon the particular rules of a specific system: it is not a *necessary* connection flowing from the very *concept* of law itself.

---

[6] *The Concept of Law*, p.204.

THE LEGAL SYSTEM

According to Hart, a legal system can be said to exist when two conditions are satisfied:

1. Officials must accept and apply a basic rule of recognition. They must "accept" the rule in the sense that they regard it from an internal point of view, as a standard that ought to be complied with.

2. The population at large must generally comply with the primary rules. But it is not a part of the concept of a "legal system" that the population should "accept" the primary rules or the rule of recognition: only the officials need take an internal point of view. This is not to deny that a legal system which did not rest on some degree of popular acceptance might be both morally objectionable and politically unstable: but these moral and political requirements are not features of the concept of "law" or "legal system" itself.

Once we have passed from a society having only primary rules to a society having a basic rule of recognition, new concepts become applicable. In a simple society with only primary rules, rules "exist" only when they are accepted and observed in people's conduct. To invoke a rule against theft (for example) in such a context is to point to a regular pattern of conduct (the external aspect) as a standard which ought to be complied with (the internal point of view). But, when there is a rule of recognition, rules can be said to "exist" in another sense. Rules which emanate from the sources identified by the basic rule of recognition are "valid"; and a "valid" rule can exist even if it is not accepted or applied by anyone. Suppose that an Act of Parliament was passed in 1800 and has never been applied in a case since then. Indeed, the judges, lawyers, and police have completely forgotten of the Act's existence. Such an Act would not be accepted or applied by anyone; the rules that it contains would not be exemplified by anyone's conduct and would have no "external aspect": but the Act, if it has not been repealed, would still be a valid Act, and the rules that it contains would be valid rules.

In this way, Hart has provided a solution for the problem of the relationship between efficacy and legal validity. Legal validity is to be distinguished from efficacy, for a rule may be totally ineffective and yet be valid. But we should not be led to detach validity completely from considerations of efficacy. We feel that the laws of Tsarist Russia are now invalid because they are no longer effective. Hart's theory shows how an ineffective rule may still be valid provided that it emanates from the basic rule of recognition: but in order to be an existing valid rule, the legal system to which it belongs must, as a whole, be an effective legal system.

The central role that Hart gives to "officials" in his theory is both striking and curious. Hart nowhere tells us just what an "official" is or how we recognize one. Since we identify the law by reference to official behaviour (in the form of the rule of recognition), it may seem that we cannot identify officials by reference to the law. Opinions differ on whether there is a way of overcoming this problem.[7]

Whatever the answer to that question, it should not escape our notice that Hart's reliance upon the centrality of "officials" brings his theory closer to that of Austin than one might at first imagine. For Austin, a rule possesses legal authority if it emanates from the sovereign; but what, we might ask, gives the sovereign authority to enact rules? Sovereign law-making authority cannot be derived from a law enacted by some higher source of law, for we could then ask how the higher source was authorised to create such a law (we would thereby become involved in an infinite regress). To derive sovereign law-making authority from a *moral* criterion would be to abandon legal positivism. Consequently, Austin treats law-making authority as a matter of observable fact: the sovereign has authority because and in so far as the sovereign's commands are habitually obeyed by the bulk of the population.

At first glance, Hart's theory looks very different. The law-making authority of a supreme legislative body is, according to Hart, not derived from a law *enacted* by some higher body, nor is it derived from morality: the authority results from a rule of recognition which is *accepted* by officials. Moreover, the fact that the officials *accept* the rule of recognition as a rule to guide their

---

[7]   See M. Kramer, *Legal Theory, Political Theory and Deconstruction* (Indiana 1991), Chap. 3. J. Raz, *Ethics in the Public Domain* (Oxford 1994), p.280n; J. Coleman, "Incorporationism, Conventionality and the Practical Difference Thesis" in J. Coleman (ed.) *Hart's Postscript* (Oxford 2001) p.99 at p.121.

conduct explains the law's normative language, which does not *describe* patterns of conduct but *invokes* rules as standards that ought to be complied with.

So far so good; but suppose we ask "What makes the rule of recognition, accepted by these officials, the rule of recognition *of a legal system?*"

Suppose that the Fellows of Corpus Christi College "accepted" a rule that treated all pronouncements of the Master of Corpus as laws governing everyone in the United Kingdom, and empowered the Fellows to enforce the Master's decrees. Their acceptance of this eccentric "rule of recognition" would not give the Master of Corpus law-making authority in the U.K. This is not because the Fellows are not "officials": for they *would* be "officials" under *this* rule. The reason why this would not be the rule of recognition of the U.K. legal system is that the bulk of the British population do not comply with the decrees of the Master of Corpus. In Hart's theory, therefore, the "official" acceptance of a rule gives rise to a rule of recognition of a legal system, only if the officials (or the regime that they support, by their acceptance of the relevant rule of recognition) can succeed in getting the bulk of the population to comply with the primary rules of conduct that result. Like Austin, Hart seems to ground law-making authority in the facts of power.

What if someone described Hart's theory as simply saying "The law is whatever the officials say it is"? Would that be a fair summary of Hart's views? Well, we must begin by appreciating that the rule of recognition is not just a regular pattern of official behaviour. It is not just what the officials regularly do: it represents a standard that they believe they ought to comply with. Since it is a genuine rule that they accept, it is possible for the officials to misapply it. Suppose that the officials accept a rule requiring them to enforce Acts of Parliament. If an official one day fails to apply an Act (because, say, he disapproves of it) we can describe him as having got the law wrong, or as having failed to apply the law. Thus it is not true that, in Hart's theory, whatever an official does or says represents the law.

In another sense, however, officials do occupy a key position for Hart. Suppose that the House of Lords and all the other senior English judges, decided that they were not going to enforce Acts of Parliament any more, but were going to enforce decrees of the Workers' Revolutionary Council. If they succeeded in doing this, and if the bulk of the population complied with the new decrees rather than with the old enactments of

Parliament, the judges would have effected a change in the rule of recognition. From the point of view of the old rule of recognition, the judges' actions would be unlawful: but then, that old rule of recognition no longer exists. So in this way official behaviour does indeed provide the bedrock criterion of legitimacy for Hart.

On some points the existing rule of recognition may give uncertain guidance or no guidance at all. When Britain first joined the EU (EEC as it was then called), the effect upon parliamentary sovereignty of our so joining was a matter for speculation: the established practice of the officials gave little assistance in the formulation of an answer. Hart's view on such uncertainties in the basic rule of recognition seems to be that the questions with which they face us are, in a sense, not really legal questions at all. Though framed in legal terms and debated as if they were legal in nature, the questions are political in nature; but, once a decision has been given by the judges, the decision establishes law on that point.

At the basis of legal authority, therefore, Hart (like Austin) discovers the facts of political power. This forms a major focus for opposition to legal positivism. Some natural law theorists would say that a governing regime cannot constitute a legal system unless its power is exercised for certain purposes, such as justice and the common good. For Hart, by contrast, legality seems to be a matter of the manner and form in which power is exercised, rather than the purposes it serves.

We will see in due course, however, that Hart also wishes to eschew an austere reliance upon considerations of pure form, and to invoke certain minimal and uncontentious claims about law's purpose; whether this undermines his positivism in any respect is a matter for debate.

ADJUDICATION

Legal positivists do not deny that judges sometimes decide cases by reference to moral values or social policy considerations. It may be necessary for the judge to do this, according to the positivists, whenever the existing rules of law fail to give a determinate answer in the specific case. In claiming that law is separate from morality, the positivists are denying that moral judgments must necessarily underpin the exposition of the existing law. Determining the content of the existing law is not always enough in itself to decide a case, however. Where the law does not give an answer, the judge must establish, by his decision, a new legal rule: and this he will do partly on the basis of extra-legal considerations of morality and social policy.

In the first half of the twentieth century, many legal scholars in the United States emphasised the apparent pliability and alterability of legal rules, and the extent to which this pliability required judges to rely upon considerations drawn from outside the legal rule itself. These scholars came to be referred to as the "American Realists".[8] Their views were very diverse, and for that reason cannot be summarised with any pretension to accuracy; but their writings tended to focus upon the way in which our interpretations of rules depend upon a host of background contextual assumptions, and the way in which rules of case law may be modified in the course of application. The Realists tended to mix their insights with a good deal of hyperbole, often asserting that rules are not binding at all, or are mere fictions.[9] At the same time, some of the most substantial figures in the movement (such as Karl Llewellyn) emphasised the stability and predictability of judicial understandings, and the consequent "reckonability" of legal outcomes.

Hart distinguishes between formalists and rule-sceptics. Formalists look upon the law as a self-contained body of standards that determine, by deductive logic, the correct answer in every case. Hart regards this as a mistaken view. Language does not pick out and classify situations with surgical precision: it possesses an "open texture". While there will generally be a range of clear cases to which a word is definitely applicable, there will also be "penumbral" cases where it is not clear whether the word should apply or not. Such "penumbral" instances are simply left open by the ordinary standards of linguistic usage. Similarly, some situations may fall within the "penumbra" of legal rules: for example, it may be unclear whether a rule relating to "vehicles" should be applied to a milk-float, a pedal car, or a pair of roller skates, since it is not clear whether these count as "vehicles". In such cases, the court has to exercise its discretion, and will have regard to policy considera-

---

[8] The two best surveys are W. Twining, *Karl Llewellyn and the Realist Movement* (London 1973), and N. Duxbury, *Patterns of American Jurisprudence* (Oxford 1995).

[9] The hyperbole is not entirely gratuitous, however: it reflects a rough and intuitive grasp of some quite deep philosophical puzzles.

tions (including the presumed policy objectives of the rule in question) and to considerations of fairness. In the majority of cases, no such exercise of discretion is necessary: a motor car, for example, is clearly a "vehicle"; but, because of the open texture of language, no set of rules can give pre-determined answers in every possible case, and formalism must therefore be wrong.

In Hart's view, rule-sceptics (American Realists) simply make the opposite mistake to the formalists. Formalists overlook the penumbral uncertainty of rules; rule-sceptics treat rules as if they have no core of settled meaning and give no determinate guidance at all. But the fact that concepts have a penumbra of indeterminacy does not mean that they are altogether devoid of meaning. Words have a core of settled meaning, rules have a core of settled application: in some cases the judges must have recourse to moral and social policy considerations, but in the great majority of cases the judge has merely to apply an established legal rule.

Hart could be read as simply pointing out that, in the great bulk of cases, lawyers will agree on the proper outcome, and may ascribe that outcome to the applicability of a settled legal rule. If this is his meaning, however, he misunderstands the objection of the rule-sceptics. Rule-sceptics would agree that outcomes are frequently predictable, and that lawyers will ascribe the propriety of the outcome to settled rules; but, they would insist, such a consensus always tends to depend upon a background of shared policy views and moral understandings. When lawyers are confronted with a case that goes beyond the limits of their background moral and policy agreement, they are likely to exhibit great uncertainty regarding the proper application of the rule. Hence, the rule-sceptics conclude, verbally formulated rules provide little real guidance if detached from a background of agreement on moral values and social policy.

If, on the other hand, Hart were to be read as claiming that verbally formulated rules prescribe determinate outcomes in most cases quite apart from any such background of shared values, his claim would be overly simplistic. The formal semantic rules of language often place only very general constraints upon the meaning of a particular text or utterance: in interpreting the statements of others we place a heavy reliance upon a host of taken-for-granted assumptions that we share with them. Thus, I have elsewhere argued that the rule "Dogs must be carried on the escalator" could, so far as the formal rules of language go, mean a huge diversity of different things (think about it): we reach univocal conclusions about its meaning because we share certain concerns and assumptions about the world.[10]

A related point was urged by Lon Fuller. Fuller argued that we always interpret rules in the light of our understanding of their purpose. Consequently, what counts as an unproblematic "core" case, or a contested "penumbral" case, depends upon our understanding of the rule's purpose at least as much as it depends upon the ordinary meaning of the words used in the rule.

Fuller offered a host of entertaining illustrations of his point. Thus, he took up Hart's example of a rule prohibiting "vehicles" from the municipal park. He pointed out that, contrary to Hart's claims, the ordinary meaning of the word "vehicle" would not be the key factor in determining what did or did not count as a straightforward or a problematic case. Thus, although a lorry is undoubtedly a "vehicle", the introduction of a lorry into the park might be a very problematic case for the rule: if, say, a group of war veterans wished to establish a lorry as a war memorial. The case would be problematic in so far as the rule is presumably aimed at eliminating the noise, pollution, and hazards of traffic from the park; but none of these purposes seem relevant to the establishment of a lorry as a war memorial.[11]

Hart's own response to Fuller's argument was to point out that there is nothing in the nature of law guaranteeing that the relevant purposes of the rules are *moral* purposes: hence, even if Fuller was correct to say that the interpretation of a rule always depends upon an understanding of its purpose, this would not establish a necessary connection between law and morality. This response, while correct so far as it goes, unfortunately misses the wider significance of Fuller's argument. Hart's intention was to demonstrate that Fuller's insights, even if sound, did not identify any necessary connection between law and morality: but there

---

[10] Simmonds, "Between Positivism and Idealism" [1991] CLJ 308. J.W. Harris takes up the same example in the second edition of his book *Legal Philosophies*, (London 1997) p.161. Harris misses the point of the example, by equating the background context of understandings with the formal semantic conventions of language (such as the rule that the furry animal which barks is called a "dog" not a "cat"). Not all shared understandings are matters of convention, however.

[11] See Fuller, "Positivism and Fidelity to Law" (1958) *Harvard Law Review* p.630, at pp.661–669.

are other important jurisprudential questions that should be considered here.

The purposes served by legal rules are often far from transparent. Even if we were to treat the intentions of the law-makers as definitive of the rule's purpose,[12] it may only be when problematic and unanticipated cases arise that the law-makers begin to appreciate the relative indeterminacy of their aims in enacting the rule, so that their "legislative intentions" fail to provide the answer we seek. Allowing for the point that the law's purposes need not be moral purposes, it would still be true to say that we are most likely to reach convergent conclusions about the applicability of our laws when we share a broad range of moral understandings and interpret the law in that light. Yet this suggests that the law's determinacy itself depends to some extent upon a background of shared values. It is often assumed that one can have an orderly society that exhibits great moral pluralism and diversity, while being held together by "the rule of law". So are such liberal assumptions flawed?

DISTINGUISHING CASES

So far, we have been chiefly considering rules that have a definite verbal formulation, such as rules contained in statutes. A further range of considerations applies to case law, where no such authoritative formulations are to be found. It is always open to a later judge to narrow the "rule" laid down in an earlier case, or to reformulate the rule by creating a new exception to it, or in some other way. There are well-established practices of legal reasoning such as the practices of distinguishing earlier cases by narrowing their rulings, and of creating unenvisaged exceptions to rules. It is not easy to explain such practices on a model of judicial decision that treats them as simply "laying down" rules by which later courts are "bound". How, we might ask, can the judges alter the rules if they are also bound by the rules? Surely, we might say, being bound by a rule means that you have to follow it, and not feel free to alter it.

Different responses to this problem are possible. Hart's solution is not very fully explained, but it appears to depend on saying that the formulation of a settled rule of case law is

---

[12] For some difficulties with this approach, see Dworkin, *Law's Empire* (London 1986) Chap.9; see also J. Waldron, *Law and Disagreement* (Oxford 1999) Part 1.

always relative to a particular context of application, and the occurrence of future cases may always render the rule to that extent unsettled.[13] Hart does not mean, of course, that courts can simply exclude individual cases from the operation of a rule on an ad hoc basis: the court must propose a reformulated rule that takes the instant case outside of the rule as originally formulated, but renders its decision consistent with the relevant precedents.

Superficially, Hart's approach might seem to rob rules of their ability to *guide* decisions: for the settled rule will not itself inform us as to whether the next case is one to which the rule should properly be applied, or one in which the rule should be modified. To understand how a verbal precept can serve as a general guide, while always being subject to qualification, we need to remember the context of taken-for-granted assumptions within which the precept functions: for it is those assumptions that help to determine the appropriateness of modification. If this is Hart's position, however, it is not clear that it is inconsistent with the claims of most rule-sceptics. While admittedly indulging in a certain amount of hyperbole, the majority of rule-sceptics were aiming to highlight the status of verbally formulated rules as general guides only, always open to modification and dependent upon context and background assumption.

A somewhat more restrictive and structured approach is offered by Raz, who argues that the judges do indeed have power to alter the rules, but the power is consistent with the rules being binding, in so far as the power is a limited power. In a first version of this argument, Raz suggested that the relevant power was limited in so far as it could be exercised only for certain sorts of reasons.[14] The problem here is that any account of the relevant reasons that is sufficiently broad to explain the practice of distinguishing and narrowing rulings is likely to encompass all of the reasons on which a court may legitimately act quite apart from the binding force of specific rules. In a later version of the argument,[15] Raz claims that the power to alter rules is limited by constraints on the *form* that the alteration can take: it must consist in the addition of a new exception to the

---

[13] Hart, *The Concept of Law* pp. 134, 139. See my discussion in "Protestant Jurisprudence and Modern Doctrinal Scholarship" [2001] CLJ p.271 at pp.297–299.

[14] J. Raz, *Practical Reason and Norms* (London 1990) p. 140.

[15] J. Raz, *The Authority of Law* (Oxford 1979) pp.186–188.

rule, such that the rule-plus-exception would justify earlier cases as successfully as the original rule-without-exception did. This version of the argument, however, fails to explain the way in which judges can fundamentally reformulate rules in a way that cannot be analysed as the addition of an exception.[16]

Another solution is to be found within Dworkin's theory of law (to be examined in the next chapter). Dworkin says that the judges alter the more specific legal rules, but do so in the implementation of deeper legal principles, and not at their discretion.

Thus, on the one hand, we have the general observation that propositions of case law are always dependent upon context and therefore subject to revision: the legitimacy and desirability of revision depends upon a host of background assumptions that expert lawyers might take for granted, but would find it impossible exhaustively to articulate. This general emphasis upon the relevance of context and background understanding was shared by many of the rule-sceptics (Karl Llewellyn being a key figure here), and such a view may have been espoused by Hart himself (Hart's criticisms of the rule-sceptics being focused upon their hyperbolic claim that rules are not binding, rather than upon their insights into the relevance of context).

On the other hand we have the approaches of Raz and Dworkin. Vague invocations of context and background understanding may seem unsatisfactory by contrast with these more structured and systematic theories, but it is wrong to assume that the neater and more articulate alternatives are always superior. In many contexts, our knowledge of what constitutes appropriate behaviour depends upon a background of understandings that we could not fully articulate in advance of the situations that call them into play. Something similar may be true of case law. When judges modify an earlier ruling, they must give reasons for doing so, and must articulate a rule, not just create an arbitrary exception; but it does not follow from this that judges (or legal theorists) can envisage and describe in advance the types of modification that can be made, or the circumstances in which they can be made. Perhaps our background understandings are never fully articulable in advance of the situations that make them especially pertinent as a basis for modifying our understanding of the rule.

---

[16] See Simmonds, "Bluntness and Bricolage" in H. Gross and R. Harrison, *Jurisprudence: Cambridge Essays* (Clarendon Press, Oxford 1992) p.1, at pp.8–11.

The dependence of our practical reasoning upon a never-fully-articulable background understanding is a most significant fact which has been explored by philosophers.[17] Contemporary legal theorists often seem to neglect the significance of this point, however, and we may legitimately ask whether this reflects their sense that a general dependence of practical understanding upon a background consensus would pose problems for some standard liberal visions of the rule of law. If written rules can have determinate meanings only given a host of shared background understandings, what questions does this pose for diverse and pluralistic societies that hope to be held together by the rule of law?

LEGAL OBLIGATION AND THE INTERNAL POINT OF VIEW

Suppose that we were convinced that all laws are posited rules emanating from authoritative sources: no rule counts as a law simply because it is just or reasonable; to count as a law a rule must be authoritatively established. Nevertheless, the truth of legal positivism would not follow from that thesis alone. For what precisely is meant by speaking of the relevant sources of law as "authoritative"? Might the "authority" of a law-making body not be a matter of the morally binding force of that body's decrees? So long as this construction of the nature of law-making authority has not been excluded, legal positivism has not been established.

Kant, for example, argued in *The Metaphysics of Morals* that, even in a system of wholly posited laws, one would still require a basic natural law that established the authority of the legislator. We saw earlier how Austin and Bentham rejected this type of argument by explaining law-making authority in terms of the facts of obedience, rather than in terms of moral legitimacy and moral bindingness; but we saw too how their approach neglected the "internal" prescriptive aspect of law, by (for example) analysing legal duty as the likelihood of suffering a sanction.

On one view the law can be spoken of as conferring rights and imposing obligations only insofar as we regard it as morally binding: a law that is not morally binding cannot impose any

---

[17] H.-G. Gadamer, *Truth and Method*, 2nd English ed., (London 1979) pp.278–289; M. Oakeshott, *Rationalism in Politics* (London 1962).

obligation on us. Since lawyers talk about the law in the language of rights and duties (rather than, say, the language of force and coercion) they are committed to a view of the law as morally binding.

Hart wants to resist such arguments and to claim that legal discourse does not assume any particular moral attitude towards the law. Judgments about the existence of legal rights and obligations leave the moral question of what ought to be done quite open. Yet Hart does not want to reduce legal discourse to some form of simple fact-stating discourse. Propositions about the existence of legal obligations, for example, are not simple predictions of the application of sanctions, or the likely reactions of courts. Judges invoke the parties' legal obligations in justification of their decisions; the language of law (rights, duties, ought, etc.) is essentially concerned to prescribe conduct, not to describe it. The problem for Hart is clear. How can a legal positivist resist the conclusion that propositions of law are a type of moral judgment without reducing them to predictive or fact-stating propositions? How can one separate law from morality unless one approaches law from a purely external point of view? How can Hart remain a legal positivist while claiming that the characteristic concepts of legal discourse derive their meaning from an "internal point of view": a point of view that regards the law as a body of standards that ought to be complied with?

One approach is offered by the legal theory of Hans Kelsen. Kelsen, like Hart, emphasised the contrast between reductive approaches to the legal order that treat it as an apparatus of systematic coercion, and the lawyer's distinctive point of view, that regards the legal order as a body of "valid" norms. To reflect the lawyer's point of view, and to make sense of his language, it is necessary, in Kelsen's opinion, to adopt the basic presupposition (or basic norm, as Kelsen called it) that the authorities in effective control ought to be obeyed. This looks at first like an abandonment of legal positivism: indeed it seems to endorse Kant's observation mentioned above. Kelsen even describes the basic norm as the minimum element of natural law without which a (non-reductionist) cognition of law is impossible. Yet Kelsen insists that this basic presupposition does not commit one to moral approval of the law, for the presupposition can be made for the strictly limited purpose of reproducing the content of the legal order as a body of valid norms. A complex debate surrounds these claims.

Hart hopes to avoid the problematic introduction of such a "basic norm". Kelsen assumes that "valid" means "ought to be obeyed", but Hart rejects this assumption. According to Hart, the judgment that a rule is valid is not a judgment that it ought to be obeyed, but a judgment that the rule "satisfies all the criteria provided by the rule of recognition."[18] The concept of "validity" is one that derives its meaning from a context characterised by the existence of a rule of recognition, and it is employed in judgments that express a conclusion about the applicability of that rule.

This argument leads Hart to reject Kelsen's theory of the basic norm, for the following reasons. When Kelsen is confronted with an ultimate constitution or rule of recognition he asks, in effect, "what makes this rule valid?" Hart sees the basic norm as Kelsen's answer to that question; but Hart rejects the question itself as meaningless. The rule of recognition provides the ultimate criterion of legal validity, but is itself neither valid nor invalid. To say that a rule is valid is to say that it emanates from the rule of recognition. Accordingly it makes no sense to ask whether the rule of recognition is itself "valid", any more than it would make sense to ask whether the metre-bar in Paris is really a metre long. "Validity" is a concept that has its proper place *within* systems of rules characterised by a basic rule of recognition: once we reach the limits of the system, we have reached the limits of applicability of the concept of "validity".

Hart's point about the concept of "validity" is a strong one, but he could nevertheless be accused of missing the fundamental point of Kelsen's theory, which is essentially to comprehend, within the context of a positivist theory, the "internal point of view". Hart himself says that concepts such as right, duty, ought, and validity are characteristic of the internal point of view, and that is a point of view which regards the law as a body of standards that ought to be complied with. Those who reject the law's demands, and are concerned only to avoid incurring sanctions, regard the law from an "external" point of view. Such people, Hart tells us, would not require the normative vocabulary of the internal point of view, but the descriptive language of "being obliged" and "being likely to suffer a sanction".[19] The existence of a legal system, however, requires that at least the officials must regard the rule of recognition as a

18 *The Concept of Law*, p.103.
19 *The Concept of Law*, p.90.

common public standard that ought to be complied with.[20]

Does it not follow that propositions about legal rights, duties, validity, and so on, express conclusions about what ought to be done? And does that not suggest that propositions of law are really a species of moral judgment, resting upon the assumption that law is morally binding?

Hart rejects any such conclusion: he has, for example, rejected the claim of Joseph Raz that judges who speak of the law as imposing obligations assume (or at least purport to assume) that the law is morally binding.[21] According to Hart, the internal point of view involves regarding the relevant rules as standards that "ought" to be complied with, and the "ought" must be expressive of a standard common to officials: yet it need not be a moral "ought", for it could be grounded in non-moral considerations such as considerations of long-term self-interest.[22] It is important to emphasise here that Hart is not addressing the question of why judges, in most actual legal systems, apply the basic rule of recognition: he is not arguing that they generally do so for non-moral reasons. His point is rather that, even if their compliance *was* grounded upon non-moral considerations, their use of the vocabulary of the internal point of view would still make perfectly good sense. Hence, one's employment of that vocabulary does not commit one to a belief in the law's moral bindingness. Propositions of law (describing the law's content in terms of validity, its imposition of obligations, its conferment of rights, and so forth) therefore need not be regarded as moral judgments: they are morally neutral.

A DIFFERENT POSITIVISM?

A positivist theory of law tends to involve a number of separable claims that should carefully be distinguished. One set of claims, for example, concerns the nature of the criteria on the basis of which we judge certain rules to be law. Another set of claims concerns the meaning of propositions that treat legal rules as

[20] *The Concept of Law*, p.116.
[21] H.L.A. Hart, *Essays on Bentham* (Oxford 1982) pp.153–161.
[22] *The Concept of Law*, pp.116, 203.

imposing obligations and conferring rights. Suppose that one rejected Hart's effort to distinguish the "internal point of view" from the judgment that the law is morally binding.[23] It would not necessarily follow that legal positivism as a whole should be rejected.

Hart claims that laws can be identified by a rule of recognition that need not include any reference to moral value. He also claims that propositions of law are not (or, at least, need not be) expressive of any moral judgment concerning the justice or the bindingness of laws: propositions of law are, in that sense, morally neutral.

Consider the following two theses:

1.   The law is never morally conclusive. Even given that the law requires that I act in a certain way, it remains an open question whether morally I ought to act in that way. The existence of the law may affect the morality of the action, but it does not conclusively determine it.

2.   The mere fact that a rule is a just and good rule does not make it a law. To be a law, it must emanate from an authorised source. Equally, the fact that a rule is unjust does not show that it is not a law, if the rule does in fact emanate from an authorised source.

These two claims are close to the heart of legal positivism, and explain much of that theory's plausibility. But they can be interpreted in a way that is consistent with the claim that the internal point of view is a judgment of the law's moral bindingness, and that propositions of law are a type of moral judgment.

If we reflect on Hart's account of the need for a rule of recognition to provide the certainty that is lacking in a society with primary rules alone, we will see that the positivist view of law as publicly ascertainable rules reflects an important moral dimension of the law. If we accept the need for publicly ascertainable rules, and we accept that legal rules are publicly ascertainable, we may feel that the whole point of having laws will be defeated if people are willing to comply with the law only

---

[23]   I am not suggesting that we *should* reject Hart's view: I express no opinion on the question. Hart's view on this and many other issues is vigorously defended by Matthew Kramer, *In Defense of Legal Positivism* (Oxford 1999).

when they consider it to be just. We can view the law as binding us morally even when we disapprove of its content. Thus, the claim that legal obligation is a type of moral obligation is quite consistent with the positivist idea that law is law, be it just or unjust. Since the basis of the moral obligation lies in law's publicly ascertainable nature, the claim is also consistent with the idea that laws must emanate from authoritative sources, and that being "just" is not enough to make a rule into a law. Since any moral obligation may be overridden by conflicting obligations, the claim that legal obligation is a type of moral obligation is also consistent with the idea that the law is never completely conclusive of what we morally ought to do: there may be circumstances when it is our moral duty to break the law.

The starting point for our discussion was the contrast between the reductive external view of the legal order as a system of power, sanctions and threats, and the internal view (of the lawyer, the judge and most citizens) of the law as imposing obligations, conferring rights, and so on. The conclusion we are now considering is that the internal point of view is best understood as a particular moral attitude towards the law: not necessarily moral approval of the law's content, but moral acceptance of the general obligation to comply with publicly ascertainable legal rules. Propositions of law are, on this view, not morally neutral. Rather, they represent a specific type of non-conclusive moral judgment: a judgment from the point of view of a specific range of considerations (considerations relating to the need for order and for compliance with rules of which we may disapprove).

When he is explaining the "practical merits" of adopting a positivist conception of law, Hart emphasises the importance of preserving "the sense that the certification of something as legally valid is not conclusive of the question of obedience".[24] Such a perspective is, of course, fully compatible with the position that we are now considering, since that position insists upon the morally non-conclusive nature of propositions of law. Hart then goes on to claim that rejection of the positivist view "may grossly oversimplify" the moral issues to which iniquitous laws can give rise. He refers to situations such as those where it must be decided whether accused persons should be punished for evil acts that were lawful under the evil statutes obtaining at the time when the acts were performed: the issues faced in such

---

[24] *The Concept of Law*, p.210.

situations will be oversimplified if (in consequence of their wickedness) we refuse to describe such evil statutes as "law".

It is difficult to see Hart's point here. The situations he speaks of could surely be described quite lucidly in terminology drawn from a non-positivist theory of law. Where a positivist might speak of "evil laws", for example, his opponent might speak of "evil governmental decrees" or "evil statutes". If, in describing a decree as "law" we make a morally neutral statement (as Hart claims), it can surely make little difference which terminology we choose: the issues are equally clear whether we speak of "evil laws" or use some slightly longer phrasing, such as "evil, but procedurally correct, decrees".

Suppose, however, that we abandon Hart's view that propositions of law are morally neutral, and we adopt the alternative view (described above) that they are morally non-conclusive judgments concerning the applicability of a particular range of moral considerations. Hart's claim that we should speak of "evil laws" rather than "evil non-legal orders" now assumes a new significance. For the positivist terminology would now (on this construction) serve to mark the division between distinct sets of moral reasons. Applying the label "law" even to iniquitous rules would acknowledge the continued force and applicability of the moral considerations stemming from the need for a body of shared publicly ascertainable rules; whereas to deny the legal character of such an iniquitous rule would be to treat it as a mere non-entity lacking in all moral significance.

Some resistance to this view can be anticipated, on the basis that it involves ascribing *some* moral force even to utterly iniquitous laws, such as laws establishing slavery. Where a law is grossly unjust, and we feel that the reasons for complying with it are clearly outweighed by other conflicting considerations, we may be unwilling to speak of it as having any moral claim upon us at all. Are we really to say, for example, that the Roman law of slavery conferred genuine moral rights upon the owners of slaves?[25]

There is, however, a difference between a set of considerations being clearly outweighed, and their being inapplicable. Our reluctance to ascribe moral force to a wicked law may stem from the recognition that any moral considerations favouring compliance with the law are clearly outweighed by other counter-

---

[25] On this issue, see H. Sidgwick, *The Methods of Ethics*, 7th ed., (1907) Chap. 2.

balancing considerations. The general impetus behind Hart's discussion of the "practical merits" of adopting a positivist account of law is to encourage the acknowledgement that moral issues are complex, and that diverse considerations can conflict. From such a perspective, we might have expected that the *refusal* to ascribe moral force to a wicked law might itself be seen as an intellectually obfuscating confusion of different issues: it amounts, in effect to the suggestion that certain reasons are inapplicable, when in fact they may be applicable but clearly outweighed. Whether a proper acknowledgement of moral complexity is best served by Hart's version of legal positivism, or by some rival version, therefore appears to be a matter on which there is ample room for disagreement.

RULES AND FORMAL JUSTICE

Any positivist theory of law should be capable of explaining how non-positivist theories have been led into error. If law really is separate from morality, why have some people thought otherwise? If law is just the rules enforced by officials, how have intelligent men and women been led to confuse it with justice and moral right? Part of the answer might be thought to be the shared vocabulary of law (legal rights and moral rights, legal duties and moral duties, etc.) but this is scarcely a sufficient explanation on its own, for it does not tell us how it is that law and morality have come to share so many of the same concepts.

Hart goes some way in exploring the features of law that link it closely to morality. These are, principally, (1) the connection between rules and the principle of formal justice, and (2) the shared content of legal systems. We shall examine the first of these features here. The shared content of legal systems will be discussed in the next section, and it proves to raise issues of extensive significance.

Hart adopts a well-known distinction between "formal" and "substantive" justice. The principle of formal justice is that like cases should be treated alike, and different cases should be treated differently. Different conceptions of justice offer different explanations of what counts as a "like" or "unlike" case. If I believe in distribution according to need, and you believe in distribution according to desert, we hold different substantive conceptions of justice. But we are agreed on the principle of formal justice: our disagreement is a disagreement about what should count as a material difference to justify differential treatment. Is need relevant, or only desert?

The two aspects of justice (formal and substantive) reflect two different problems of justice in the law. On the one hand, the law may be criticised as substantively unjust. An egalitarian may disapprove of laws based on a Nozickean theory of justice; a Nozickean would disapprove of the law of a Rawlsian community. But on the other hand, whether we approve or disapprove of the substantive conception of justice on which the law is based, we may scrutinise the legal system from the point of view of formal justice. Justice in its formal dimension is essentially a matter of the consistent application of rules. Formal justice requires that, given the criteria of likeness and difference which are established in the law, these criteria should indeed be the determining element in judicial and official decisions applying the law.

Since Hart treats law as a body of rules, it is easy for him to fit the value of formal justice into his theory. If judicial decisions are concerned with the application of rules, the value of formal justice will have an immediate relevance to the moral scrutiny of such decisions. This, in Hart's view, is enough to explain the close connections often thought to exist between the concepts of law and justice.

What Hart does not seem to perceive is the way in which conceptions of formal justice could be developed much more extensively in ways that would erode legal positivism quite fundamentally.[26] For example, if the consistent application of rules is a requirement of justice, then litigants presumably have a moral right that the rules should be applied consistently. Is it not possible that that moral right is just what their legal rights amount to? In other words, could one not argue that legal rights are really a variety of moral rights, based on the value of formal justice? And if formal justice is a matter of consistency, could not that requirement of consistency extend beyond the application of posited black letter rules? Might it not require that judges, in introducing new legal rules, should do so only by reference to the concepts and criteria implicit in the existing law? And would this not suggest that the account of legal reasoning as the application of pre-existing rules interspersed with moral or policy decisions is itself inadequate? In examining the legal

---

[26] An argument to block such moves is offered by Kramer, *In Defense of Legal Positivism* Chap. 2.

theory of Ronald Dworkin, in the next chapter, we will be turning to a line of thought that develops such suggestions into a basic rejection of legal positivism.

THE MINIMUM CONTENT OF NATURAL LAW

One idea that we might associate with natural law theory is the claim that a truly unjust or wicked decree, issued by those in authority, cannot be a valid law. Another, somewhat more subtle, claim is that, to count as law, the governmental ordering of society must at least be *aimed at* justice or the common good. On this latter view, individual laws may be unjust and yet be valid; perhaps an entire system of law may be unjust, while its rules are nevertheless valid. There is a difference, however, between good faith errors concerning justice (the law-makers are trying to do what is just, but are misguided), and a form of governance that is not aimed at justice at all.

Suppose that the Mafia gains complete control of the United Kingdom, overthrowing the established government, demolishing the apparatus of courts, police forces, and so on. In the place of these institutions they issue their own decrees, which they enforce by their own officials. The Mafia's decrees are not aimed at justice or the common good, but at exploitation and profit, and the new "lawmakers" make no attempt to justify their enactments in terms of justice: if questioned, they simply "explain" the laws by reference to their own self-interest. Old laws protecting the citizen from violence are left unenforced. Complicated "tax" provisions determine how much each person should pay to the Mafia; the level of "tax" being determined, not by some theory of justice and the common good, but by reference to what can be extracted without wholly destroying the nation's economic life, thereby killing the goose that lays the golden egg.

Would this count as a "legal system"?

One traditional answer says that it would not. According to this view, it is essential to the concept of a legal system that the apparatus of rules, courts and government, is aimed at the common good, or is intended to implement some conception of justice. A regime intended only to exploit the civil population cannot be properly described as a legal system no matter how many of the institutional arrangements of rules and officials it deploys.

To the legal positivist, such a response is likely to seem an unnecessary confusion of law and morality. The concepts of law and legal system, the positivist will argue, should be explicated in terms of purely factual, non-moral criteria. Legal systems can be put to good purposes or to bad: the enforcement of justice, or the extermination of Jews. Our account of what a legal system is must therefore be formulated in morally neutral terms that make no reference to the good or bad purposes of the system.

In consequence of this desire to explicate law in morally neutral terms, some legal positivists (Kelsen being an example) have concentrated upon law's *form* at the expense of its *content*. It would be very easy, on a superficial reading, to equate Hart's own theory with this type of approach. For does not Hart explain the nature of law by reference to formal features such as a rule of recognition and a body of primary rules which are, for whatever reason, generally complied with? The existence of such features would seem to be consistent with a legal system possessing any content whatever.

In fact, Hart tells us that theories that approach law "in purely formal terms, without reference to any specific content or social needs" have proved to be inadequate.[27] Thus, a part of Hart's argument for distinguishing between duty-imposing and power-conferring laws points to the differing social functions of the two types of rule. Whereas a more formal positivist such as Kelsen is content to demonstrate that such laws can be analysed in a single canonical form, Hart regards Kelsen's approach as purchasing analytical uniformity at the price of distorting the law's diverse social functions. Similarly, Kelsen's purely formal analysis of the structure of law obscures (in Hart's opinion) the difference between a law imposing a tax and a law creating a crime with a financial penalty.[28]

Philosophers distinguish the "necessary" from the "contingent". Traditionally, philosophy has concerned itself with what is necessarily the case, leaving merely contingent truths to the investigation of other disciplines, such as history or the natural sciences. Truths which flow from the very concept of an entity are said to be "necessary": not only are they true of all instances of the entity, but they *must* be true (it could not be otherwise). Thus, it is a necessary truth that all bachelors are unmarried, since it is part of the concept of a "bachelor" that he is

[27] *The Concept of Law,* p.199.
[28] *The Concept of Law,* p.39.

unmarried. On the other hand it might be a contingent truth that all bachelors are sad: even if this is indeed true of all bachelors, it is still not a necessary truth, for it does not flow from the very concept of a "bachelor" that he is sad (we could imagine a happy bachelor, even if none such actually exist).

Jurisprudence as pursued by Hart is concerned with the "concept" of law; it is therefore primarily concerned with "necessary" truths about law, in the sense of truths that flow from the concept of law. When Hart asserts that law is separate from morality, he means that the concept of law does not entail anything about the moral goodness or justice of law: his claim might be sound even if (remarkably) all actual instances of law were indeed just and good. On this criterion, therefore, the shared content of legal systems is simply a "contingent" fact, lying beyond the scope of philosophical interest.

Nevertheless, there is a high degree of convergence in the rules that legal systems contain. They all contain rules imposing some prohibitions upon acts of violence and theft, defining and regulating property and agreements, and governing relationships within the family. This convergence of content is not, in Hart's view, a coincidence. It does not just "happen to be the case" that legal systems have these rules; to that extent we may feel uncomfortable saying that these are contingent facts without philosophical interest. Although "contingent" in terms of the distinction explained above, they are dictated by such fundamental features of human nature and circumstance that they may be said to be "necessary" in a different sense: they are, Hart says, "natural necessities".

If, says Hart, we assume that legal systems consist of rules which will make human survival possible, the basic facts of human nature and human circumstances make rules of the kind outlined essential. Thus, the typical content that we associate with legal systems is not a superficial feature; but nor is it a logical feature of the concept of "law". The shared content of legal systems is a natural necessity. It is a necessary feature of legal systems, given certain basic facts of human nature and circumstances.

It does not follow from this that law must, as a matter of "natural necessity", aim at justice or serve the common good. The aim of survival is a minimal assumption indeed, and its pursuit is entirely consistent with the most wicked forms of governance that human history has seen. An understanding of what Hart calls the "core of good sense" in natural law theory will, however, help us to avoid making extravagant claims to the effect that "law can have any content whatever". This in turn will lead us to realise that the desire to analyse legal concepts in purely formal terms is misguided.

What justifies Hart in invoking the value of "survival" in this context? Minimal it may be, but survival is not a value shared by everyone (some people avidly seek their own extinction; others might pursue the extinction of some hated race even at the cost of their own lives). Hart gives two replies to this question. The less interesting of these two replies says that survival is simply presupposed by the terms of our inquiry into law, since "our concern is with social arrangements for continued existence, not with those of a suicide club." The more interesting reply is to the effect that the structures of thought through which we comprehend "the world and each other" themselves presuppose the general value of survival.

Hart discards "as too metaphysical for modern minds" the notion that survival or any other value "is something ante-cedently fixed which men necessarily desire because it is their proper goal or end." Thus "we may hold it to be a mere contingent fact which could be otherwise, that in general men do desire to live, and that we may mean nothing more by calling survival a human goal or end than that men do desire it."[29] He immediately qualifies this, however, by the following thesis:

"For it is not merely that an overwhelming majority of men do wish to live, even at the cost of hideous misery, but that this is reflected in whole structures of our thought and language, in terms of which we describe the world and each other. We could not subtract the general wish to live and leave intact concepts like danger and safety, harm and benefit, need and function, disease and cure; for these are ways of simulta-neously describing and appraising things by reference to the contribution that they make to survival which is accepted as an aim."[30]

One might suggest that this attributes to the value of "survival" the status of an objective good. The value is inextricably bound up with our entire outlook upon the world and our relations with other human beings. Consequently, it is not clear that any

[29]   *op. cit.* p.192.
[30]   *loc. cit.*

alternative outlook is available to us: the value is a constitutive feature of "our" world.

Seen in this way, Hart's argument might be thought to resemble the argument of a natural lawyer such as Finnis. Finnis seeks to demonstrate the existence of certain objective goods by showing how they are presupposed by all of our practical reasonings and practical understandings: they provide our intellectual access to the entire world of human life and action. Hart could be said to do the same with the more minimal value of "survival". Once we see the similarity, at this point, between the arguments of Hart and Finnis, we are led to ask a series of interesting questions. Are there, for example, other values apart from survival that are "reflected in whole structures of our thought and language"? May we not in this way arrive at a somewhat richer notion of human flourishing, going beyond mere survival? And may that not in turn justify the construction of a more contentious concept of law, including elements that go beyond or supplement Hart's focus on public ascertainability?

THE NATURE OF CONCEPTUAL ANALYSIS

It is common to think of Hart's theory as a contribution to "analytical jurisprudence", a form of inquiry that might be contrasted with the discussions of the nature of law to be found in the great classics of political philosophy, such as Hobbes' *Leviathan* or Aristotle's *Politics*. Hobbes and Aristotle reflected upon law in the context of broader philosophical inquiries, intended to improve our understanding of how the institutions of law and government might serve human well-being. "Analytical jurisprudence" by contrast, is thought of as an enterprise of "conceptual clarification". Its claim to a morally neutral, descriptive, status suggests a concern with the pre-liminary clarification of ideas, rather than an attempt directly to address fundamental questions of political philosophy.

Hart's discussion of the "minimum content of natural law" serves to draw his work much closer than one might at first imagine to the historic tradition of political philosophy. For, at this point in his argument, he departs from claims about conceptual necessity, and reflects upon the law's relationship to the general circumstances of human nature and the human condition. We may neverthless wonder whether the discussion plays a significant part in Hart's theory, or is its position as one small part of one of the later chapters of *The Concept of Law* indicative of its merely marginal role?

This question is quite distinct from asking whether the "minimum content of natural law" represents a significant concession to the opponents of legal positivism: it is clear that it does not, for even the most wicked systems could satisfy the requirements of Hart's "minimum content". Nevertheless, it would be a mistake to treat the discussion as marginal to Hart's project.

In the first place, we have already seen how Hart links the "minimum content" thesis with the role that he gives to law's purpose and content, and his rejection of theories that focus exclusively upon law's form. Thus, he explains that his "simple truisms" concerning human nature and the requirements of survival "are of vital importance for the understanding of law and morals" serving to explain "why the definition of these in purely formal terms, without reference to any specific content or social needs, has proved so inadequate."[31] This acknowledgement, that the "simple truisms" on the human condition "are of vital importance" to the theory of law, should not be overlooked. There are numerous ways in which law's groundedness in the needs of social life underpins Hart's detailed analyses. More to the point, Hart's general account of law's role in the human condition forms the background for his commitment to a legal positivist account of law. For, as we shall see, Hart's somewhat sketchy remarks concerning the nature of concepts and conceptual analysis suggest that claims concerning the presence or absence of "necessary" conceptual connections between law and morality cannot be self-standing, but depend upon a prior exercise of selection and regimentation that must be informed by wider considerations of law's general role and importance.

As we have repeatedly pointed out, legal positivism's denial of necessary connections between law and morals, is a denial of connections grounded in the *concept* of "law". Positivism does not deny the existence of many *contingent* connections between law and morals, even connections that might be found in all actual legal systems. The terms "necessary" and "contingent" are laden with philosophical baggage, and they pose very

---

[31] *op. cit.*, p.199.

complex problems.[32] For present purposes, however, doubts and complexities can be ignored: we can take the distinction to be adequately illustrated by a simple concept such as the concept of a "bachelor". Thus, as we explained a little earlier, the proposition "All bachelors are unmarried" expresses a necessary truth, because it is part of the *concept* of a "bachelor" that he is unmarried. We cannot even imagine a world where not all bachelors are unmarried (if you think you can, you are really imagining a world where the word "bachelor" has changed its meaning). On the other hand, the proposition "All bachelors are sad" is (even supposing that it is true) clearly not a *necessary* truth. "Being sad" is no part of the concept of being a bachelor. Even if all existing bachelors are in fact sad, we can easily imagine a world where some of them are happy. Hence the world-wide misery of bachelors, if it is a fact, is only a *contingent* fact that could conceivably have been otherwise.

A simple concept such as the concept of a "bachelor" may be defined by a set of necessary and sufficient conditions. We can identify those conditions by reflecting upon our ordinary understanding of the word; we can then say which truths about bachelors are "necessary", by referring to our set of defining conditions. It seems clear, however, that Hart does not think that the concept of "law" is open to simple definition in terms of a set of necessary and sufficient conditions, discernible by reflection upon our settled semantic intuitions governing proper usage of the word "law". Indeed, the object of the analysis is not to regulate our use of the word "law" but to "clarify the general framework of legal thought".[33]

In some cases, philosophers and legal theorists find themselves puzzled by concepts that can be applied uncontroversially in their day-to-day use: thus, lawyers may employ with complete confidence the concepts of "contract" or "corporation", but may be thrown into bewilderment if asked to explain, in general theoretical terms, what exactly a contract or corporation really is. The confusion may be the product of a tendency to equate all uses of language with a familiar paradigmatic use. Thus, if we assume that language is invariably used to *describe* observable

---

[32] There are ample grounds for doubting conventional distinctions between the "necessary" and the "contingent". Such doubts could undermine the entire enterprise of "conceptual analysis" as pursued by many of Hart's admirers. The matter raises issues too complex to discuss in this context, however.

[33] *The Concept of Law*, Preface.

features of reality, we will try to analyse "contract" and "corporation" as descriptive terms, and will offer various conflicting theories about the features of the world that they supposedly describe. Here what is needed is a realisation that language can relate to the world in other ways: a concept may have a specific role within a certain body of practices, for example, so that it is to be understood by elucidating the context that gives it its point, and then clarifying its role within that context. Perhaps the word "contract", or "corporation", does not refer to any entity (either real or fictitious) or state of affairs, yet nevertheless has a meaningful role within certain practical contexts.[34] Thus, to say that a statute is "valid" does not *describe* the fact of its enforcement by officials or anyone else (a valid statute may be left unenforced, for example): the concept of validity is used, within the context of a rule of recognition, to draw conclusions about the applicability of the rule of recognition to the circumstances of the statute's enactment.

Clarification of "the framework of legal thought" cannot always be achieved by purely analytical insights of this sort, however. Hart warns us that insights into the nature of language will not help to solve all of the problems of legal philosophy. In particular, he explains:

"The methods of linguistic philosophy which are neutral between moral and political principles and silent about different points of view which might endow one feature rather than another of legal phenomena with significance ... are not suitable for resolving or clarifying those controversies which arise, as many of the central problems of legal philosophy do, from the divergence between partly over-lapping concepts reflecting a divergence of basic point of view or values or background theory ... For such cases what is needed is first, the identification of the latent conflicting points of view which led to the choice or formation of divergent concepts, and secondly, reasoned argument directed to establishing the merits of conflicting theories."[35]

Hart is here saying that some of the problems of legal philosophy

---

[34] See H.L.A. Hart, *Essays in Jurisprudence and Philosophy*, (Oxford 1983), Essay One.

[35] H.L.A. Hart, *Essays in Jurisprudence and Philosophy*, (Oxford 1983) p.6.

require an elucidation of the way in which certain concepts ("contract", "corporation") are used; and such an elucidation need require no attention to wider perspectives upon law that "endow one feature rather than another of legal phenomena with significance". Other problems, however, arise from precisely such a divergence between different points of view (or "values" or "background theory"), and in these cases it will be necessary to offer "reasoned argument" aimed at establishing the merits of the different broader theoretical perspectives (points of view, values, background theories).

It follows from this that Hart's denial of any necessary connection between law and morals is not dictated by any settled rule of language governing the concept of law. Hart is saying that, when we regiment the various facets of the concept of law in an enlightening way, we will find that the central elements (by reference to which the whole is ordered) do not include any elements of morality: everything turns, therefore, on *how* we choose to regiment the concept, and *what* we select as being the central elements. In a sense, Hart's "concept of law" is one that he *constructs*, not one that he simply *discovers*. This is not to say, of course, that his construction is arbitrary; but it is to say that his construction is informed by a broader "point of view" or "background theory" that endows "one feature rather than another of legal phenomena with significance."

Suppose that we ask Hart "Why should we be legal positivists?" Hart's answer would *not* be that rival positions will inevitably lead to contradiction or incoherence, or something of that sort, nor is he claiming that our well-established semantic intuitions are sufficient to dictate a positivist concept. Hart presumably sees his version of legal positivism as conducive to intellectual clarity in so far as it reflects and emphasises the most *important* features of the phenomena of law. His emphasis upon the importance of secondary rules, and the way in which they remedy the defects of the regime of primary rules, suggests that he regards the provision of publicly ascertainable rules as the most important and distinctive feature of the general phenomena of law. Some theorists, by contrast, might regard the ascertainability of legal rules as less important (or no more important) than the law's coercive enforcement; or they might think that the lawyer's focus upon matters of principle and authority manifests a concern for formal justice and fairness, rather than a concern for the ascertainability of rules (after all, how "ascertainable" are the rules of the common law?).

The notion of "importance" turns upon evaluative criteria. These need not, of course, be *morally evaluative* criteria, but they must nevertheless amount to some perspective from which importance can be judged. We may therefore ask what broader perspective underpins and explains Hart's emphasis upon the public ascertainability of rules.

A little re-arranging of Hart's book is sufficient to reveal that Hart's views on human nature and circumstance provide an appropriate perspective from which the public ascertainability of rules might be judged to be the most "important" aspect of the phenomena of law. In his discussion of "the minimum content of natural law" Hart tells us that, human nature and circumstances being what they are, we must have shared rules regulating certain areas of social life, if we are to survive. In his discussion of the function of "secondary rules" (including the rule of recognition)[36] he tells us that a society of any complexity can have shared rules only if it has a basic rule of recognition. Given that we inhabit a complex society, it follows that, if we are to survive, we must have a body of publicly ascertainable rules identified by a basic rule of recognition. This is what reveals the importance of the public ascertainability of law; and it is this perspective that is fundamental to the "importance" of legal positivism.

We can now see that, whatever his focus upon questions of necessary conceptual connection, Hart's analytical theses concerning conceptual necessity are not self-supporting: they depend in part upon a deeper set of claims grounded in the "natural necessities" of human nature and circumstance, rather than in conceptual truths. We have examined the way in which Hart needs to justify a focus upon public ascertainability as the central, or most important, aspect of the general phenomena of law; and we have seen how he might invoke for this purpose his claims about the "natural necessities" of human nature and circumstance, and the "minimum content of natural law".

HART'S THEORY AS POLITICAL PHILOSOPHY

The object of the greatest political philosophy has not been to set forth a utopian vision, but to attain a reflective understanding of the practices and forms of community that we inhabit. Nor need

---

[36] *The Concept of Law*, Chap.5.

the focus of such inquiry be upon abstract concepts, or upon modes of conduct common to the whole of humanity: for, even when the aspiration is to understand universal human goods, it may be accepted that such goods can find expression only in specific forms that vary from one community to another.[37] Thus, from Aristotle's *Politics* to Hegel's *Philosophy of Right*, the great classics of political philosophy have reflected upon the major institutions of political communities because they have found in them an expression of our human nature, and a clue to possibilities for human flourishing. One does not come to understand one's own character by introspection, but by reflecting upon one's actions in the world. Similarly, human nature may find its clearest expression in the various forms of community that have evolved in response to the demands of human nature and circumstance.

While Hart is not seeking to extract moral injunctions from his insights into the nature of law, his inquiries could be seen as a contribution to this broader tradition. To view his work in this way is to ask whether his basic picture of the human condition is soundly based, and whether it goes far enough. Hart expresses scepticism about the possibility of discovering a rich and well-founded notion of human flourishing, or the "good for man";[38] but his own perspective is informed by the value of survival, which he says is presupposed by "whole structures of our thought and language, in terms of which we describe the world and each other."[39] Could not further values be underpinned by a similar argument? The possibility cannot be ruled out in principle. The fact of disagreement about goals (upon which Hart places some emphasis) is not decisive here: for (as Finnis might point out) values may have an axiomatic role within our practical reasoning (the structures of thought whereby we understand each other) even though they would not win express assent from everyone: thus, the fact that some people hold knowledge to be only an instrumental (not an intrinsic or objective) good does not in itself demonstrate that knowledge is *not* an objective good.[40]

---

[37] "The shape which the concept assumes in its actualisation ... is essential for cognition of the concept itself." G.W.F. Hegel, *Elements of the Philosophy of Right*, translated by H.B. Nisbet, (Cambridge 1991), para. 1.
[38] *The Concept of Law*, p.191.
[39] *The Concept of Law*, p.192.
[40] See Chap. 4 above.

Hart's concept of law is underpinned by an account of human nature and circumstances, in conjunction with the value of "survival". His argument for the latter value (as providing an appropriate perspective) seems to point to the value being "objective" in the only sense, perhaps, that values ever can be "objective" (the value is presupposed by our thought and language, and by the way we comprehend each other). An argument of this type, however, might possibly establish the objective status of further values.[41] If our basic perspective were to be informed by values richer than that of survival, or by a different account of human nature and circumstances, might we not reach different conclusions about the nature of law?

A couple of examples will help to clarify the point.

(i) *Sanctions*

Hart's theory of law does not give a central role to sanctions. He regards sanctions as in general necessary for the effectiveness of law, but they are not an integral part of the concept of law. In this respect, Hart's theory differs from some rival positivist theories, such as the theories of Bentham, Austin and Kelsen. Kelsen, for example, regards every law as a direction to officials to apply sanctions, a view that Hart rejects on the basis that it purchases analytical uniformity at the price of distorting law's social functions.[42] A focus upon sanctions suggests a concern for the bad man, who is simply coerced into obedience: but "Why should not law be equally if not more concerned with the 'puzzled man' or 'ignorant man' who is willing to do what is required, if only he can be told what it is?"[43]

Here we see how Hart's theory of law flows smoothly from his general account of human nature and circumstances, which emphasises the need for shared rules, and the problems of uncertainty in discovering the content of those rules. Hence the perspectives of the puzzled man and the ignorant man are, for Hart, at least as important as that of the bad man.

---

[41] For further examples of this general type of argument, see P. Strawson, "Freedom and Resentment" (1962) *Proceedings of the British Academy* (reprinted in Gary Watson (ed.), *Free Will*, Oxford 1982). See also Hart and Honore, *Causation in the Law*, 2nd ed., (Oxford, 1985) p.lxxvii-lxxxi.

[42] *The Concept of Law*, pp.38–42.

[43] *The Concept of Law*, p.40.

Those who give a central role to sanctions in their theories of law, however, might invoke a slightly different picture of the human condition. Bentham, for example, holds that sanctions are a central element in law's nature, because it is a major part of law's role to achieve a convergence between individual self-interest and the general welfare. As we saw in Chapter 1, Bentham holds that we always act out of self-interest; as rational self-interested agents, we will see that the establishment of a system of shared rules is in our joint interest; but compliance with the rules so established, on the other hand, will not always be in our individual interest. Thus we may all be able to see that we will be better off if there are laws against theft, but we will not necessarily find it in our own interest to refrain from stealing. The best situation, from my point of view, is one where you observe the rules prohibiting theft, and I do not; I will be aware, however, that everyone is in a similar situation with regard to compliance, so that general compliance cannot be expected if the rules are not enforced by sanctions. It is therefore in our interests to establish a system of sanctions, in order to ensure that breaking the law is not in the individual's interest. The point of law is not simply to provide guidance for the "puzzled" man, but to ensure that the puzzled man's self-interest coincides with the requirements of the general welfare.

Bentham's theory of law is one wherein sanctions are no less important than the public ascertainability of rules. We can go further, however, and can easily imagine a viewpoint from which sanctions are of far greater importance than the issue of public ascertainability. Suppose we believed that people possess in their hearts a knowledge of certain moral standards (perhaps the knowledge has been planted by God; or perhaps it is part of our genetic make-up, produced by natural selection). In spite of this knowledge, people are weak and selfish, and many deviate from standards to which they know they ought to adhere; or perhaps they simply fear that their compliance with moral standards will expose them to the predations of the wicked, and so are prepared to comply only if the wicked are coerced into compliance.[44] If we thought this way, we might think of law as a coercive apparatus aimed at inducing people to comply with

[44] See Hobbes, *Leviathan*, Chap.15.

standards of which they already have an adequate knowledge. Our theory of law would then focus upon sanctions rather than upon the need for public ascertainability. The Kelsenian view that every law prescribes a sanction might then be seen as highlighting law's social function, rather than obscuring it. The shared content of legal systems (discussed by Hart in connection with the "minimum content of natural law") might also be seen as a central conceptual feature of law, reflecting the relevant moral standards that law serves to enforce. The concept of "law" might be constructed in terms of sanctions, and the characteristic content of legal systems, rather than in terms of the rule of recognition and public ascertainability.

Hart's readers could be forgiven for concluding from his discussion of Austin that an emphasis upon sanctions springs from simple conceptual error: but in fact this is not the case. Theories of law that have emphasised the centrality of sanctions have generally done so in consequence of deeper accounts of human nature and moral value that made such a focus seem appropriate. In their disagreement about the centrality of sanctions to the concept of law, Hart and his predecessors are not fighting a battle that can be confined to purely analytical points (about the difference between "having an obligation" and "being obliged", for example). While Bentham and Austin were inclined to link their emphasis upon sanctions to misguidedly reductionist accounts of law, this is not a necessary feature of a focus upon sanctions, as the example of Kelsen should make clear: Kelsen espouses a non-reductionist theory that views laws as prescribing the official application of sanctions. Nor does the distinction between primary and secondary rules in itself entail rejection of a focus upon sanctions. The distinction is quite compatible with the claim that every law is a direction to officials to apply sanctions, since the rule of recognition could itself be viewed as an instruction to apply sanctions only in accordance with rules emanating from certain sources; other secondary rules (such as rules providing for the making of wills) could be expressed as fragments of wider sanction-stipulating norms.[45]

Thus Hart's rejection of sanction-based theories cannot ultimately be based upon his opposition to reductionism, or

---

[45] For the latter point, see *The Concept of Law* pp.35–38.

upon any other purely analytical consideration: it stems from his theory of human nature and the human situation.

(ii) *Justice*

When a case goes to an appellate court on a point of law, there must be lawyers on both sides who have advised their client that the law is on their side. From the perspective of Hart's theory, this shows that the case is a "penumbral" case, where the settled legal rules do not give a clear cut answer. In such cases, Hart tells us, the court will have regard to diverse considerations: analogies (or the lack of them) between the existing case and cases clearly covered by the rule; the overall coherence of the law; the policies served by the law; considerations of justice and fairness. These arguments do not really concern the question of what the law currently is, so much as the question of how it should be developed to deal with the penumbral case before the court.

Lawyers, however, do not offer their legal arguments as proposals for how the law should be developed: they offer them as claims about what the existing law is. This apparent mismatch between Hart's theory and the assumptions that we ordinarily make flows directly from his concern with public ascertainability, and therefore from his background account of human nature and circumstance. Suppose, therefore, that we adopted a different background account.

In Book 1 of *The Politics*, Aristotle tells us that man is the only animal possessed of speech. He informs us that mere "voice", such as is possessed by animals, serves only for the expression of pleasure and pain; whereas "the power of speech is intended to set forth . . . the just and the unjust." Hence Aristotle's view at this point seems to be that mankind realises its true nature and potential by participating in the articulation of standards of justice. This is an activity that is only possible in a political community; hence man's true nature can be realised only in such a community. Indeed, Aristotle informs us that "justice can exist only among those whose relations to one another are governed by law".[46]

For Hart, deliberation over rival principles in penumbral cases is a relatively marginal feature of the phenomenon of law: the most important aspect of law is revealed in the

---

[46] Aristotle, *Nicomachean Ethics*, Book 5, Chap. 6.

multitude of ordinary situations where the content and applicability of the rules is not in doubt. By contrast with Hart's view, let us focus for a moment upon the remarkable fact that many human communities seek to resolve disputes, not by reference to the unstructured preferences of the people in power, but by articulating highly general principles that, it is felt, should command the support of reasonable people in virtue of their intrinsic justice. If, like Aristotle, we were to regard the capacity to articulate standards of justice as the most distinctively human capacity, we might not share Hart's desire to marginalise the legal debates in problematic appellate cases. Indeed, the effort to decide disputes by reference to articulable principles of justice and fairness, after discussion of such principles in the public space of the courtroom, might seem to be the very essence of law. A court might be seen as pre-eminently a "forum of principle",[47] and the law might be thought of as revealing its nature most fully in the elevated context of appellate decisions.

Each of the above examples is aimed at showing that our account of law's nature would differ from that offered by Hart *if* we worked from a basic value richer than survival, or we adopted a different account of human nature and human circumstances. Remember that we are not trying to show that Hart's theory of law is false: we are trying to show that his account depends upon an account of value, human nature and the human situation. Consequently, it does not matter whether you consider the values and accounts of human nature, discussed above, to be plausible.

It should be noted that I am not suggesting a relationship of one way dependence here. Theories of law's nature depend upon deeper accounts of human nature; but, at the same time, we can understand our nature only by reflecting upon the institutions and practices in which it is given expression. To test the views of human nature set out above, we would need to see how successful they can be in offering a plausible account of human institutions such as government, the family, property, literature, art, science and many others, including law. If we found that the Aristotelian view (for example) would yield only a contrived and implausible account of law, that would count

[47]   Ronald Dworkin, *A Matter of Principle* (Harvard 1985) Chaps. 1 and 2.

against the theory as a whole (it would not be decisive if the theory was highly succesful on other fronts).

LEGAL DOCTRINE AND LEGAL THEORY

Hart's rejection of purely formal approaches to the under-standing of law, and his insistence that legal theory needs to take account of the social function of laws, might seem to align his approach to jurisprudence with theories of social science that emphasise the purposive character of social practices and political institutions, and the consequent need to understand such practices and institutions by reference to their purposes.[48] For such theories, the values served by an institution are not an external imposition upon the nature of the institution, but are an integral part of its nature. Goals and values are multiple, however, and are often contested by the participants. Perhaps it is true, for example, that the nature of "democratic government" cannot be elucidated simply by reference to the existence of formal mechanisms such as elections, without also referring to the presumed *point* of those mechanisms; but the point of such mechanisms is likely to be contested by those who participate in them, and the debate between rival accounts of the relevant purposes and values is likely to form one important aspect of the life of the democratic institutions. It is for this reason that theories emphasising the goal-directed character of institutions frequently reject any outright separation between the descriptive understanding of such institutions and the normative debates that characterise their actual working.

In offering a theory of the nature of such a social practice as law, is jurisprudence adopting the perspective of the participants in that practice, for whom disagreement about the nature and point of law may be an important aspect of the operation of legal institutions (just as democratic politics often encompasses argument about the nature of democracy)? In the next chapter we will find that one of Hart's most formidable critics views legal theory in precisely this way. According to Dworkin, judicial disagreements concerning the details of legal doctrine not infrequently reflect and embody broader disagreements con-cerning the nature of law; legal theory is an attempt to intervene

---

[48] For a brief, lucid, discussion see R. Geuss, *History and Illusion in Politics* (Cambridge 2001) p.113.

in such debates, which are essentially internal to the practices of law: "Jurisprudence is the general part of adjudication", he tells us.

Hart's view, by contrast, appears to be that jurisprudence can usefully reflect upon the character of law from a perspective that is not internal to the practices under investigation. Legal theory, in Hart's view, should take account of the attitudes of participants (such as the "internal point of view") but need not itself *adopt* those attitudes, nor become a contribution to the debates of those who share them. The wish to remain aloof from such participant debates presumably helps to explain Hart's austere reliance upon a very minimal account of human nature and value as the basis of his claims concerning law's function: he hopes to transcend contentious theses regarding law's proper role, rather than engage in such controversies.

The trouble with this approach is that it fails to take seriously the debates between participants concerning the nature of law. For the Hartian legal theory is presented as *revealing* law's nature, by reference to a very austere and minimal account of law's purpose. Having understood law's nature by reading Hart, how then are we to understand the various non-Hartian claims concerning law's nature that are offered by participants in the practice of law, as part of that ongoing practice? To view them as simply *false*,[49] in virtue of their non-Hartian character, does not seem to be an option: for one cannot claim to have offered a theory that is disengaged from the internal debates, while simultaneously treating that theory as having falsified the claims made within those debates. One must therefore adopt the expedient of reconstruing those claims about the nature of law that are made in the course of debate between legal participants: we could view them as complex forms of legal argument, applying the criteria of legal validity specified in the particular system's "rule of recognition"; or we could regard them as open-ended moral or political debates which, for some curious reason, are by convention conducted in the form of a debate about law's nature.[50] However we view them, we of necessity fail to construe

---

[49] It might be suggested that such analytical theories are neither true nor false, but are to be evaluated in terms of their usefulness, or their clarificatory power. Whatever the dimension of assessment, however, one can scarcely claim to be disengaged from internal debates whilst simultaneously offering an implicit evaluation of the positions adopted in those debates.

[50] See T. Honore, *Making Law Bind* (Oxford 1987) p.32.

them as they are viewed by participants: that is, as debates about law's nature.

Imagine a similar approach to the nature of democracy. The theorist would begin by disavowing any intention to engage in normative debate concerning the goals or values of democracy, such as might be engaged in by citizens and lawmakers with a view to advocating this or that path of development for the democratic institutions. A theory would then be constructed, from an austerely "external" viewpoint, and would be offered as revealing the "nature" of democracy. The multiple contentious claims, regarding the nature of democracy, offered by citizens and lawmakers would then be said to be something other than what they purport to be: not claims about the nature of democracy (for that nature is supposedly best revealed by a disengaged theory constructed from an "external" viewpoint) but proposals for how democracy ought to be changed or defended from change.

Given the multiple and contested nature of the goals and values that social institutions may be understood to serve, an understanding of those institutions from an "external" viewpoint cannot, without distortion, be achieved by working from very minimal and uncontentious values. This is the way that Hart seems to approach the problem, but the approach ends by distorting the phenomena under consideration. If we really wish to characterise law's nature while remaining disengaged from the disputes of participants, the most important fact to record might be the very fact that Hart's theory tends to suppress or distort: that it is a part of law's nature that its nature should be continuously disputed.

Hart might well deny the general proposition that it is a part of law's nature that its nature should be continuously disputed. In Hart's view, legal theoretical dispute concerning the nature of law is as an entirely different kind of enterprise from the interpretation and application of legal doctrine in adjudication: legal doctrinal thought for Hart does not involve questions of legal theory, but is a matter of rule-application bounded by a basic rule of recognition.

Hart's view probably reflects the circumstances in which his theory was written. In the middle decades of the twentieth century, English law had long had well-established rules defining the sources of law, and had enjoyed a stable and shared framework of ideas for up to a century; in addition, the basic temper of English law was and is fundamentally pragmatic and sceptical of "theory" of any kind. In such periods of settled practice, legal theory may seem to be a matter of external reflection upon the law, rather than an integral part of the operation of the legal order. Things do not, however, always go so smoothly. In a host of circumstances, such as when states wrestle with new constitutional settlements,[51] or when supra-national organisations evolve in the direction of becoming states,[52] fundamental juridical questions are raised that cannot be resolved by reference to a well-established rule of recognition. Something similar is true when a basically a-theoretical legal culture finds some of its most prominent lawyers proclaiming a need to order the law by reference to highly general principles, or abstract doctrinal categories.[53] Even the resolution of a technical issue of labour law may depend upon a choice between different conceptions of a "right", which may in turn depend upon dramatically contrasting visions of the nature of law.[54] It is in contexts such as these that questions concerning the nature of law are likely to be addressed.

When questions concerning the sources of law are not resolvable by reference to the basic rule of recognition, Hart regards them as amounting, in substance, to political questions where "all that succeeds is success".[55] The intellectual and

---

[51] See A.J. Jacobson and B. Schlink (eds) *Weimar: A Jurisprudence of Crisis* (California 2000).

[52] See P. Eleftheriadis, "The European Constitution and Cosmopolitan Ideals" (2001) 7 *Columbia Journal of European Law* p.21.

[53] For example, a judge committed to searching for highly general principles in the law can reach quite eccentric conclusions about the meaning of a statutory provision. See for example the decision of Goff J. in *B.P. Exploration v. Hunt* [1979] 1 W.L.R. 783. The assumption that a statutory provision *must* embody some general principle is one that could be defended (if at all) only on the plane of legal theoretical debate concerning the nature of law.

In the nineteenth century, many common lawyers advocated a more "principled" approach to legal doctrine, by appealing to the Kantian conceptions of law that had exerted a powerful influence in Germany. See Mathias Reimann, "The Common Law and German Legal Science" in R. W. Gordon (ed.) *The Legacy of Oliver Wendell Holmes Jr.* (Edinburgh 1992).

[54] I have argued elsewhere that Lord Lindley's judgment in *Quinn v. Leathem* was informed by assumptions drawn from nineteenth century German jurisprudence. See Simmonds, "Rights at the Cutting Edge" in M. Kramer, N.E. Simmonds, and H. Steiner, *A Debate Over Rights* (Oxford 1998).

[55] *The Concept of Law*, p.153.

theoretical aspect of legal practice is therefore treated as lying somehow beyond law, in the realm of discretion where judges must draw upon a rag-bag of ideas in order to fill gaps in the system of rules. Hart here seems to adopt a Procrustean approach to complex realities that is plausible only when such open-ended debates can be confined to the periphery of the legal system. As modern legal systems confront increasingly diverse and unprecedented challenges, however, such intractable "penumbral" questions can proliferate.

We noted above that Hart seems to deny the possibility of offering a definition of "law" in terms of necessary and sufficient conditions: but he nevertheless believes that we can identify certain elements as central to the concept. A more radical denial of the possibility of definition can be found in the work of Friedrich Nietzsche. Nietzsche observes that "only that which has no history is definable."[56] Long standing practices (Nietzsche's example is the practice of punishment) have a certain continuity that survives and underlies considerable changes in the *meaning* attached to the practice. In time, the practice comes to resemble a complex palimpsest through which the various historical layers of significance are simultaneously visible; it becomes impossible to say what the point or object of the practice truly is. Consequently, the concept of "punishment" comes to be one in which "an entire process is semiotically concentrated", rendering the concept indefinable.[57]

Those situations where reflection upon the nature of law erupts into the practice of doctrinal legal argument both manifest and contribute to the semiotic complexity of law: they demonstrate the way in which legal practice results from, and is always suspended within, a perpetually contested landscape of philosophical ideas. They might therefore be regarded as significant moments, that we marginalise only at the cost of greatly impoverishing our understanding.

From a Nietzschean standpoint, Hart might be thought to ignore the layers of semiotic complexity that make up the practices of law: he is, in effect, seeking to "define" the historically shaped concept of "law", at least to the extent of selecting certain elements as central, and ordering other aspects around their centrality. This process of selection, however,

---

[56] Friedrich Nietzsche, *The Genealogy of Morals*, 2nd essay, section 13
     (various editions and translations).
[57] *loc. cit.*

requires an unflinching willingness to impose one's preferred regimentation upon complex historical realities, rather than an alert sensitivity to the various layers of significance that may be found within them.

For some practical purposes, a strong desire to regiment complex realities, ordering them around a very simple model, may be entirely appropriate. Even Nietzscheans need not deny the value or the possibility of attempts to achieve univocality in our practices. Any such attempt, however, must be seen as an *intervention* aimed at advancing certain strands at the expense of others. The internal dynamic of complex human institutions frequently consists of such attempts to reconstrue the purpose and significance of the institution. Hart is misguided if he sees himself as discovering an essence or central case of law that enjoys intellectual priority over the numerous other facets of significance exhibited by the actual practice under investigation. He is misguided also in imagining that an account of the practice's core significance can be constructed from the disengaged standpoint of an external observer. If one eschews the participants' desire to replace semiotic complexity with univocality, one can only record the multiple layers of significance to be found within the practice, and perhaps offer a "genealogical" reconstruction of the history that produced such multiple meanings.

Selected reading

H. L. A. Hart, *The Concept of Law* (1961), 2nd edition (1994).
H. L. A. Hart, *Essays in Jurisprudence and Philosophy* (1983).
M.H. Kramer, *In Defense of Legal Positivism* (1999).
N. MacCormick, *H. L. A. Hart* (1981).
R. Sartorious, "Hart's Concept of Law" in R. Summers (Ed.) *More Essays in Legal Philosophy* (1971).

Chapter 6

DWORKIN

In the Introduction to Part 2, I explained that legal theorists disagree not only about the nature of law, but also about the nature of legal theory. What exactly is one doing in constructing a theory of law's nature? Should such a theory be a conceptual analysis devoid of contentious moral presuppositions and implications (as Hart would say)? Or should a theory of law be grounded in a deeper moral philosophy, and be aimed at revealing (or denying) law's moral claims upon us, and perhaps at prescribing the conduct of judges and citizens?

Jurisprudence is often seen as divided into "normative jurisprudence" and "analytical jurisprudence". For those who accept this distinction as a fundamental watershed, theories of justice of the type that we examined in Part 1 would be seen as falling within "normative jurisprudence", because they seek to offer normative guidance as to what ought be done. Theories of law such as that offered by Hart would be seen as falling within "analytical jurisprudence" insofar as they aim to clarify our understanding of the concept of "law", without offering any normative guidance as to how we ought to behave or what institutions should be supported as just and right. Several theorists regard the analytical/normative distinction as misleading, however. They believe that an understanding of law's nature will inevitably be bound up with moral and political understandings that have normative implications. Indeed, they may take the view that, if detached from such a normative project, legal theory would be a pointless activity.

Ronald Dworkin began by offering a critique of Hart's account of law's nature that did not fundamentally call into question Hart's conception of legal theory; but he was ultimately to deepen his position into a critique of Hart's entire conception of the enterprise of jurisprudence. To understand how this came about, it will be helpful to begin by describing Dworkin's earlier writings, before going on to a discussion of his later, and more fully developed, theory.

RULES AND PRINCIPLES

Hart claims that we can work out what the existing law is by reference to the basic rule of recognition. The rule of recognition identifies certain sources, such as statutes and judicial decisions, as sources of law: a rule counts as "law" if it emanates from such a source. Sometimes it will be unclear whether or not a rule applies to a given case. This is because of the "open texture" of language. For example, it may be unclear whether a rule relating to "vehicles" should be applied to a milk-float, a pedal car, or a pair of roller skates, since it is not clear whether these count as "vehicles". In such cases, the court has to exercise its discretion, and will have regard to policy considerations (including the presumed policy objectives of the rule in question) and to considerations of fairness. But in the majority of cases, no such exercise of discretion is necessary: a motor car, for example, is clearly a "vehicle".

Dworkin challenges this general picture of law and legal reasoning. He discusses a United States case, *Riggs v. Palmer*, although he tells us that almost any case in a law school casebook would serve his purpose equally well. In *Riggs v. Palmer* a murderer claimed that he was entitled to inherit under the will of his victim. The will was valid, and was in the murderer's favour. The existing rules of testamentary succession contained no exceptions relating to such a case. The court decided, however, that the application of the rules was subject to general principles of law, including the principle that no man should profit from his own wrong. They held that the murderer was not entitled to the inheritance.

Riggs v. Palmer shows us, according to Dworkin, that the law does not consist entirely of rules: it also includes principles. Principles differ from rules in a number of related ways:

1.   Rules apply in an "all or nothing" fashion. If a rule applies, and it is a valid rule, the case must be decided in accordance with it. A principle, on the other hand, gives a reason for deciding the case one way, but not a conclusive reason. A principle may be a binding legal principle, and may apply to a case, and yet the case need not necessarily be decided in accordance with the principle. This is because principles conflict and must be weighed against each other: see points 2 and 3 below.

2.   Valid rules cannot conflict. If two rules appear to conflict, they cannot both be treated as valid. Legal systems have doctrinal techniques for resolving such apparent conflicts of valid rules, *e.g.* the maxim *lex posterior derogat priori*. Legal principles, on the other hand, can conflict and still be binding legal principles.

3.   Because they can conflict, legal principles have a dimension of weight which rules do not have. Rules are either valid or not valid: there is no question of one rule "outweighing" another. But principles must be balanced against each other.

This analysis may at first seem hard to square with Dworkin's own discussion of *Riggs v. Palmer*: for was that not a case where a principle came into conflict with a rule (the statutes regulating testamentary succession)? And does not Dworkin's analysis suggest that principles conflict only with other principles, and not with rules?[1] The answer would seem to be that *Riggs v. Palmer* is in fact, despite appearances, a clash between principles, not between rules and principles. The rules of testamentary succession were binding on the court by virtue of certain underpinning principles, such as the principle that "the enactments of the legislature should be enforced according to their clear wording". This principle (or one like it) came into conflict with the principle that "no man shall profit from his own wrong". The court, in deciding that the latter principle was decisive, was not deciding that that principle would always outweigh the principle about enforcing statutes. Rather, they were deciding that the effect of allowing a murderer to inherit from his victim would be such a serious infringement of the values protected by the "no profit" principle, that that principle should prevail in those circumstances. In consequence, the statutory rules on succession were to be construed as subject to an implicit proviso, rather than being enforced according to their surface meaning.

   This analysis enables us to see how the courts can change the law while applying the law. At first this seems paradoxical: one might argue that if the courts change the law they must do so by deviating from the strict application of the law. However, we can see from the example of *Riggs v. Palmer* that a court may create a new exception to the established rules, but do so on the basis of

---

[1]   See the objection put by Hart, *The Concept of Law*, 2nd ed., p. 262.

legal principles. Thus, *Riggs v. Palmer* created a new exception to the general rules on testamentary succession ("a murderer may not inherit under the will of his victim") but justified that exception by a legal principle ("no man shall profit from his own wrong").

PRINCIPLES AND POSITIVISM

Suppose that we accept Dworkin's analysis of *Riggs v. Palmer*. What does this have to do with legal positivism? It is not enough merely to point out that Hart does not mention legal principles, for that does not show that they are in any way inconsistent with his theory. Why shouldn't we treat Dworkin as simply making a useful addition to Hart's theory?

One might at first think that *Riggs v. Palmer* would not even qualify as a hard case in Hart's theory. Hart's discussion of the "open texture" of language can give the impression that he thinks *all* legal uncertainties flow from such indeterminacy in the meaning of words; but *Riggs v. Palmer* was not concerned with any uncertainty about the exact range of applicability of the concepts "valid will", "profit", "wrong" or anything else. We need to remember, however, that Hart is concerned with *necessary* features of law, not *contingent* features that may be exhibited by this or that legal system. Indeterminacies stemming from the open texture of language are necessary features of law that could not conceivably be avoided; but a focus on such necessary features does not deny the possibility of other, contingent, sources of indeterminacy that may or may not be present in a particular system. Thus, Hart could acknowledge that it is possible for legal standards to conflict with each other, and that, when this occurs, it produces a type of uncertainty in the law not encompassed by his discussion of the "open texture" of language. There seems to be nothing inconsistent with legal positivism here.

The importance of the analysis as an attack on positivism can be appreciated only when we come to Dworkin's account of how legal principles are identified as part of the law: for he claims that legal principles cannot be identified by anything resembling Hart's rule of recognition. A principle may already be a legal principle although no court has ever formulated it or laid it down as a principle. For example, suppose that no lawyer or judge has ever mentioned the principle that no man shall profit from his own wrong. It might still be possible to demonstrate that that principle is an existing legal principle (Dworkin tells us) if one could show that the principle provides an appropriate justification for a range of established black letter rules and decisions (*e.g.* a gambler cannot sue for his winnings; a prostitute cannot sue for her earnings; a person injured in an illegal enterprise cannot claim compensation; a party cannot rely on a mistake induced by his own fraud in order to avoid or enforce a contract). Thus we cannot identify principles simply by consulting certain sources, but only by engaging in a moral or political discussion of what principles should be invoked to justify the black letter rules of law.

Two strategies for reconciling principles with positivism may be contrasted. On the one hand, the positivist may argue that principles are indeed a part of the law, but that they can be identified by some version of the rule of recognition. On the other hand, the positivist may concede that principles cannot be identified by a basic rule of recognition, but may argue that this is because they are not in reality a part of the law: they are extra-legal moral considerations that are applied by the courts, in the exercise of their discretion, when the legal rules fail to give a clear and determinate answer. We shall examine each of these two responses in turn, starting with the latter response.

Discretion and rights

Positivists could claim that Dworkin's "principles" are simply moral considerations that the judge may have recourse to, in the exercise of his or her discretion, in cases where the law does not give a clear answer. It could then be argued that an inability to identify principles by a basic rule of recognition does not refute legal positivism in general or Hart's theory in particular. To produce a refutation of positivism, Dworkin must offer compelling reasons for treating principles as a part of the existing law.

Dworkin does endeavour to produce such reasons. To understand the strongest of those reasons fully, let us begin by noting one initial difficulty for the positivist. If we treat principles as a part of the law, we can see why *Riggs v. Palmer* was a hard case. This was not because of any vagueness or "open texture" in the relevant rules, but because it involved a conflict between different legal standards: the principles requiring the enforcement of statutes according to their clear wording conflicted with the principle that no man should profit from his own wrong. But if principles are not part of the law, *Riggs v. Palmer* did not involve any conflict of legal standards. Nor did it involve any vagueness, uncertainty, or "open texture": the legal rules were clear and unambiguous. So why was it a hard case? If the law consists only of rules, *Riggs v. Palmer* was a case where the legal rules conflicted with desirable social policies or moral values. If the positivist takes that view of the case, he must hold one of two things. On the one hand, he may hold that *Riggs v. Palmer* was wrongly decided (we would then have to consider Dworkin's claim that almost any other case from a law school casebook would have served his argument equally well). On the other hand, the positivist may hold that judges may legitimately alter the legal rules where they conflict with desirable social policies or moral values. But, if a judge can alter a rule whenever that seems best on the whole, he cannot be said to be bound by the rule.[2] The upshot of this argument is that, if we refuse to regard principles as a part of the law, we will be forced to conclude that judges may set aside the established law whenever they think it best on the whole to do so. But if that is so, judges are never bound by rules at all, rules are of no real importance, and our "legal positivism" collapses into a version of rule-scepticism.

Dworkin offers an argument closely related to the above when he points out that courts in most jurisdictions now have the power to depart from their own earlier decisions. If principles are part of the law, we may regard the court's decision to depart from earlier precedents as itself regulated by legal principles. On this view, a court may alter the established rules only in the implementation of legal principles: even in altering the legal rules, the judge is applying the law. But if we hold that principles are not a part of the law, we must say that judges may depart from earlier decisions when, in the exercise of their discretion, they think it best to do so. If, however, judges can alter established rules in this way whenever they think it best (on moral or social policy grounds), they cannot be said to be bound by the rules at all. Thus, Dworkin argues, if principles are not part of the law, rules are not binding. Once again we are led to the conclusion that a rejection of the idea of legal principles

---

[2]   Raz argues that a power to alter the rules is consistent with being bound by the rules, provided that it is a limited power. Raz has considerable difficulty, however, in offering an acceptable account of the nature of the limitations upon the relevant judicial power. See above pp.147–148.

leads, not to the positivist view of law as black letter rules, but to a thoroughgoing "rule-scepticism".

The view that principles are not a part of the law, but are extra-legal considerations applied in the exercise of discretion, is incompatible (according to Dworkin) not only with the idea of binding rules, but also with the idea that courts enforce the parties' rights. We regard courts, not as deciding to benefit the plaintiff at the defendant's expense (or vice versa), but as enforcing the plaintiff's or the defendant's rights. But if principles are not part of the law, it follows that courts in hard cases (which would certainly include many of the cases that reach an appellate level) are exercising discretion; and if the court has a discretion about how it will decide the case, the parties cannot have a right to any particular decision. Suppose that I am the trustee of £1,000 under a discretionary trust, and that you are one of six beneficiaries. If I have a discretion about how the money is distributed, it cannot be the case that you have a right to the whole £1,000. If you have a right to the whole sum, I cannot have a discretion about how it is distributed. Similarly, if a court has discretion about how it decides a case, neither the plaintiff nor the defendant can have a right to a decision in his favour. If courts in hard cases are exercising discretion, they cannot be enforcing pre-existing rights. But we ordinarily do think of courts as enforcing rights, and that is presupposed by the characteristic form of legal arguments. So we can refuse to admit principles as part of the law only by radically revising the way that we think and speak about law.

Some positivists are happy to accept this conclusion. They argue that people really only have established legal rights in clear cases. In hard cases, a court is not enforcing rights but exercising discretion on moral or social policy grounds. Lawyers and judges certainly talk as if they are concerned with the enforcement of pre-existing rights, but (it is argued) this form of speech is purely rhetorical and traditional, devoid of any real significance.

Whether or not this response is available to the positivist depends, of course, on the success or failure of the earlier argument that, if principles are not part of the law, rules are never binding. If the latter argument is correct, the discretion that positivists find in hard cases cannot be confined to hard cases, but will characterise *all* cases: the conclusion would have to be that we possess no legal rights at all.

THE RULE OF RECOGNITION AND THE SOUNDEST THEORY

Dworkin does not argue that all moral principles are *ipso facto* legal principles. Some principles are legal principles and others are not. We might therefore attempt to argue along the following lines:

"Dworkin accepts a distinction between legal and non-legal principles. He therefore must hold that there is some criterion that distinguishes legal from non-legal principles. But the idea that, in each legal system, there is some such basic criterion is the essential core of Hart's theory of the rule of recognition. Dworkin's theory therefore itself depends upon some notion of a basic rule of recognition."

Dworkin's response is to point out that Hart's theory of the rule of recognition cannot simply claim that there is a criterion distinguishing law from non-law. Hart must claim, according to Dworkin, that laws are identified by pedigree not by content, *i.e.* a rule counts as a law not because it is just or fair (a matter of its content) but because it has been laid down or established in a statute or a case (a matter of source or pedigree). The whole point of having a rule of recognition, according to Hart, is to provide a body of rules which will be publicly ascertainable, in the sense that we can work out what the rules are without falling back on our judgments about justice or moral right. According to Dworkin, this general thesis only makes sense if the rule of recognition identifies the law by criteria of pedigree. To the extent that the rule said something like "all those rules which are just are legal rules" it would provide no greater certainty than do our differing views of justice. Legal positivism must hold that laws are identified by their pedigree (their source of enactment) and not by their content.

Legal principles, however, are not identified by their pedigree, Dworkin informs us. It is not necessary that a principle should have been laid down in a statute or a case. The judge who first formulates a legal principle formulates it as an existing part of the law and not as a legislative innovation of his own. In general, principles are identified by showing that they are embedded in the established rules and decisions, in the sense that the principle provides a suitable justification for the black letter rules. Thus, one would seek to show that the principle "no man shall profit from his own wrong" is an existing principle of the law by showing how a number of the specific legal rules embody the principle, in the sense that they appear to be specific applications of the principle to diverse contexts: the principle might be invoked as a general justification for the content of those rules.

Dworkin describes an imaginary judge, called Hercules. Since he possesses superhuman powers, Hercules is able to carry out his judicial function in a far more thorough-going and articulate manner than could any actual judge. Nevertheless, the procedures and methods of argument employed by Hercules represent the form of decision-making that is presupposed by the methods of more fallible judges. Hercules does fully and explicitly what normal judges do in a more piecemeal and less self-conscious manner. When Hercules decides a hard case, he must begin by constructing a theory of law applicable to his jurisdiction. This theory of law will consist of an elaborate moral and political justification for the legal rules and institutions of the jurisdiction. For example, Hercules's jurisdiction may contain settled rules about legislative supremacy, and about the binding force of precedent. Hercules will need to work out a body of principles that will justify these rules. He must ask "What moral principles would serve to justify the doctrine of legislative supremacy? What moral principles underlie the doctrine of precedent?" Hercules must also consider the moral and political theory that seems to be at the basis of the substantive law of contract, tort, property, criminal law, welfare law, and so on. If Hercules carries out this task properly, the result will be a complex and integrated body of principles.

Now the criterion that, according to Dworkin, distinguishes legal from non-legal principles is this: a principle is a legal principle if it forms a part of the soundest theory of law that could be offered as a justification for the established legal rules and institutions in a particular jurisdiction. Constructing such a theory is, inevitably, a highly controversial matter involving complex and intractable issues of moral and political theory. It differs fundamentally from the process of identifying laws by reference to their sources in the way that seems to be envisaged by Hart's account of the rule of recognition.

There is a further respect in which Dworkin's theory differs from Hart's notion of the rule of recognition. In Hart's theory, we identify the law by reference to the basic rule of recognition; but we identify the basic rule of recognition by reference to the empirical facts of official behaviour: in this way, the content of the law can be established by a purely empirical inquiry, without asking any controversial moral questions. But this assumes that a judge, called upon to apply the rule of recognition, will apply the rule that is accepted by his fellow judges. This is fundamentally different from the position of Hercules. Hercules does not seek to apply the theory of law that is accepted by his judges: he seeks to apply the soundest theory of law, whether or not that theory is accepted by the other judges. Hercules must decide for himself which body of principles provides the best justification for the established laws. He is faced by a controversial question of political theory, not an empirical question about the behaviour of his colleagues on the bench.

Dworkin holds that his account of law and adjudication accords more closely with our experience than does that of Hart. For example, we know that even very basic constitutional issues and questions concerning the sources of legal validity can be controversial: different lawyers may take different views on such questions. If, however, the law was based upon a rule of recognition that existed as a shared practice of officials, it could not be controversial in this way: if judges disagree about the fundamental sources of law, this cannot be in consequence of some *uncertainty* in the rule of recognition, for the very fact of disagreement establishes that there is no shared practice amongst the judges.[3] What we find at the foundation of a legal system, therefore, is not a shared practice or rule of recognition, but a diversity of partially overlapping theories of law held by different judges.

Dworkin's picture of adjudication looks dramatically different from the one we seem to find in the pages of Hart's *Concept of Law*. We need to remember, however, that Hart is concerned to deny the existence of *conceptually necessary* connections between law and morality: he is not denying the existence of contingent connections to be found in this or that system of law. Legal validity, according to Hart, is dependent upon criteria established by the practices of officials in each legal system: specifically, by a rule of recognition. Nor does Hart claim that

---

[3] Dworkin's assumption (at this stage in his career) that a practice cannot have an uncertain content was unsound. I pointed out that practices may possess an uncertain content, in so far as the practice needs to be interpreted, and rival interpretations may be offered. See Simmonds, "Practice and Validity" (1979) *Cambridge Law Journal* 361.

The idea that practices may be the focus of interpretative disagreement became the basis for Dworkin's later theory.

the rule of recognition *must* identify rules by pedigree not content, or by essentially non-moral facts such as the source of enactment. He expressly acknowledges that "In some systems, as in the United States, the ultimate criteria of legal validity explicitly incorporate principles of justice or substantive moral values."[4]

It therefore seems that the first round of Dworkin's attack on positivism partially misfired: for it is not clear that his claims are really inconsistent with legal positivism as conceived by Hart. Dworkin insists that positivism must identify the law by "pedigree" not content; but Hart does not share this view. Even if Dworkin's account of Herculean adjudication does capture the character of legal thinking in Britain and America (and perhaps other countries), Hart is not denying the existence of connections between law and morality that depend upon the particular features and practices of this or that legal system, for these would be purely *contingent* connections. Hart is concerned to deny the existence of *necessary* connections between law and morality, grounded in the *concept* of law.

Dworkin's response to this misfire was to deepen the nature and focus of his attack. This he did in his book *Law's Empire*,[5] which represents the most mature statement of his legal theory. To the views expressed in that book we now turn.

CONSTRUCTIVE INTERPRETATION

In Hart's view there is a fundamental contrast between the intellectual enterprise of interpreting and applying the law, on the one hand, and the enterprise of offering a legal theory, on the other. When a judge forms a view of the existing law and applies it to an individual case, basic criteria of legal validity specific to that particular system are being followed. When a legal theorist offers a jurisprudential analysis of the nature of law, by contrast, claims are being made about what is involved in the very concept of law. The legal theorist might point out, for example, that the concept of "legal validity" is internal to systems

---

4   *The Concept of Law*, p.204. Dworkin argued, at one point, that Hart could not adopt this view consistently with the general philosophical commitments of his theory. For the problems with Dworkin's argument, see Kramer, *In Defense of Legal Positivism* (Oxford 1999) pp.152–161.

5   (London 1986)

possessing a basic rule of recognition; the judge *applies* such a rule to decide an individual case, but need not offer or hold any general views on the concept of "law" or "legal validity" as such.

For Hart there is also a fundamental distinction between "analytical" and "normative" jurisprudence. An example of "analytical" jurisprudence is Hart's own theory of law: it is aimed at clarifying the "concept" of law, not at prescribing our conduct by telling us what is good or bad, just or unjust. An example of "normative" jurisprudence would be Rawls' theory of justice, for this is aimed at prescribing the way in which our institutions ought to be reformed.

In *Law's Empire* Dworkin simultaneously rejects both of these distinctions. He claims that legal theory, if it is to be a worthwhile intellectual activity, will be inseparable from the process of interpreting and applying the law, and will be aimed at offering us prescriptive guidance, rather than simply at "clarifying" our "concepts".

Let us cast our minds back to Hercules. Hercules decides cases by offering a sweeping moral or political theory that serves to justify the existing legal materials of statute and precedent. He is looking for a set of general principles that will "fit" the bulk of the statutes and cases, but will also present them as justifiable from the viewpoint of justice. Dworkin now takes this account of the Herculean project and deepens it into an account of the nature of legal theory. For legal theorists, according to Dworkin, are not in substantial reality concerned to analyse concepts, but to interpret the practices of law in the Herculean style.

We are familar with the idea of "interpreting" texts or utterances. What is it to "interpret" a practice?

To interpret a practice, Dworkin tells us, we must not adopt the perspective of an external observer who merely records what people typically do: we must take up the viewpoint of the participants in that practice. Interpretation is essentially concerned with the question of how the practice should be followed and applied, and these are questions that arise for participants, not for external observers. This does *not* mean, however, that we must simply report the understandings of participants in the practice. For the participants in a practice may disagree about the nature and meaning of the practice (just as lawyers disagree about the nature of law), and when they do so disagree, they are not arguing about the content of each other's intentions: they recognise a distinction between the true meaning of the practice, and the beliefs that participants have about that meaning.[6] Thus, I may be aware that many other participants in the practice disagree with my view of its meaning, but this knowledge would not show my view to be false: otherwise, it would be hard to see how participants ever could disagree about the point or meaning of a practice.

The underlying significance of Dworkin's view is not hard to appreciate. Hart seems to regard legal theory as a reflection upon the social phenomenon of law from the viewpoint of an external observer. Legal theory must take account of the attitudes of participants in the practices of law (*e.g.* the internal point of view), but it is not concerned to endorse those attitudes; nor is legal theory concerned to engage in the disputes conducted by participants. Indeed, Hart would in all probability say that the disagreements in which participants are involved address wholly different questions from those addressed by legal theory. Participants (such as judges and lawyers) disagree, for example, about what the existing law requires. Legal theorists, are not disagreeing about the rules of this or that jurisdiction: they are disagreeing about law in general, or the "concept" of law. Dworkin, by contrast, is claiming that the questions of legal theory are really interventions in the disputes between participants; that, when judges and lawyers disagree about the specifics of legal doctrine, their disagreements are generated by more basic disagreements concerning the meaning of the general practices in which they are engaged. Playing tennis may not involve intellectual debate about the *nature* of tennis; but engaging in the practice of law *is* in part a matter of debating the point or meaning of that practice.

Adopting the perspective of a participant involves viewing the practice as one that we might wish to support and continue. For that reason, we seek to work out what the practice requires of us. Some participants may simply follow traditional observances slavishly, without reflecting upon their point: Dworkin regards such people as guilty of what he calls "runic traditionalism". Questions about the meaning of a practice arise, however, when the participants adopt the "interpretive attitude".[7] Those who

---

[6] *Law's Empire*, p.63.
[7] *Law's Empire*, p.46, *et seq.*
      In place of the word "interpretative", Dworkin persists in using a word of his own invention: "interpretive". No difference in meaning seems to be intended by this eccentric (but very sensible) variant. I shall follow Dworkin's usage in the rest of this chapter.

adopt the interpretive attitude assume that the practice has some general point or meaning, and they assume that what exactly the practice requires is a function of that point. Rather than unthinkingly accepting all aspects of the customary observance of the practice, they assume that what the practice truly requires of them depends upon its point. Consequently, it is only when they have formed an interpretation of the meaning of the practice, that they can intelligently reach conclusions concerning what the practice requires.

Being informed by a disposition to support and continue the practice, interpretation must be "constructive".[8] To interpret a practice, Dworkin argues, is to offer a "constructive interpretation". Constructive interpretation aims to present the object of interpretation (whether it is a practice or, say, a work of literature) in its most appealing light: we must present it as the best thing of its kind that it can be. This means that interpretation requires us to draw upon our values, and these may be aesthetic values if we are interpreting a work of literature, or moral values if we are interpreting social practices such as law.

Suppose that we are concerned to offer a general interpretation of *Hamlet*. We must first agree on the text of the play: we cannot have a sensible debate if, by "Hamlet", I mean a Shakespeare play and you mean a children's comic that happens to have the same name. Having identified the text, we must now look for an overall understanding of the point or significance of the play. The interpretation we are seeking must satisfy two criteria: it must be an adequate "fit" for the given features of the play; and it must have "appeal, in that it presents the play as the best play of its genre (the best tragedy, presumably) that it can possibly be, consistently with the requirement of "fit".

An interpretation need not be a perfect fit: if one scene is inconsistent with my "Freudian" reading of *Hamlet*, there is

---

8 The word "constructive" is one with resonances that it may be helpful to understand. For Dworkin, interpretation is "constructive" in the familiar sense that it seeks to move matters in a positive direction, and to put things in their best light; but it is also "constructive" in a more philosophical sense. "Constructivism" in philosophy is the view that the objects of knowledge in some field of inquiry (*e.g.* mathematics, morality) are "constructed" by the intellectual practices of the inquirers, rather than discovered as entities with a wholly independent existence. Constructivists deny that this undermines the objectivity of the relevant areas of knowledge.

room for me to say that that particular scene is just a mistake from the viewpoint of the play's overall meaning. But an interpretation must be an "adequate" fit: it would not do to offer an interpretation that fails to fit the entirety of the play's second-half. We can only engage in a sensible interpretive debate if we have criteria for how good a fit an interpretation must be, but these criteria will vary with the type of interpretive dispute in which we are engaged.

Dworkin tells us that an interpretive dispute can be divided into three analytically distinct stages. He calls these the "pre-interpretive stage", the "interpretive stage" and the "post-interpretive stage". We can see what these distinctions signify if we use Dworkin's own example of a dispute about the practices of "courtesy".

Imagine that you and I are disagreeing about the point or meaning of the traditional practices of courtesy. To conduct a sensible interpretive debate, we must have a rough and provisional agreement on the practices that we are referring to: thus we may agree that we are talking about such practices as raising one's hat, saying "How do you do?", and so forth. Dworkin styles this the "pre-interpretive stage". It requires, not acceptance of a general criterion for what counts as "courtesy", but simply a degree of agreement upon a range of instances.

Now we need to find an interpretation that best satisfies the twin criteria of "fit" and "appeal": this constitutes the "interpretive stage". You and I will debate various ideas about the "point" or "meaning" of the practice of courtesy. Each of us will try to form a view about which interpretation is an adequate "fit", while presenting the practice in its morally most appealing light.

Finally, at the "post-interpretive stage", we may revise our original conception of what counts as "courtesy", in order more accurately to reflect our new interpretation of the practices of courtesy.

You may conclude, at the interpretive stage, that the practices of courtesy express our feelings of respect for people. In the light of this interpretation, you may decide, at the post-interpretive stage, that courtesy does not require you to raise your cap to the local squire, but it does require you to raise your cap to the soldiers returning from a war. I, on the other hand, may conclude that the whole point of courtesy is to enable us to deal with others in a non-judgmental way that does *not* evince our feelings either of respect or the lack of it. I may therefore decide not to follow your example, but to continue raising my cap to everyone that I meet.

The debates of legal theory, according to Dworkin, are interpretive disputes of this type. We have a rough provisional agreement on what counts as "law" (the pre-interpretive stage); but suppose that we have to decide some such question as that raised in *Riggs v. Palmer*. This is not really a matter that can be resolved by reference to a basic rule of recognition, for there may be no established rule that settles the issue. The question is really one concerning the nature of the judge's duty to apply the law: what is meant by "law" in the context of that duty? . Does "law" consist only of the published and established rules, so that the duty to apply the law entails a duty to follow the statutes on testamentary succession regardless of the fact that they would let a murderer profit from his own wrong? Or does "law" contain unstated but implicit principles of justice so that our conclusions as to what the law is should always be controlled and constrained by those requirements of justice? These are matters on which judges and citizens might legitimately disagree, and their disagreement would rapidly project them into a debate about the nature of law. When jurisprudence offers theories of law's nature, it intervenes in precisely such debates, and every piece of adjudicative reasoning tacitly presupposes an under-lying legal theory: "Jurisprudence is the general part of adjudication, silent prologue to any decision at law."[9]

Dworkin's claim that "Jurisprudence is the general part of adjudication" could easily be misunderstood. Legal theory as conceived by Hart is an elucidation of the *concept* of law: the intention is to cast light upon legal institutions *universally*. He sees legal theory as a reflection upon law's nature from the viewpoint of an external observer, rather than an engaged participant. Such reflection upon law's nature is considered by Hart to be valuable insofar as law is an important social phenomenon that we might seek to understand for a host of diverse reasons. Dworkin, by contrast, sees legal theory as reflecting upon the nature of law not as part of some general intellectual inquiry, but as part of our reflections upon the scope of a presumed duty to obey and apply the law. Legal theory is the most abstract plane upon which participants in a legal system seek to determine what "law" means in the context of such a duty to comply with the law. Consequently, legal theory

---

[9]   *Law's Empire*, p.90.

is local and culturally specific in its ambitions: "Interpretive theories are by their nature addressed to a particular legal culture, generally the culture to which their authors belong."[10] The judge is concerned to construct a theory, not of law in general, but of the law in his particular system. We might expect an adequate theory also to apply to those systems that are similar to ours in their general legal and political culture; but we should not expect such a theory to apply to politically remote cultures, simply in consequence of their possession of legal institutions.[11]

When *Law's Empire* was first published, one came across many people who were inclined to dismiss the book's argument by suggesting that it did not really contradict Hart's theory at all. For had Dworkin not acknowledged that interpretation must begin with the pre-interpretive stage, at which we agree upon the object of our interpretation? And does that not mean that we must begin with something like a rule of recognition, by which we identify the rules of law, before we go on to interpret them in the Herculean way? Readers who responded to Dworkin's argument in this way felt that he needed to rely upon something like Hart's theory, at the pre-interpretive stage, to get interpretation started. His own theory of interpretation was not, therefore, a true rival to Hart's theory, but a mere supplement to it. Hart offered a theory of law's nature, but he did not offer a prescriptive theory of adjudication (that is, a theory telling judges how they ought to decide cases): Hart's positivism is simply neutral on such prescriptive issues. Dworkin, by contrast, offers a prescriptive theory of adjudication; he then simply mistakes it for a theory of law. Dworkin, it seemed, had simply lost the plot.

These criticisms were misguided. Dworkin's pre-interpretive stage refers to rough and provisional agreement upon a range of instances as instances of law. It is not a matter of agreement upon some general *criterion* for what counts as law, such as a rule of recognition. We might, for example, agree that statutes and precedents are law, without possessing any general view as to what makes them law, or as to what the precise limits of law and the basis of legal validity might be. From this rough initial agreement, we seek to construct by interpretation our general criteria for law. In this way judges may arrive at slightly different conceptions of the fundamental criteria (the "soundest theory of

[10] *Law's Empire*, p.102.
[11] *loc. cit.*

law"), even though they share broad agreement upon a range of instances. Such disagreements will permeate and inform their views in hard cases such as *Riggs v. Palmer*, making such doctrinal disagreements inseparable from deeper disagreements in legal theory.

There is of course another way in which one might conclude that Hart and Dworkin are not really disagreeing: they have such completely different views about the nature of legal theory that their rival accounts of the nature of law do not seem directly to engage with each other. To dismiss the appearance of disagreement as bogus, however, would be a mistake. Dworkin does not simply pursue a different project from Hart's: he suggests that the project of legal theory, as conceived by Hart, is at worst philosophically misguided, and at best a pointless waste of time. We shall pursue this matter a little further in the next section.

SEMANTIC THEORIES

We have seen how Dworkin rejects the distinction between doctrinal reasoning and legal theory. But in what sense does he also reject the analytical/normative distinction?

Dworkin characterises theories such as Hart's as "semantic" theories of law. Such theories assume that we have implicit criteria governing our use of the word "law", but that the criteria exhibit a degree of "penumbral uncertainty" stemming from the open-texture of language. In situations falling within the penumbra of uncertainty, we will find disagreements about what law really "is". Semantic theories seek to address these disagreements by setting out the semantic criteria explicitly, and seeking to reduce penumbral uncertainty by refining the relevant criteria at the borderline.

According to Dworkin, semantic theories rest upon the assumption that one cannot have sensible disagreements without shared criteria. If you and I are disagreeing about how many "banks" there are in North America, our disagreement is a meaningful one only if we have a shared criterion for what counts as a "bank". If our criterion suffers from extensive penumbral uncertainty, we may need to specify it more closely. If, on the other hand, we have totally different criteria in mind (as where I am speaking of savings banks and you are speaking of river banks), our disagreement is a nonsensical one.

Dworkin holds these assumptions to be false. In the first place, he argues, the semantic view confuses "borderline disputes" with "pivotal disputes". If you and I agree on some general conception of "art", but disagree how far that conception applies to photography, we are engaged in a borderline dispute. In such a case, we have a shared criterion, but are disagreeing about its applicability: you think that photography satisfies our shared criterion sufficiently well to entitle it to the appellation "art", while I think that it departs from the criterion too significantly. In other cases, however, the disputing parties may have no shared criterion. Suppose that you and I have dramatically different conceptions of what art is. Here, our disagreement about photography will not concern the degree to which photography satisfies a shared criterion: rather, photography may be simply the context in which our broader disagreement has been forced to the surface. Yet, according to Dworkin, we may still have a perfectly sensible debate about whether photography is an art, in spite of the absence of any shared criterion. This latter type of debate, where there is no shared criterion, is a "pivotal" dispute, because the instance of photography is being used as the pivotal issue in terms of which we choose between two much more general conceptions of art.

Legal theories are concerned with pivotal disputes, not borderline disputes. Consequently, they are not attempts to explicate or refine a shared criterion that exhibits some border-line indeterminacy: they are attempts to choose between quite different criteria or conceptions of law. Such debates can be perfectly meaningful even though they are not structured by the acceptance of a shared criterion: what holds the debate together (preventing it from being a nonsense debate like our example of savings banks and river banks) is a shared *object of interpretation*.

Much of Dworkin's argument here seems to rest upon a fairly gross mischaracterisation of Hart. Hart repeatedly points out that he does *not* see legal theory as concerned with the "borderline" of the concept of law: indeed, he insists that such borderline questions do not raise interesting philosophical issues.[12] Nor is the contrast between "core" and "penumbra" in Hart's theory in any way inconsistent with Dworkin's notion of "pivotal disagreement". Thus, in his *Essays in Jurisprudence and Philosophy*, Hart describes the central controversies of legal

---

[12] For example, Hart tells us that "what may be called the borderline aspect of things is too common to account for the long debate about law". *The Concept of Law*, p.4.

philosophy as arising from "partly overlapping concepts reflecting a divergence of basic point of view or values or background theory".[13] These remarks suggest a contrast between the settled usage of the core and the divergence within the penumbra that is the product of an overlap between divergent perspectives or criteria, rather than the product of simple vagueness in a shared criterion.[14] The image we seem to be presented with is one of beams of light cast from different directions upon the flat surface of a floor or wall. The beams produce a bright central patch of overlap, and an area of less bright partial overlap gradually fading into darkness. When penumbral uncertainty manifests this type of criterial overlap, rather than criterial vagueness, any reduction in the area of penumbral uncertainty will require a choice between different perspectives. The resulting disputes will be as "pivotal" as Dworkin might wish.

There is, however, one sense in which Hart's theory might perhaps be characterised as "semantic": the theory seeks, not to regulate our conduct, but to improve our grasp of a concept.[15] Thus, Hart does not tell the judge that rules flowing from the rule of recognition ought to be applied in preference to general standards of justice or fairness. Hart would say that *that* is a moral question that should be addressed separately. However, in reflecting upon that moral question, Hart suggests, the judge will find his deliberations clarified if he thinks of the positive rules as "law" regardless of their justice or injustice. The theory is aimed at improving our ways of thinking, not our ways of acting (except in so far as clarified thought will contribute to the latter).

Dworkin's view is that the Hartian enterprise of conceptual clarification lacks a genuine intellectual point, unless and until it is connected to questions concerning our moral duty to obey the law, and related issues. Thus, when a judge or citizen asks "what is law?", the question derives its point (according to Dworkin) from the assumption that we have some general obligation to obey the law, and that judges in particular have a duty to follow and apply the law. A full political theory, according to Dworkin, must include answers to two sets of questions. One set concerns

---

[13] Hart, *Essays in Jurisprudence and Philosophy* (Oxford 1983) p.6.
[14] I drew attention to this point in my essay "Bringing the Outside In" in (1993) 13 *Oxford Journal of Legal Studies* 147 at p.156.
[15] One should of course not neglect Hart's insistence that an improved conceptual analysis will sharpen our understanding of the phenomena that the relevant concepts describe: *The Concept of Law* p.14.

the *grounds* of law: what exactly is law? When are propositions of law true and false? The other set concerns the *force* of law: How far are we obligated to obey the law? How far can law justify the use of coercion? Answers to the two sets of questions must be mutually supportive, but a provisional division of labour is possible, with legal theorists concentrating on the grounds of law, and political theorists concentrating on questions concerning its force. Legal theorists therefore abstract from the question of force sufficiently to enable a concentration on the question of grounds. In other words, when they ask "what is law?" they take it more or less for granted that law does indeed have some moral claim upon us such that, in general, it ought to be obeyed.[16]

It follows that, for Dworkin, inquiry into the nature of law (a theory of the "grounds" of law) is ultimately intended to guide our conduct, and the conduct of judges, by being reconnected to a theory of the "force" of law. In the absence of some such guiding normative intention, jurisprudence would be, Dworkin tells us, "an orphan of scholasticism".[17]

For this reason, an interpretive theory of law will be intended to guide conduct, and not simply to clarify the conceptual framework with which we reflect upon what we ought to do. However, because a theory of the "grounds" of law is not a full theory of law's "force", the guidance will be provisional. A theory of law will tell us what we ought to do, on the assumption that we ought to obey the law. Of course, *that* way of putting the point may make it seem that Dworkin's conception of legal theory is not so different from Hart's after all. Hart too could say that his theory tells us what we ought to do, *if* we ought to obey the law. The difference is that Hart's theory is intended to clarify our understanding of law's nature while disengaging from moral debate: Hart does not intend us to draw upon contentious moral considerations in selecting one theory of law in preference to another. Dworkin, by contrast, sees our deliberations on law's nature as inextricably linked to our moral understandings.

Suppose that a student comes up to me and asks "would it be discourteous for me to walk out of Professor X's lecture before the lecture has finished?" In answering such a question, I will probably assume that the student wishes to act courteously, and I will therefore draw upon my general moral understanding in order to answer his question. I might say "No, not really. It

[16] *Law's Empire*, p.110–111.
[17] *Law's Empire*, p.112.

would be polite to warn Professor X of your intention to leave early, and to apologise. But if you get no opportunity to do so, I do not think that you need feel that you have acted discourteously." My answer is, if you like, based on my interpretation of the practice of courtesy, and is informed by my own moral understandings. In reaching my conclusion, I take account of a great diversity of considerations: the possible good reasons that the student may have for leaving early; the worthiness of his desire to hear Professor X's lecture, rather than skipping the whole thing; the difficulty of securing a chance to speak to Professor X before he begins his lecture; and so forth. Assessing various considerations of this type is an uncertain matter. I may be well aware that others, who hold different moral views to mine, would have given the student different advice on the requirements of courtesy: my advice was not intended as a morally neutral "analysis" of the "concept" of courtesy, but as a substantive moral opinion.

At the same time, I have not actually told the student what he should do. My advice was offered on the assumption that the student is seeking guidance as to how best to act in compliance with the practice of courtesy; but my own opinion may be that considerations other than courtesy are more important in this particular context. I may feel that he should be (discourteously) expressing his disapproval of Professor X's lectures, given the Professor's failure to support my campaign to save the centipede; but the student did not ask "what should I do?", he asked (in effect) "what does courtesy require?" And that is the question that I answered.

Now consider a slightly different scenario. This time the student has been replaced by a visiting anthropologist from a little known part of the world that possesses practices very unlike our own. I am aware that he never attends lectures, and that he is making a study of British practices of courtesy. He asks me "Would it be discourteous to walk out of Professor X's lecture before the lecture has finished?" Given the circumstances, I will not assume that I am being asked for guidance on what he ought to do (if he is to behave courteously), but on what most British people might think. I may feel unsure of the correct answer to that latter question, and might even ask a few of my colleagues for their responses before replying. I could then say "We disagree amongst ourselves over this issue. Many of us think it is not discourteous, but equally many think it is." Given the nature of the anthropologist's particular interests, this seems a perfectly good reply. I might elaborate my reply by providing some examples of the types of arguments pro and con offered by my colleagues, but I would not feel that an adequate reply required me express an opinion on which of the arguments I considered to be most weighty.

What of questions about the nature of law? Are they like the questions of the student asking for guidance? Or are they more like the questions of the visiting anthropologist?

Suppose someone says to me "Is law just a body of rules laid down in statutes and cases? Or is it more like the conception of justice implicit in those rules, so that legality requires the rules always to be applied in the light of underpinning considerations of justice?"

Imagine me replying, "Well, some lawyers and judges take one of those views, and others take the other view." I have answered the question on the assumption that it is analogous to the anthropologist's question above. But such an answer would not amount to a theory of law. The various judges and lawyers who take the rival views described are adopting rival positions within legal theory. For my reply itself to constitute a contribution to legal theory it would have to take sides in the debate, not simply note the existence of the debate. Does that not suggest that the questions of legal theory are more akin to the student's question about courtesy than to the anthropologist's?

Dworkin takes Hart and other defenders of analytical jurisprudence to be holding that there is a third type of question, seeking a clarification of the concept of "law" (or of "courtesy") independently of any moral, or straightforwardly factual, investigation. The assumption is that, when we proceed to engage in practical debate or empirical inquiry, we will find such a clarified concept invaluable. Dworkin doubts the value, or perhaps even the possibility, of this third type of inquiry. He sees the questions of legal theory as similar to those asked by the student: they are raised from the perspective of one who wishes to know what would be count as the best and most appropriate way to follow or comply with the practice. Hence, legal theories should offer, not merely "conceptual clarification", but practical guidance to the judge.

SOME SCEPTICISMS

Dworkin discusses two forms of scepticism that he feels his

theory of "constructive interpretation" must confront. He labels these "internal scepticism" and "external scepticism". We will consider each of them in turn.

The internal sceptic does not contest Dworkin's general account of interpretation, but is concerned to challenge its applicability to a particular object. In the context of law, the internal sceptic might be suggesting, for example, that the law is just too disorderly, chaotic and morally incoherent to be interpreted as expressing some grand overarching moral or political theory. Dworkin believes that such internal sceptics often confuse the complexity of law with moral incoherence. The law embodies a rich multiplicity of values and moral principles, many of which can, in certain circumstances, compete with each other. It is a mistake, however, to assume that such competing values amount to a situation of moral contradiction or incoherence.

Internal scepticism represents an interesting challenge to Dworkin's theory of law, but it is difficult to decide on its soundness in abstraction from particular attempts to produce overarching "interpretations" of areas of legal doctrine, and ultimately of the system as a whole. There is surely ample room for suspecting that the Dworkinian form of constructive interpretation can be made to fit the disorderly realities of a modern legal system only if the criteria for adequacy of "fit" are unacceptably lax.[18]

External scepticism represents a more abstract and fundamental attack upon Dworkin's position, because it challenges the entire account of interpretation on the basis of a sweeping philosophical thesis, to the effect that values are essentially "subjective". Dworkin's theory of interpretation holds that the correct interpretation is intimately bound up with values, for we must choose the interpretation that satisfies criteria of both "fit" and "appeal". When considering the "appeal" of an interpretation, we must draw upon our moral (or, in the case of a work of literature for example, aesthetic) values. The external sceptic claims that this shows interpretation to be purely subjective: there are no objective moral or aesthetic values, so there are no "correct" interpretations, only "different" interpretations.

External scepticism of this sort is so much a part of popular

---

[18] For some more specific problems see Simmonds, "Bluntness and Bricolage" in *Jurisprudence: Cambridge Essays*, edited by H. Gross and R. Harrison, (Oxford 1992).

culture that it can sound like an obvious truism; one therefore faces an uphill battle in trying to show that it may, in fact, be misguided. We first need to break the common assumption that subjectivism of this sort is supportive of tolerance, and that one who asserts the existence of "objective" values is claiming an infallible knowledge of such values, and is perhaps intolerant of those who disagree. I explained in the Introduction to Part 1 that these assumptions are almost the opposite of the truth, and readers should refer back to my remarks at that point (p. 12).

Dworkin's answer to "external scepticism" is complex, but it centrally turns upon the thesis that there is no difference between the statement that (for example) slavery is wrong, and the statement that it is true that slavery is wrong.

To understand Dworkin's point, consider a situation where I am giving a lecture on justice, and have remarked that slavery is unjust. A student's hand goes up:

Student: "What you are saying is completely subjective! It is not a 'fact' or a 'truth' that slavery is wrong!"

Me: "Oh. So you don't think slavery is wrong?"

Student: "Certainly I think slavery is wrong. But I do not think it's *true* that slavery is wrong."

Has the student just contradicted himself? It would seem that he has, if "slavery is wrong" and "it is true that slavery is wrong", simply mean the same thing.[19] Hence, one cannot make moral claims with apparent seriousness while denying that those claims are true. Moreover, the only arguments we can offer to show that it is *true* that slavery is wrong, are the very same arguments we would have offered to show that slavery is wrong. So if, on the basis of those arguments, the sceptics accept that slavery is wrong, they have accepted all that needs to be accepted.

Whatever posture sceptics adopt while defending their scepticism, they must perforce abandon that posture upon returning to ordinary engagement in moral debate. Thus, Dworkin says that sceptics, having articulated their scepticism,

---

[19] The view that they do mean the same thing, and that this tells us all that there is to know about the nature of truth, is sometimes called the "disquotational" or "redundancy" theory of truth. See if you can work out why the theory bears those names.

must finally "return to their knitting", in accepting and resisting moral arguments in the normal way.[20]

THE "THRESHOLD OBJECTION"

A further general objection to Dworkin's project should be considered before we move on. Dworkin imagines what he calls "a threshold objection" to his idea of constructive interpretation.[21] The objection claims that a proper understanding of law's nature should place law in a broader social or historical context. Dworkin's engagement in interpretive dispute concerning the practices of legal doctrinal argument is denounced as misguided: legal theorists pursuing Dworkin's agenda look, from this point of view, "like anthropologists sucked into the theological disputes of some ancient and primitive culture."[22]

Dworkin's response is that law is an argumentative social practice: that is, it consists in the offering of arguments. To write the sociology or history of law we need to have a grasp of what would count as good or bad legal arguments: to ignore such questions concerning the internal character of legal arguments, in order to focus on sociological or historical issues, would be like trying to write an innumerate history of mathematics.

If Dworkin is simply saying that an understanding of the character of legal arguments is an essential pre-requisite for an adequate sociology or history of law, we need hardly disagree with him.[23] His writings are, however, strikingly devoid of any informed reference to the history or social context of the practices that he discusses; it is possible that he takes his reply to "the threshold objection" as licensing such a narrowness of focus. If so he is misguided, for reasons that I will now explain.

(i) *Negative interpretations*
   In the first place, many theories might view the social context of a practice as very relevant to its meaning. This is especially true of interpretations that propose a sinister or

---

20   *Law's Empire*, p.85.
21   *Law's Empire*, pp.11–15.
22   *op. cit.* p.13.
23   One might, however, point out that what is required is only a grasp of what would count as a good or a bad argument within the practice: one would not need to resolve substantive controversies within the practice.

negative meaning for practices that seem superficially benign. Consider, for example, a possible feminist interpretation of the traditional male practices of courtesy (standing up when ladies enter the room, opening doors for them, offering them one's seat on the bus, and so forth). We can imagine someone saying that, looked at in isolation, these practices may seem harmless enough; but when we locate them in the context of a hierarchical male-dominated society, they take on a different significance: they then appear to convey a negative image of women as useless ornamental objects, incapable of performing simple tasks (like opening a door) or exhibiting ordinary physical resilience (like that required by standing up on the bus).

Dworkin might say that interpretations such as this are not "constructive": they do not present the practice in its best light, and can only be shown to be adequate interpretations if no more appealing interpretation will fit.[24] Yet it is hard to see why the odds should be stacked so heavily against negative interpretations. Why should it be necessary to show that *no* more positive view will "fit"? Why should a very powerful and enlightening negative interpretation not be preferred to a positive interpretation that is a barely adequate "fit"? Negative interpretations can be enlightening when they draw out deep, and otherwise overlooked, affinities and resonances between various practices composing the social context: the significance attributed to the practices of law or courtesy (for example) may be echoed and reinforced by meanings that can be plausibly attributed to a host of other practices.

It might be thought that negative interpretations necessarily abandon the perspective of the participant, and adopt that of an external observer of the practice. After all, participants are primarily concerned to interpret the practice in order to determine what would count as compliance with its requirements: so does it not follow that they will wish to construe the practice in an attractive, rather than a repulsive, way?

The short answer is "No, that does not follow." Participants in a practice presumably view their compliance with its requirements as conditional upon it being a worthy and meritorious practice: if they became convinced that the

---

[24] *Law's Empire*, p.421, n.12.

practice's true significance was malign, their compliance would be called into question. The participant's commitment to the adoption of a "constructive" interpretation, that presents the practice in its best light, is best thought of as provisional upon there being grounds for regarding the practice as deserving support. Practices do not merit our support simply in virtue of there being an interpretation of them that is suitably appealing, while being a barely adequate fit. We must also discount any "negative" interpretations that may be offered, for it is conceivable that some such interpretations may be of great intellectual power and plausibility. The evaluation of such interpretations will demand reference to the wider social context.

Law's social context is particularly relevant to Dworkin's project, given his ultimate conclusions about law's nature. For Dworkin informs us that law expresses a deep conception of equality, and thereby makes the society that it governs into a genuine community. Marxists would agree that law involves a "discourse" of equality: people appear in front of the court as equal citizens possesssed of equal rights, and their relationships are seen as governed by impartial principles that apply in the same way to everyone. The Marxist would go on to point out, however, that this discourse of equality takes on a different significance when located in the context of a society founded upon domination and inequality. Rather than being a source of genuine community, the law is then perceived to be a mystificatory attempt to misrepresent the nature of social relations (as founded on equality rather than domination). Dworkin does not exclude or deny the value of sociological investigation, of course; but when we reach the end of *Law's Empire* we have heard no mention of capitalism, or class, or social exclusion, or the market. In spite of this lack of concern for law's social context, Dworkin nevertheless feels entitled to reach conclusions about the nature and reality of true "community".

(ii) Sources of interpretive dispute
The business of interpreting the point of a practice is grounded, according to Dworkin, in what he calls "the interpretive attitude".[25] The interpretive attitude is a stance that we can adopt towards practices, whereby we regard the

<hr>

[25] *Law's Empire*, pp.46–48.

exact requirements of the practice as being dependent upon the overall "point" of the practice. He contrasts the "interpretive attitude" with an intellectual posture towards practices that he describes as "runic traditionalism". The difference seems to be as follows: the runic traditionalist simply does what the practice has traditionally been thought to require, without reflecting upon the overall point of the practice, or upon how particular aspects of its traditional requirements might (or might not) be related to that point; the person who adopts the "interpretive attitude", by contrast, believes that we cannot know what the practice *really* requires without forming a view (by means of "constructive interpretation") of its point. Thus, the runic traditionalist may simply go on raising his hat to the squire, because that is what everyone always has done; whereas one who adopts the "interpretive attitude" will ask what the *point* of courtesy is, and may on that basis decide to raise his hat to the returning soldiers instead.

Dworkin tends to identify adoption of the interpretive attitude with things we might value, such as intellectual awareness and reflection; practitioners of "runic traditionalism" come across in Dworkin's pages as lacking in intellectual insight and understanding. All of this, however, may be very misleading. A more accurate picture might be that, when our practices are working smoothly and unproblematically, we never think about their point: we adopt the stance of runic traditionalism. Only when something in the intellectual, social or political environment of the practices starts to disrupt or undermine their normal working, are we forced to reflect upon their point and adopt what Dworkin calls "the interpretive attitude".

If this is so, then a knowledge of the history and social context of an interpretive dispute might be essential if we are to engage in that dispute in an enlightened way: otherwise, we do not really understand the significance of the debate in which we are engaged. The practices that we inherit are not univocal: they are composed of multiple layers of meaning, suggestive of quite different rationales.[26] Much of the time this does not pose a problem for us, and may even be a virtue. When an "interpretive" dispute flairs up, however,

---

[26] See Friedrich Nietzsche, *The Genealogy of Morals*, second essay, section 13 (various editions and translations). See above p.178.

we really need some understanding of how this has come about, and that demands a historical perspective. To imagine that the interpretive dispute can be pursued in isolation from such a perspective is to be a victim of intellectual blindness and lack of self-awareness.[27]

CHOOSING A LEGAL THEORY

We have been explaining the account offered, in *Law's Empire*, of the nature of legal theory. When we put forward a theory of law, Dworkin says, we are proposing an interpretation (satisfying the standards of "fit" and "appeal") of the practices that compose the workings of a legal order. Dworkin will now apply this conception of legal theory, by considering rival interpretations of law's nature and selecting the best one.

Three rival theories of law are considered. Dworkin calls these "conventionalism", "pragmatism" and (his own favoured theory) "law as integrity". Some people have been irritated by the new terminology he introduces, and it is true that "conventionalism" broadly resembles legal positivism, while "pragmatism" broadly resembles rule-scepticism. So why does he not stick to the familiar labels?

Actually, the change in terminology is amply justified: for it marks the fact that we are now discussing interpretive theories, not semantic or analytical ones. Whereas Hart's positivism offers a morally neutral analysis of the "concept" of law, conventionalism is a theory constructed on the (provisional) assumption that we have a duty to obey the law, and it is aimed at elucidating the content of that duty. Consequently, conventionalism does not aim at moral neutrality: it aims to present law in its morally most appealing light. Acceptance or rejection of legal positivism will determine the conceptual categories in terms of which one addresses a moral problem, but will not prescribe an answer to such problems; conventionalism, by contrast, aims to prescribe the conduct of judges and citizens. Thus, the vision of law offered by conventionalism is recommended as being

---

[27] I have made attempts at a more "genealogical" understanding of legal theoretical debates in several of my writings. See, *e.g.* Simmonds, *The Decline of Juridical Reason* (Manchester 1984); "Between Positivism and Idealism" (1991) *Cambridge Law Journal* 308; "Protestant Jurisprudence and Modern Doctrinal Scholarship" (2001) *Cambridge Law Journal* 271.

morally informative, not simply as being analytically clearer. Conventionalism is, if one wishes, positivism translated into an interpretive rather than an analytical guise.

Dworkin tells us that it will help to structure discussion if the lawyers who engage in legal theoretical debate can agree on some of law's general features, for this will enable them to focus more clearly upon the precise nature of their disagreements. The area of agreement might be said to amount to a shared general "concept" of law, while the rival theories constitute differing "conceptions" of that concept. (Readers may recall that a similar distinction between "concept" and "conception" is employed by Rawls: p.50 above). As a shared concept of law, Dworkin proposes the idea that "the most abstract and fundamental point of legal practice is to guide and constrain the power of government" by insisting "that force not be used or withheld ... except as licensed or required by individual rights and responsibilities flowing from past political decisions about when collective force is justified." Rival theories of law can then be presented as offering different explanations of what the point of this constraint might be, and of what precisely it signifies.[28]

The principal idea can be conveyed quite simply like this. We can all accept, Dworkin thinks, that law constrains the government's use of force by requiring it to be used only in ways that "flow from" past decisions of, say, judges and legislators. When sanctions are ordered against citizens, we expect this to be justified by pointing to some established law. But, we might ask, what is the *point* of this? Is the object to give fair warning of the circumstances where sanctions might be ordered, so that citizens could discover the risk of sanctions in advance of their action? Or is the point rather to see that, when sanctions are used, citizens are being treated equally in the sense that the sanctions are required by general standards that apply to everyone? And what exactly is it for a decision to "flow from" or "be required by" the law? Must it be expressly stipulated by a verbally formulated authoritative rule? Or is it enough if it is in keeping with the deep principles that may be said to underpin the system as a whole?

Conventionalism offers a reply to these questions that turns upon the notion of "fair warning". According to the conventionalist, judges should decide cases in accordance with rules identified by reference to a basic convention (a rule of

[28] *Law's Empire*, p.93–94.

recognition); they should stick to the explicit content of the rules, and should not treat as law ideas that they consider to be implicit in the system of rules as a whole. The point of this form of adjudicative practice is to ensure that citizens have been given "fair warning" of the circumstances where sanctions will be used against them, and to protect expectations formed in reliance upon the warnings so given.

To understand Dworkin's critique of conventionalism, we must bear in mind that he holds interpretive theories of law to account against the two criteria of "fit" and "appeal". It is by moving between these two criteria that he rejects conventionalism. The main line of argument goes something like this.

If conventionalism is really concerned to give fair warning and avoid the defeat of expectations, the conventionalist should be a "unilateral" conventionalist. The unilateral conventionalist proposes that, where plaintiffs can invoke a clear rule in their favour they should win; but where they cannot, they should lose. This will eliminate the defeat of expectations, because it will eliminate cases where sanctions are deployed unexpectedly against defendants in innovative cases where there was no clear rule favouring the plaintiff's case.

Unilateral conventionalism might or might not be an attractive strategy: but it clearly does not fit the existing character of law, Dworkin says. We know that courts do grant new remedies in innovative cases, where no clear and well-established rule favoured the plaintiff's case. So, even if the theory is appealing, it does not fit.

The response from conventionalism, Dworkin suggests, might be a revised version of the theory. He calls it "bilateral conventionalism". Bilateral conventionalism holds that fair warning is important, but is not the *only* important value for law: other things are important too, such as the capacity of law to respond to new demands and grant new remedies. Thus we have to strike a balance between flexibility and the protection of expectations. We do this, the conventionalist claims, by the following adjudicative practice: if the plaintiff has a clear rule in his or her favour, the plaintiff wins; if the defendant has a clear rule in his or her favour, the defendant wins; if neither side has a clear rule in their favour, the court can have regard to considerations of flexibility, and can (if it is thought desirable) innovate by granting a new remedy.

The bilateral conventionalist picture might be a rough (very rough, in Dworkin's view) fit for the practices of law; but it fails for lack of appeal. This is because it proposes an unattractive way of balancing the two values of flexibility and predictability. Bilateral conventionalism does this by confining the value of flexibility to those cases where neither side can invoke a clear rule in their favour, allowing the value of predictability to govern the other cases. If, however, we are to balance these two values, it would be better (Dworkin claims) to do so case by case. We would then think of predictability and flexibility as competing in every decision. In each case, arguments for predictability would favour the enforcement of the settled rules; but, in each case, it would also be possible for arguments of flexibility to kick in, suggesting that it might be best to abandon the established rules. We would have to balance the values against each other and do what was best all things considered.

The judge who considers competing values in this way, and is always prepared to set aside the rules if the arguments for upholding them are outweighed by competing values, is a pragmatist. Hence we may say that conventionalism collapses into pragmatism.[29] (Notice how this resembles Dworkin's earlier argument that, without background legal principles, positivism collapses into rule-scepticism.)

The pragmatist judge may attach great weight to rules, and may believe that there are powerful reasons, in the great bulk of cases, for sticking by the rules. Yet the pragmatist does not think of the rules as strictly binding, for pragmatist judges will set aside the rules if that is for the best all things considered. They are concerned to give decisions that will have the best outcomes, and rules are important only in so far as they have a bearing upon that issue (compare utilitarianism).

Pragmatism, Dworkin holds, does not fit. Judges regard themselves as bound by pre-existing law, not just as having some good reasons for following the law in most cases. Moreover, the pragmatist's theory is inconsistent with parties having genuine legal rights: if the judge can give whatever decision he thinks will have the best consequences, the parties cannot have a right to this or that decision.

We must therefore consider the next alternative, which is Dworkin's own theory of "law as integrity".

---

[29] For an explanation of why the argument does not work, see Simmonds, "Why Conventionalism Does not Collapse into Pragmatism" (1990) *Cambridge Law Journal* 63.

LAW AS INTEGRITY

If we were to describe someone as "a person of integrity", one thing we might mean would be that they hold and adhere to a consistent set of moral principles: they do not invoke one principle when it serves their interests, and then deny that principle when it threatens their interests, for example. It is some such notion of "integrity" that underlies Dworkin's theory of law: "integrity" is ascribed, this time, not to an individual, but to the system of law as a whole.

It should be easy for you to get a general grip upon the main idea here, because you have already encountered it *twice* in this chapter: once when we looked at the Herculean approach to adjudication, and once when we looked at Dworkin's account of legal theory as an "interpretive" exercise. For the Dworkinian judge must look for an overall theory of the legal order as a whole, in the sense of an ordered set of principles and values under which the great bulk of the established statutes, cases and doctrines could be subsumed. The construction of such a theory demands attention to criteria of "fit" and "appeal": one must find an account of the law that is an adequate "fit", and that presents the law in its morally most appealing light. This resembles Dworkin's account of the nature of legal theory because it is exactly the same as that account. As you will remember, Dworkin takes the view that jurisprudence (legal theory) is but the first stage of adjudication; if, at that first stage, the judge selects "law as integrity" as the best theory, the second stage (of application of the theory of law) will follow on in an unbroken process of interpretation.

Let us get clear about this. Hercules must first decide (let's call this "stage one") upon a theory of law. Here he will consider such possibilities as conventionalism, pragmatism, and law as integrity. He will choose the theory that, in his opinion, best satisfies the criteria of fit and appeal. Having chosen a theory at stage one, he will then proceed (at stage two) to apply the law *as identified by the theory selected*. Thus, if he chooses conventionalism at stage one, that theory tells him to apply explicit rules identified by a basic convention. If, however, he chooses "law as integrity", he will simply continue the process of interpretation in which he has already, thus far, been engaged: he will take the law to be identified by that set of values and principles that provides the most appealing general account adequately to fit the existing statutes and cases.

Given that we must choose legal theories (according to Dworkin) on grounds of both "fit" and "appeal", it is reasonable for us to ask what is "appealing", from a moral point of view, about law as integrity. It is easy to see the importance of law being *just*, but integrity is not the same thing as justice at all: the judge must find a set of principles that fits the existing statutes and cases, and this may diverge in significant respects from the set that he would consider to be perfectly just. We may also see the importance of law being clear and publicly ascertainable, even if it is less than perfectly just. Unlike conventionlism, however, "law as integrity" does not emphasise public ascertainability as an overriding value. The totality of the law is not, according to "law as integrity", available in an explicit form, for law includes principles that are merely implicit, and that can be discerned only by an exercise of private moral judgment. So, if "law as integrity" does not directly serve values of justice or public ascertainability, what is the basis of its appeal? Why should it matter whether law exhibits "integrity" in Dworkin's sense? Why should it matter whether law can be represented as embodying a coherent moral or political theory?

Dworkin's ultimate answer to that question is framed in terms of equality and community. When we are governed in accordance with the requirements of integrity, we are treated as equals, for the same principles are applied to all of us; and, when we are so governed as equals, that form of governance makes us into a community. Law's power to obligate us is dependent upon its status as the foundation of our community, and law can be foundational to a political community only when it embodies integrity. Before developing his answer in terms of equality and community, however, Dworkin seeks to convince us that, whatever we might at first think, we do already value integrity, even if we have not previously had a name for that value. He tries to convince us of this point by means of an ingenious example.

Suppose that we disagree about abortion. Some people think that abortion should be permissible in certain circumstances, while others deny this. Suppose that the electorate includes 52 per cent who are pro-choice, and 48 per cent who are pro-life (I shall use these crude, if misleading, labels). Now suppose that, instead of enacting either a pro-life or a pro-choice statute, the legislature enacted a "checkerboard" statute, under which women born in odd-numbered years could get abortions when they wanted them, but women born in even-numbered years could not. We could even imagine more refined statutes, that would tailor the numerical balance between "parties-entitled-to-an-abortion" and "parties-not-so-entitled" so that it exactly reflected the proportion of votes cast in a referendum on the issue.

Dworkin's point is this. We feel that a checkerboard statute would be wrong. Yet such a statute might be recommended by some of our more familiar political values. For example, checkerboard statutes would foster a more equal distribution of political power (a value that Dworkin refers to as "fairness"), insofar as the possibility of such statutes might mean that every vote cast (on both sides) could make a real difference to the outcome. Checkerboard statutes might also be recommended by considerations of justice: a pro-life voter might consider a checkerboard statute to be preferable on grounds of justice to a pro-choice statute, for example (likewise in reverse for the pro-choice voter). So, Dworkin asks, if checkerboard statutes might be recommended by considerations of both justice and fairness, why do we still feel them to be wrong?

His answer is that justice and fairness are not the only values in play here: we also value integrity. The checkerboard statute lacks integrity because one would have to invoke some principles to justify some parts of it that you would have to deny in order to justify the other parts (pro-choice principles would have to be denied when one was justifying the denial of any entitlement to abortion for women born in even-numbered years). Someone who claims not to value integrity must either explain why the checkerboard statute is wrong quite apart from integrity, or they must say that they find nothing objectionable about such checkerboard statutes. The checkerboard statute alerts us to the value of integrity, because only that value can explain our intuition that checkerboard statutes are wrong.

Are you convinced? The abortion example is perhaps a little misleading, because it gives us a checkerboard where (so to speak) the squares are people: the statute creates two classes of women, one class being entitled to an abortion and the other class not so entitled. Thus the statute violates some rather familiar intuitions about "equality before the law". Is this why we find it so morally objectionable? Or is Dworkin right that it is the statute's lack of moral coherence that is at the heart of our objections? One very knowledgeable legal scholar has suggested that unprincipled compromises, apparently lacking in integrity, are not uncommon in constitutions and legislation: "they represent the most that people can agree upon at a particular moment of history."[30]

Dworkin's theory of law places its main emphasis upon the role of judges and adjudication. The court is, for him, a potential "forum of principle" in which the most fundamental political values of the community are articulated. Consequently, his theory naturally tends to emphasise moral coherence and deep consistency in principle. Other approaches, however, might give greater centrality to legislation, where reasonable compromise between different moral perspectives may be an integral part of the process.[31] Indeed, some theorists might see it as a virtue of law that it can often establish general standards that are capable of commanding wide support *without* needing to address the issues of basic principle about which the community may be seriously divided.[32]

We see here a tendency for Dworkin to take for granted the unproblematic continuance of a peaceful and orderly society within which debates of fundamental principle can be conducted: but the law's central task is surely not the resolution of such fundamental debates so much as the maintenance of a shared fabric of rules that can command the support of diverse groups and individuals.

At a number of points in *Law's Empire*, Dworkin seems to acknowledge the need for some degree of agreement in a community, if his model of constructive interpretation is to have any application. Thus he tells us that people must share a vocabulary, and must have sufficient similarity of interests and convictions to be capable of making sense of each others, acts and utterances.[33] They must also have "a very great deal of consensus" about what counts as law in the rough "pre–interpretive" sense that serves to identify the shared object of rival legal interpretations;[34] and they must have shared convictions about how good a "fit" an interpretation must be.[35] What Dworkin's theory signally fails to address, however, are the mechanisms whereby the law may help to sustain the back-

---

[30] G. P. Fletcher, *Basic Concepts of Legal Thought* (Oxford 1996) p.32.

[31] See J. Waldron, *Law and Disagreement* (Oxford 1999)

[32] See Simmonds, "Bluntness and Bricolage" in *Jurisprudence: Cambridge Essays*, edited by H. Gross and R. Harrison (Oxford 1992); C. Sunstein, *Legal Reasoning and Political Conflict* (Oxford 1996).

[33] *Law's Empire* pp.63–64.

[34] *op. cit.* p.66.

[35] *op. cit.* p.67.

ground of shared values upon which the law's own stability and determinacy may depend.[36]

One could imagine a conservative version of *Law's Empire* that highlighted all the points at which Dworkin acknowledges the need for agreement and convergence, and marginalised the points at which the need and scope for individual judgment is acknowledged. Dworkin, however, chooses to present his theory as an expression of "Protestant" individualism.[37] A perspective that reveals the dependence of law upon a background community of shared values would, in that very respect, be uncongenial to Dworkin, who wishes to offer a theory of law that is compatible with liberal pluralism. Liberal pluralism, however, requires that people be given clearly demarcated entitlements based on shared rules. The question then becomes one of how a community can share rules and entitlements when it shares little besides. Positivism gives us one type of answer. Dworkin's answer remains unclear.

One response that Dworkin might offer would amount to saying that a liberal community can be held together by the sharing of a liberal theory of justice: the conception of justice found to be implicit in the law of a liberal society then becomes the shared public conception of justice that binds the society together. It is this possible aspect of Dworkin's theory that leads some critics to find in the theory an aspiration towards "closure", shutting off the political community's openness towards social experiments that depart from any standardly liberal vision.

Thus, Roberto Unger has described traditional forms of legal reasoning as a "context-oriented practice of analogical reasoning" which "must be guided by the attribution of purpose to the interpreted materials, an attribution that can often remain implicit in situations of settled usage." He sees in the Dworkinian vision,[38] however, a "drive towards systematic closure and abstraction" that transforms ordinary purposive

---

[36] Contrary to initial assumptions, there is nothing problematic about the idea that law may help to sustain a background that in turn supports the law's own determinacy. See Simmonds, "Between Positivism and Idealism" (1991) *Cambridge Law Journal* 308; Simmonds, "The Possibility of Private Law" in John Tasioulas (ed.) *Law, Values and Social Practices* (Aldershot 1997).

[37] *Law's Empire*, p.413.

[38] He speaks of "rationalizing legal analysis", but we must assume that he refers to Dworkin along with many others.

judgments into "prescriptive theory-like conceptions of whole fields of law and social life".[39] Hence Unger sees the relatively a-theoretical practices of traditional legal reasoning as more open to political change than is the Dworkinian interpretation of those practices. Dworkin's theory, from this perspective, resembles an attempt to preclude political change by translating a currently dominant ideology onto a level of juridical abstraction.

ORDER, THEORY AND COMMUNITY

Let us assume that a major part of the point of law is the provision of a shared set of rules. In a simple and morally homogenous society, we might co-exist on the basis of shared moral rules (what Hart would call a "regime of primary rules"); but in more complex societies, characterised by some degree of moral disagreement and diversity, we will need laws. If the law is not to be infected by the very moral disagreements that necessitate its existence in the first place, it must be possible to ascertain the content of the existing laws in some relatively uncontentious manner: by consulting the rules laid down in certain sources, such as statutes and cases, for example.

The above paragraph seems to represent a plausible line of argument; but can Dworkin's theory of "law as integrity" meet the simple requirements of that argument? Of course, the Dworkinian judge will have regard to sources of law such as statutes and cases: the account of law offered by such a judge must be an adequate "fit" for such material. But the precise way in which such sources feature will depend upon the overall interpretation adopted by the judge; and the interpretation adopted will depend upon the judge's moral viewpoint. Each judge must be guided by his or her own moral views, whether or not those views coincide with those of their fellow judges. If, therefore, the judges as a whole reflect the moral diversity and moral disagreement of their communities, will the law not fail to provide the requisite degree of certainty and stability? Will it not simply reproduce the moral diversity that it was established to overcome?

One might at first think that the requirement of "fit" provides the basis for an answer to this question. If the judge's

---

[39] Roberto Mangabeira Unger, *What Should Legal Analysis Become?* (London 1996) p.114.

interpretation must "fit" the statutes and cases, there must be a limit on how diverse reasonable judicial opinions can be; and that limit must be considerably tighter than the limits upon possible moral opinions. We must remember, however, that the "fit" need not be perfect, but merely "adequate", and it is far from clear what the criteria for adequacy of fit might be. Moreover, a proliferation of Dworkinian judges adopting this approach to adjudication might well produce (over the long-term) a more diverse and loosely integrated body of decisions, reflecting to that extent their diverse moral viewpoints. The more diverse the precedents become, the looser the "fit" that can realistically be required of an adequate interpretation of the law.

Dworkin holds that there are "right answers" to difficult questions of law. Each judge must seek the theory of law that both "fits" and presents the law in its morally most attractive light; but this is not to say that legality is a matter of subjective opinion. Quite apart from the requirement of "fit", there are right answers to legal questions precisely because there are right answers to moral question.[40] You and I may disagree about which account of tort law is correct, and we may disagree about tort law because we disagree about morality (and hence about which account presents tort law in its morally best light); but this does not show that we are simply articulating subjective preferences. Moral views may be true or false; if we disagree about morality (and therefore about tort law), at least one of us must be wrong. The possibility of right answers does not overcome the present problem, however, for Dworkin acknowledges that such answers will be intensely controversial. So why should judges not wind up with radically different views as to what the existing law requires?

Dworkin acknowledges that "Law would founder if the various interpretive theories in play in court and classroom diverged too much in any one generation"; but he believes his theory of law to be capable of explaining how judges can reliably converge on a shared, and for the most part settled, system of rules. He draws our attention to a diversity of factors that help to prevent the legal system from spinning apart. These factors include "the general intellectual environment", and "the common language", as well as "the inevitable conservatism of formal legal education, and of the process of selecting lawyers for judicial and administrative office". Finally, an appeal is made

---

[40] See Dworkin's reply to the "external sceptic", discussed above.

to a shared sense of the danger that too great a degree of diversity would indeed lead to disaster.[41]

Such arguments will seem puzzling to anyone who is genuinely troubled by the problem that Dworkin is purporting to address. Take the last point first: that a shared sense of danger might protect us from the centrifugal forces of "protestant" interpretation. Dworkin simply ignores the fact that such a shared sense of collective danger would always compete with the individual advantages to be gained by offering innovative interpretations of the law. Litigants would have a strong incentive to proffer interpretations of law that served to advance their own interests (this is so whether we conceive of these individuals as having egoistic or altruistic preferences). Individual judges would have similar reasons for endorsing some such interpretations. In each case, endorsement of a new interpretation might yield great gains for some political position (or personal interest) that the judge holds dear. Each judge's willingness to forego such gains in order to avert the danger of interpretive meltdown would be undermined by his awareness that he could not guarantee similar self-restraint on the part of his fellow judges. Everyone might be well aware of the dangers inherent in too great a tolerance and endorsement of innovative interpretations, yet they might be powerless to do anything to arrest the slide into a chaos of conflicting interpretations. Thus, a slide into legal indeterminacy might be highly likely even in the face of a full appreciation of the danger.

Dworkin might say that co-operative strategies could be adopted to prevent this from happening; but (apart from the difficulty of showing that such strategies will be attainable and sustainable) such strategies would almost certainly have to take the form of conventions constraining the acceptable forms of interpretation and argument. Such conventions would resemble a Hartian "rule of recognition" rather than a Dworkinian model of individualistic interpretation constrained only by the requirement of "fit". In other words, Dworkin would then be "defending" his theory only by abandoning it.

The other considerations mentioned by Dworkin can be disposed of more easily. Even a shared language is perhaps not something one can take for granted within a state committed to liberal tolerance, still less a shared culture; and there is nothing "inevitable" about the conservatism of formal legal

[41] *op. cit.* pp.88–89.

education, as the recent history of some U.S. law schools (particularly those excited by the prospects of interpretative freedom) should have made clear. As for the conservativism of selection for office, might we not expect a community committed to tolerance and diversity to select its officials from as broad a range of cultural and intellectual backgrounds as possible? Would this not be especially important within a legal culture that encouraged constructive interpretation, since that form of interpretation gives such a key role to the interpreter's own moral position?

Selected reading

R. Dworkin, *Taking Rights Seriously* (revised ed., 1978).
R. Dworkin, *A Matter of Principle* (Harvard 1985).
R. Dworkin, *Law's Empire* (London 1986).
S. Guest, *Ronald Dworkin* (Edinburgh 1992).
M. Kramer, *In Defense of Legal Positivism* (Oxford 1999) Chap.6.
Special Issue of *Law and Philosophy*: "Dworkin's Law's Empire" (1987) *Law and Philosophy* Vol. 6 No. 3.

Chapter 7

FULLER

FACTS, VALUES AND PURPOSES

In Chapter 5 I posed a problem in the following terms. Suppose that the Mafia gained control of the United Kingdom, even to the extent of removing the government and the existing apparatus of law and law enforcement. In place of these institutions, the Mafia established a new "legislature", and new "courts" which enforced Mafia decrees. Would this amount to a legal system?

Two approaches to the problem can be distinguished at the outset. On the one hand are theories that treat the concepts of law and legal system as having certain moral dimensions: on this view, a body of rules might be said to count as a legal system only if (for example) it is aimed at the common good or the enforcement of justice. The other approach, which is character-istic of legal positivism, offers an account of law and legal systems that is morally neutral in character. Legal systems are characterised, on this view, by the existence of certain types of institutional arrangement rather than by the moral purposes that they may or may not serve. Thus, in Hart's theory, a legal system exists if there are officials who accept and apply a rule of recognition, and if the primary rules identified by the rule of recognition are obeyed by the bulk of the population.

The starting point for Fuller's theory is the suggestion that formal characterisations of human institutions, independently of their purposes, must be illusory and inadequate. Consider the way in which we would describe a human artifact such as a chair or a spoon to some alien being who had never encountered such objects. We might try to describe a chair (for example) in terms of its purely formal characteristics, without reference to its purpose. We would say something like "a chair consists of a more or less flat surface about 18 inches to three feet above the ground, usually supported by four legs, with a vertical surface rising from one edge of the flat horizontal surface". Such a description would be an uncertain guide, because chairs are so very various in appearance. Moreover the description would not really convey any understanding of what a chair is: to understand that, we would need to know what a chair is for. Once we understand what sitting is, and we know that a chair is for sitting on, we have a much better understanding of the concept of a chair.

We might think that positivist accounts of the nature of a legal system resemble the "formal" description of a chair. In both cases, the element of purpose seems to be studiously neglected; and in both cases, the formal regularities exist for description only by virtue of the purpose that renders those formal features intelligible. In Fuller's opinion, the characteristic features of legal systems that have provided the focus for legal positivists exist as characteristic features only because they are related to the purpose of legal systems. Once we have a clear understanding of the purpose of legal systems, we will see that it is an inherently moral purpose, a moral aspiration. Thus an understanding of what law is cannot finally be separated from an understanding of what law ought to be, because understanding what law is involves a comprehension of moral aspirations that are implicit in the very concept of law itself.

Fuller's strategy of argument is as follows. He begins by identifying eight features of law that constitute minimum conditions, in the sense that a social formation that completely lacked any one of the eight would not normally be regarded as a legal system. He then seeks to demonstrate that the eight minimum conditions, taken collectively, amount to an intelligible moral ideal which can be seen as explaining the purposive features of law. All legal systems will fall short of this ideal to a greater or lesser extent, but once we have understood its nature, we can grasp the significance of the many disparate activities and forms of reasoning that compose the operation of a legal system. In this way we can attain a reflective understanding of the practices in which, as lawyers, we have unthinkingly been engaged.

Legal positivists generally hold that there is a fundamental distinction between facts and values. The question of whether or not something is a legal system is a question of fact; the question of whether it is a good or bad legal system is a question of value. This suggests that two different sets of criteria are involved: one set of criteria is applied to determine whether something counts as a legal system, and the other (evaluative) set is applied to determine whether it is a good or bad legal system. So far as a great many questions about the justice or injustice of the law is concerned, Fuller does not dispute this view; but he seeks to delineate a range of moral values where the fact/value distinction breaks down in its application to law. In relation to these values, we apply the same criteria in determining whether or not something counts as a legal system that we apply in determining whether it is a good or bad legal system. The eight minimum conditions represent, when perfectly complied with, a moral ideal towards which the law should strive to approximate.

The concept of law may once again be compared with spoons and chairs. We do not have one set of criteria for deciding whether something counts as a spoon and another set for deciding whether it is a good or a bad spoon. In both cases, the test is a purposive one. We understand what spoons are only by reference to their purpose. The formal features of spoons (the bowl, the handle, etc.) are intelligible only in the light of the spoon's purpose. A spoon that serves its purpose well is a good spoon. A spoon that serves its purpose badly is a bad spoon. At some point, the "spoon" may perform so badly that we would refuse to describe it as a spoon at all (a handle with no bowl, a bowl made of paper). Similarly with legal systems. There are purposes that render the formal features of legal systems intelligible. Unlike the purpose of spoons, the inherent purpose of legal systems is a recognisable moral aspiration. It amounts to an "inner morality of law".

GOOD AND BAD PURPOSES

The comparison between legal positivism and the formal description of a spoon or a chair is misleading in one respect: it is simply not true that Hart ignores the purposes of the institutions he is describing. In fact, he explains the nature of the institutions by reference to their purposes: thus, he explains the nature of a rule of recognition by explaining how rules of recognition overcome some of the problems inherent in a regime of primary rules; and such explanations are located in a wider account of human nature and circumstances and the requirements of survival. Hart believes, however, that the concept of law need not be understood by reference to any *moral* standard or moral purpose. Law, in Hart's view, can be used for many different purposes, some of them good and some bad: if we had to describe some purpose which is a *necessary* feature of law, it would have to be something highly general and morally neutral such as (for example) "the provision of rules for the guidance of conduct". Thus, Hart writes in the Postscript to *The Concept of Law*:

"Like other forms of positivism my theory makes no claim to identify the point or purpose of law and legal practices as such; ... I think it quite vain to seek any more specific purpose which law as such serves beyond providing guides to human conduct and standards of criticism of such conduct."[1]

Such a purpose as this is not really self-explanatory or fully intelligible. A desire to establish rules for the guidance of conduct would be very puzzling if we could not connect it with some further point or rationale (compare the man in Chapter 4 who wants a saucer of mud[2]). The natural law tradition of thought would supplement such an explanation of law's purpose with an account of how rules serve justice or the common good or other values: once we have seen how the provision of rules overcomes certain problems inherent in the human condition, we have understood law's nature. This type of approach is exemplified by the work of Finnis, and also by Fuller. Hart would resist this line of argument by suggesting that the institutions of law may be just as serviceable for wicked goals as for justice and the common good: it is not that the establishment of rules lacks a point, but that it may serve a huge diversity of different purposes.

Much of the debate relating to Fuller's theory, and Hart's criticisms of that theory, revolves around rival assertions regarding the probable or possible behaviour of wicked regimes. Would they have good reasons for establishing and respecting the institutions of law? Or does a concern for legality make no sense when detached from broader moral commitments to such values as justice and the common good?

THE EIGHT PRINCIPLES

In his principal book, *The Morality of Law*, Fuller tells an allegorical tale about a certain king "who bore the convenient, but not very imaginative and not even very regal sounding name of Rex". Rex wished to be a law-maker for his people. Unfortunately his efforts at law-making go astray in various ways, and he never succeeds in making any laws at all! I will not attempt to summarise Fuller's entertaining yarn. But the point of

[1]   *The Concept of Law*, p.249.
[2]   See p.99 above.

the story can be briefly explained, in two main points.

(1) Law-making is a purposive activity which can fail in its purpose. Like any other purposive activity, law-making requires attention to certain practical precepts related to the ultimate purpose of the activity. In relation to law-making there are eight such precepts. The basic object of law-making is to subject human conduct to the governance of rules. If this object is to be achieved:

   (i)   there must be rules;
   (ii)   they must be prospective, not retrospective;
   (iii)   the rules must be published;
   (iv)   the rules must be intelligible;
   (v)   the rules must not be contradictory;
   (vi)   compliance with the rules must be possible;
   (vii)   the rules must not be constantly changing;
   (viii) there must be congruence between the rules as declared and as applied by officials.

(2) The eight precepts represent eight ways in which the enterprise of law-making can go astray. They point to eight minimum conditions for the existence of anything that we would regard as law or a legal system. For example, a system where *all* the rules were kept secret, or where *all* the rules were retrospective, would not normally be thought of as a legal system. Complete failure to comply with any one of the eight principles results in something that is not law at all.

Fuller describes his eight principles as an "inner morality of law", and this claim has generated much confusion. The majority of critics have been unable to see any justification for treating the eight principles as "moral". We shall consider these criticisms later. For the present, we must pursue Fuller's argument a little further.

Fuller draws a distinction between what he calls "the morality of duty" and "the morality of aspiration". These two types of morality, or areas of morality, differ from each other both in logical structure and in rationale. The morality of duty is a matter of rules or standards which are regarded as obligatory. Compliance is seen as a duty, and one either complies or one does not; there are no questions of degree. The morality of aspiration is not structured in terms of rules but in terms of ideals: here, acting morally is a matter of striving to approximate to or emulate certain ideals or aspirations. Everything here is a question of degree. No one can expect to achieve completely the ideal requirements; but one must strive for the nearest approximation one can manage.

According to Fuller, the inner morality of law resembles a morality of aspiration. He means by this that the eight principles should not be thought of individually, as moral principles compliance with which is a duty; rather they should be thought of collectively as representing a moral aspiration for legal systems. No legal system can comply perfectly with all of the eight principles; but, for every legal system, compliance should be pursued strenuously and seriously.

It is easy to see that Fuller's eight principles correspond to the idea of "the rule of law" (or at least to one aspect of that idea), long regarded as an important regulative ideal for Western legal systems. But Fuller is not simply trying to describe one possible value or ideal for legal systems: he is claiming that this ideal is implicit in the very concept of law itself. An understanding of what a "spoon" is involves an understanding of what spoons are for, and that in turn implies certain criteria for good and bad spoons. Similarly, to understand what "law" is we must have some understanding of the purpose of law and thus of the evaluative criteria that are relative to that purpose.

LAW AND PURPOSE

"But", we may ask, "can't law have any purpose? Can't law be used for good purposes and bad?" This question reflects the criticism of Fuller's argument which has come to be most widely accepted, a criticism that was first formulated by Hart. Hart argued that Fuller had simply described eight principles for effective law-making. But law is an instrument that can be used for good purposes and for bad: its efficacy is not identical with morality. In Hart's view, Fuller had no real justification for calling the eight principles a "morality" of law. We might describe certain principles for effective poisoning (*e.g.* administer a dose that is large enough to kill, but not so large that it will cause vomiting; choose poisons which cannot be traced, etc.) but, Hart says, it would be absurd to describe these as an "inner morality of poisoning".[3]

---

[3]   H.L.A. Hart, *Essays in Jurisprudence and Philosophy* (Oxford 1983) Essay 16.

Is it true that the eight principles are mere principles of efficacy? First, we should notice that there is something question-begging in the description of them as principles of effective law-making. The question we are addressing is that of whether law is inherently moral. If law *is* inherently moral, then principles of effective law-making may well be moral principles. To say that the eight principles are *not* moral principles but *merely* principles of effective law-making assumes the very point at issue.

If Hart had said that the eight principles were principles of effective social control there would have been obvious objections to his claim. If social control is merely a matter of preventing widespread violence and revolutionary dissent, it is unlikely that Fuller's eight principles will be a good guide to the most effective techniques. A regime of terror where officials act unpredictably or on the basis of secret directives is much more likely to succeed in quelling opposition. Where clear rules are published, the citizen is given advance notice of those areas of conduct where he can act without fear of official interference. In the absence of such rules, any action that worries or annoys the officials is likely to be interfered with: the only way of avoiding interference is to maintain a compliant and totally conformist attitude and lifestyle.

To say that the eight principles are principles of efficacy is therefore unhelpful, unless the object for which they are "effective" is more closely specified. The eight principles will not be a good guide to the effective techniques of mass coercion; and to describe them as principles of effective law-making begs the question of what law is and how it differs from organised coercion.

KRAMER'S CRITICISMS (PART ONE)

In support of Hart's claims, and in criticism of the above arguments (which I offered in the first edition of this book), Matthew Kramer has urged that evil regimes will need to maintain a rule-based system of coercion if they are to survive and to advance their evil goals in the long term.[4] To ensure that

---

[4]   Kramer readily concedes that an evil regime's compliance with Fuller's principles does not undermine Fuller's theory if the regime complies only in order to conceal its wickedness and present a morally benign exterior to the world: for compliance of this sort is not inconsistent with Fuller's thesis that the eight principles are of intrinsically moral import.

citizens comply with the regime's coercive mandates, and to co-ordinate the actions of the regime's own officials, the regime will need to comply with Fuller's eight principles. The type of regime described in my argument above could be effective only in the short term; beyond that, Kramer tells us, "there will typically be ample prudential reasons for wicked rulers to govern in accordance with Fuller's precepts."[5]

In my own opinion, evil regimes will not *invariably* need to rely upon anything resembling a legal order: much depends upon the character of their wicked goals. If those goals are sufficiently well-understood by the relevant population, and they are of a character that can be advanced without complex co-ordinated actions on the part of the population, a pure regime of terror may work perfectly well. Suppose, for example, that a group of religious fundamentalists has the sole aim of discouraging the propagation of atheism, being content to leave all other aspects of social life (such as the operation of markets and the protection of property rights) to be sustained (or not, as the case may be) by informal customary practices unsupported by official rules and sanctions. Unregulated brutality towards anyone suspected of sympathy for atheism would serve such a regime perfectly well. Atheists and potential atheists would be deprived of the opportunity to exploit the interstices of liberty that are inherent in any meticulously enforced set of rules; they would know that the only way to be safe was to avoid doing anything that might annoy the regime's supporters, or arouse their suspicions.

Kramer might very well reject this line of defence, however. For he may consider that it would be sufficient for him to demonstrate that it is *possible* to have prudential or even wicked motives for complying with Fuller's eight principles. It is therefore not necessary for him to show that evil regimes will *invariably* have good reasons for complying with the eight precepts: only that it is *possible* for them to have such reasons, in circumstances that are not too far-fetched. As we shall see, however, even this claim may be contested.

Kramer concentrates much of his attention upon the need for published rules and official conformity to them if a system of coercion is to be maintained. Only in this way, he argues, can a wicked regime be sustained in the medium-to-long term; only in this way can citizens be given stable incentives for conformity, and official actions be co-ordinated. To pursue Kramer's

---

[5] Matthew Kramer, *In Defense of Legal Positivism* (Oxford 1999) p.70.

argument, let us concede that our religious fundamentalists are unlikely to abandon the regulation of ordinary social life to the informal customs of the community, unsupported by official rules and sanctions. Consequently, let us also concede that the regime will indeed have to establish a system of rules that are reliably enforced. Nevertheless, Kramer fails to establish any convincing reason why the evil regime should confine the application of force to circumstances where a rule has in fact been breached. He therefore fails to demonstrate that a wicked regime could have sound prudential reasons for complying with Fuller's eight principles.

It is certainly true that atheists will on the whole be deterred from propagating their views if there are rules prohibiting such atheistic activities, and if sanctions are rigorously applied to those who break the rules. But why should the regime treat as *immune* from officially organised violence those atheistic activities that do *not* violate any published and prospective rule? After all, some atheistic activities may emerge in forms not anticipated by the religious regime, but they may be just as obnoxious to the regime (and just as much to be discouraged) as those activites that were indeed anticipated and prohibited. By ordering or permitting ad hoc official violence against the perpetrators of such obnoxious activities, the regime would not only discourage the particular activities in question, but would also discourage the expenditure of intellectual effort in dreaming up further innovative forms of atheistic practice aimed at escaping the existing prohibited categories. The same considerations apply to retrospective laws: if our evil regime has too many squeamish officials who dislike the idea of unregulated brutality against rule-conforming atheists (and other weirdos), they might be encouraged by retrospective regulation of the annoying forms of behaviour in question.

Kramer suggests that "if people often undergo punishment even when they have conformed closely to the prevailing legal norms ... the inducements for them to abide by those norms will be markedly sapped."[6] This claim seems to be straightforwardly false, however. What would undoubtedly undermine incentives for compliance would be a situation where compliance failed to *reduce* either the probability of one's suffering punishment, or the quantum of punishment suffered. But such a situation would not be brought about by the scenarios that I have described above;

---

[6]   Kramer, *op. cit.* p.60.

nor does the avoidance of such an undermining of incentives require compliance with Fuller's eight principles. To grasp this point accurately, we need to consider the following two situations:

(i) Citizens are punished for violating the rules; but they also suffer, on a very frequent but irregular basis, random acts of violence perpetrated by officials of the regime.

(ii) Citizens are punished for violating the rules; but, with equal frequency, they are also punished for activities obnoxious to the ruling powers, although not prohibited in any published and prospective rule.

In neither of these situations would incentives for compliance with the rules be reduced by the occurrence of official acts of violence not provided for in the rules, or provided for only in retrospective rules. For, by violating the rules, I would be greatly increasing my chances of incurring a punishment, or my chances of incurring an additional punishment. Even if unregulated official violence is so widespread that citizens can all expect to be its victims from time to time, it is difficult to see how this would undermine their motives for complying with the rules. The fact that you will beat me if I break the rules gives me a good reason for complying with them even if you frequently beat me at random: after all, the beating in consequence of breaking the rules will be an additional beating that I could have avoided by compliance.

The one situation where Kramer's argument has some apparent force is that where a citizen has to choose between two ways of pursuing his obnoxious atheistic activities, one of which complies with the rules, and one of which does not; if both forms of activity are equally likely to incur punishment, the citizen has no incentive to prefer the rule-conforming mode to the rule-violating mode; but, by the same token, the citizen has an equal incentive to abstain from *both* forms of activity. I can see no reason why an evil regime would be troubled by this situation; indeed, such a situation would in all probability be highly desirable from the viewpoint of such a regime. Consequently, I can see no force in Kramer's argument.

The conclusion we must draw is that evil regimes would not have any obvious reason for complying with Fuller's eight precepts. They would have good reasons for publishing rules and enforcing them; but not for restricting official violence to circumstances where the published rules had been violated. A regime that makes an assiduous effort to follow Fullerian precepts is motivated by a moral aspiration, not by a desire to advance wicked goals with maximum efficiency.

THE POINT OF LAW

According to Fuller, law is "the enterprise of subjecting human conduct to the governance of rules". Stated baldly, this hardly describes anything that we would regard as an intelligible purpose. Suppose that you met someone who wanted to have rules that governed every aspect of human conduct: he had discovered, for example, that there were no rules governing the way people laced up their shoes, and he wanted to see this matter regulated as quickly as possible. When asked for a reason for having rules regulating the lacing up of shoes he simply replied "It is my purpose to subject human conduct to the governance of rules". Such a "purpose" would look more like a mental illness! What is required from Fuller is a much better account of why rules matter, of why it is a good thing to subject conduct to the governance of rules rather than (say) to the governance of terror and coercion or to no governance at all.

Fortunately, such an account can be reconstructed from Fuller's arguments, and it casts considerable light on his notion of the eight principles as an "inner morality of law". As we have seen, the moralities of duty and of aspiration are distinguished by their differing logical forms: one is framed in terms of obligatory rules, and the other in terms of ideals. But they are distinguished also by their point or rationale. The morality of aspiration fundamentally concerns the questions "How should I live? What goals and aspirations should I pursue?" It is in this sense that the morality of aspiration can be said to concern the "good life". But the questions posed by the morality of aspiration make sense only in a context where people can meaningfully formulate and pursue personal projects and ideals. If, for example, I am a slave whose every waking hour is absorbed in labour under the direction of others, it makes but little sense for me to ask "What goals and aspirations should I pursue?" Similarly, if social life is so lacking in order and regularity that I am likely at any moment to be murdered, imprisoned, or coerced, it makes little sense for me to formulate long term plans and projects for my life. In order for the morality of aspiration to have any application at all, it is necessary for there to be some degree of order and regularity in social life. This order and regularity is provided by the rules that comprise the morality of duty. Observance of the basic rules against killing, stealing, and so on, makes possible that degree of order and personal integrity that is an essential pre-condition for the meaningful confrontation of the demands of the good life, the morality of aspiration. The eight principles described by Fuller resemble the morality of aspiration in their logical structure: they collectively represent an ideal towards which legal systems should strive but from which they will inevitably fall short. But the eight principles resemble the morality of duty in their rationale: their object is to provide that degree of regularity and order which is the context within which the morality of aspiration has application. This is the real meaning of Fuller's description of law as "the enterprise of subjecting human conduct to the governance of rules". Only when human conduct is subjected to the governance of rules can we (in Fuller's words) "rescue man from the blind play of chance and . . . put him safely on the road to purposeful and creative activity".

We are now in a position to see the fallacy that is involved in treating Fuller's eight principles as mere principles of efficacy. For us to speak meaningfully of efficacy, it must be possible to distinguish means from ends. Thus, there could be principles of effective poisoning because there is a definite end in view (a dead victim) and certain steps calculated to achieve that end (the right dose). But Fuller's eight principles are not related in this way to any independent end. Observance of the principles is valuable not because it is effective in the attainment of some goal, but because it is constitutive of that situation that we describe as "the rule of law".[7] We value the rule of law because we value the projective capacities of men and women: we value "purposeful and creative activity" and we know that this is possible only within the context of a social order based on the observance of clear and declared rules.

INTERNAL AND EXTERNAL MORALITIES

Fuller distinguishes between the internal (or "inner") morality of

[7]   For Matthew Kramer's criticism of this argument, see *op. cit.* p.50.

law, which is represented by his eight principles, and what he calls the external morality of law. The latter concerns the familiar question of whether the law is just or unjust, good or bad. But what does Fuller mean by the contrast between internal and external moralities?

The basic point is this. You and I may disagree about justice and about which laws would be just. There may or may not be ways of rationally resolving our dispute; but, as between our two views of justice, the concept of law will be neutral. The law could appropriately be used to implement either conception of justice. With the values represented by the eight principles, the position is different. These values are internal to the law in the sense that they form a part of the concept of law itself. We understand what law is only by reference to its purpose; and its purpose is an ideal state of affairs (the rule of law) represented by the eight principles. Every legal system will fall short of the ideal to some extent but (as the allegory of Rex demonstrates) too great a failure results in something that cannot be called a legal system at all. Law is not the only possible form of governance or social control: one might employ organised coercion, behavioural conditioning, or mediation and compromise, for example. But the use of law as against those other forms of ordering carries with it certain moral commitments. It carries a commitment to the idea of man as a rational purposive agent, capable of regulating his conduct by rules, rather than as a pliable instrument to be manipulated; and it carries a commitment to the values of the rule of law as expressed in the eight principles.

Because the eight principles are internal to the concept of law itself, the part that they can play in legal reasoning is quite different from the part played by values such as justice or equality. A judge who invokes some conception of justice as a justification for his decisions may be exposed to the criticism that his job is to apply the law, not to resolve controversial issues about justice which should be resolved democratically. But, since the eight principles form a part of the concept of law itself, the judge's duty to apply the law includes a duty to be guided by the eight principles. Thus, when lawyers and judges interpret laws in such a way as to make them clear and to remove apparent contradictions, they can justifiably claim to be exhibiting fidelity to law, rather than an unprincipled willingness to interfere with democratically enacted rules. Indeed Fuller insists that it is important not to confuse fidelity to law with mere deference to constituted authority. Fidelity to law involves a commitment to the eight principles, which therefore serve as general guidelines for the purposive activity of maintaining, applying and advancing a legal system.

Given the contrast between internal and external moralities, it should be clear that compliance with the eight principles does not guarantee that the law will be just. It is logically possible for a government to comply with the eight principles to a very high degree and nevertheless enact unjust laws. This is presumably what leads Hart to say that Fuller's inner morality of law is "compatible with very great iniquity".

Fuller would probably say that compliance with the eight principles is logically consistent with the pursuit of evil aims in very much the same way that armed robbery is logically consistent with a scrupulous concern for paying one's debts. They are indeed logically consistent, but they are very unlikely to be found together. An evil regime which is likely to meet opposition from its subjects will not choose to operate through the rule of law. An evil regime that has the massive support of its populace (say, because it persecutes only a small minority group) may find it easier to comply with the eight principles; but even here such compliance would be problematic. Evil aims such as racist persecution could be pursued through the law, in Fuller's opinion, only by means of laws employing inherently vague and uncertain concepts of "race": this would violate the principles requiring clarity, and congruence between declared rule and official action. In any case, Fuller argues, the eight principles make sense only in the context of a commitment to the value of man as a rational and purposive agent, a commitment that is likely to be absent in the worst varieties of tyranny.

If respect for the eight principles makes extreme forms of oppression improbable, it does not resolve the host of problematic questions about the justice of the law. Different views of justice are of course compatible with respect for the rule of law. But even here, Fuller argues, greater concern for the eight principles can help to resolve some controversial issues. There has, for example, been a long-running debate about the legal enforcement of personal sexual morality, laws against homosexuality being the most common example. Fuller argues that such laws should be removed from the statute book where they still exist because they lead to too great a deviation from the eight principles, particularly the principle requiring congruence between the declared rule and official action. Enforcement of such laws would be so sporadic and uncertain that a gulf would be created between the law as it appears in the books and as it is actually enforced.

These arguments of Fuller's are not without merit; but they serve to divert attention from a more obvious weakness in Hart's line of attack. For the fact that compliance with the eight principles is compatible with injustice does not demonstrate that such compliance is not a genuine moral value. We should readily concede that justice is one potential virtue in law, and compliance with the "inner morality" is another, and that the two virtues are to some extent independent. The fact that the law complies with Fuller's eight principles will not guarantee that it is just; indeed, it is conceivable that a high degree of compliance with the eight principles might co-exist with gross injustice. Yet none of this even begins to show that compliance with the eight principles is not a moral virtue in law.

Consider an analogy. Honesty is one potential virtue in people, while kindness is another. Now honesty may be compatible with serious shortcomings in regard to kindness: indeed, honesty may be compatible with great cruelty. This does not, however, show honesty not to be a virtue. The fact that honesty is "compatible with great iniquity" is an important fact, but not one that negates honesty's status as a virtue. Similarly, the fact that compliance with the eight principles is "compatible with great iniquity" is in no way inconsistent with the thesis that the eight principles represent a virtue in law.

Imagine two regimes, A and B, both equally guilty of violating human rights of various kinds; regime A operates by clearly declared rules, consistently and scrupulously enforced, while regime B operates with the aid of retrospective legislation, unlawful acts of violence by officials, secret trials, secret laws, and so forth. Is there any moral value attaching to regime A's commitment to the rule of law? Clearly there is. Where the government acts in accordance with the eight principles it makes its behaviour both public and predictable. This means that the citizen who wishes to avoid official interference knows just how far he can go without meeting that interference; this provides the degree of order and regularity which is the necessary framework for purposeful and creative activity; moreover (and more importantly from the point of view of an evil regime) it gives the citizen areas of freedom which may be exploited in order to actively oppose the regime.

These are familiar facts, and they reflect a belief that is as justifiable as it is widespread. Questions of due process and the rule of law are so far from being mere matters of "efficacy" that we ordinarily think of them as constraints on government power. But if Hart's arguments were correct, this approach would be fundamentally misconceived.

KRAMER'S CRITICISMS (PART TWO)

Matthew Kramer has forcefully attacked the above argument. In his view, when we are assessing the respective moral merits of different regimes, everything turns upon questions concerning the content of the laws, and the nature of any official deviations from the laws. Benign deviations from wicked laws may be morally desirable, and enforcement of those laws may be morally abhorrent; conversely, malign deviations from good laws may be abhorrent, while enforcement of those laws may be highly desirable. If we imagine regime A in my example to be preferable in any respect to regime B, we are in all probability focusing upon malign deviations from the law by regime B: but it is not the fact of deviation that is morally pertinent here, but the fact of the deviation's malignancy.[8]

My original argument (set out above) was that compliance with the eight principles is a morally desirable feature of a legal regime because, amongst other reasons, it provides interstices of liberty within which the citizen can act freely, without the risk of interference. This not only provides the necessary framework for purposeful and creative activity, but also provides secure areas of freedom which may be exploited for the purpose of opposing the existing regime (which is, of course, one reason why evil regimes are unlikely to favour Fuller's principles).

The flaw in Kramer's response to my argument is that it over-simplifies the issues involved, by ignoring the fact that my actions may be impinged upon by the acts of other citizens, and the ability of other citizens so to interfere with my liberty is in part dependent upon the regularity with which the law is enforced. It follows from this that one may pay a moral cost even when wicked laws are left unenforced, or are enforced only sporadically; official deviations from legality may have con-sequences adverse for liberty even when they are motivated by benevolence.

Suppose, for example, that I am an opponent of the existing

---

[8]   See Kramer, *op. cit.* p.56 *et seq.*

regime, but that all my near neighbours are loyal Party members. If I choose to pursue anti-governmental activities such as distributing leaflets and putting up posters, the ordinary laws against assault and damage to property will afford me a measure of protection from the resulting hostility of my neighbours, consequent upon their discovery of my subversive outlook. My liberty is here protected by the regular enforcement of laws that are in themselves just and benign; but my liberty might *also* be protected by laws that are in themselves wicked.

Let's say that I am unwilling to incur the hostility of my neighbours because, even though they cannot lawfully assault me or damage my property, they could seriously disrupt my life by getting local shopkeepers to refuse to serve me. I therefore wish to carry on my subversive activities without the knowledge of my neighbours. Each evening, I execute a subversive leaflet drop by means of specially-trained carrier pigeons that I release from my window. My neigbours are upset by the leaflets that appear on their lawns, but do not realise that I am their author and source. They are unable to discover this fact because the regime imposes a 7 p.m. curfew upon all citizens, thereby ensuring that no one will be wandering around in the street to see me release pigeons from my window.

A 7 p.m. curfew is a very oppressive and unjust restraint upon liberty. Nevertheless, even in the case of such a law, the regular enforcement of the law enables me to form stable expectations about the conduct of my fellow citizens; and those stable expectations are an important bulwark of my freedom. Benevolent judges may be strongly tempted to deviate from the strict requirements of an oppressive law such as the curfew, and they may be right, on balance, to do so; but such benign deviations come at a general moral cost, in so far as they undermine the ability of law to encourage stable mutual expectations, such stability being itself a precondition for the pursuit of individual projects.

Of course, laws can reduce personal security as well as protect it. The same regime that imposes the 7 p.m. curfew may also confer upon Party members a right to search my home, and may enact laws prohibiting me from offering any physical resistance to their actions. If the judges deviate from a law of this type (whether by penalising the Party members or by refusing to punish me for my resistance to their actions) they will to that extent respect and protect my security on this occasion. Precisely in being unregulated, however, such official deviations are unpredictable. They consequently fail to provide me with any domain within which I can confidently feel free from potential interference. A system of law that satisfies Fuller's eight principles, by contrast, will (simply in virtue of being such a system of laws) inevitably provide the citizen with certain domains where interference is predictably excluded.[9]

It is important to remember that Fuller is claiming that compliance with the eight principles is a moral virtue in law: but it does not follow from this that compliance with the eight principles will always lead to morally preferable outcomes. Analogously, honesty is a moral virtue; but telling the truth does not always lead to the best outcome, nor is it always the right thing to do (*e.g.* a mad axeman, with obvious intent, asks me for your whereabouts). To demonstrate that honesty or promise-keeping or kindness is a virtue we need to show that human nature and circumstances being what they are, things will generally go better if the truth is told, promises are kept, and kindness exhibited. Sometimes, it is right to tell a lie, break a promise, or cause pain that could have been avoided. In each such case, however, something of moral importance is sacrificed; the situation that makes a lie necessary is to be regretted and avoided if at all possible.

It is much the same when we consider the virtues of institutions. If Fuller is right that a commitment to the eight principles is inherent in our concept of "law", he has good grounds for saying that such commitment is a moral virtue of law. The fact that compliance with the principles will not invariably yield the best results does not distinguish this virtue from any other. Human nature and human circumstances being what they are, things will generally be best when we have clear, published, prospective rules that are consistently enforced. Only in this way can we enjoy domains of liberty secure from official interference, and the interference of other citizens; only in this way can we form reliable expectations about the conduct of others that are sufficient to permit the formulation and pursuit of individual plans and projects.

---

[9] What of a body of laws that extended to some class of individuals (some minority racial group, perhaps) no protection of any kind? I have argued elsewhere that such individuals would not stand in legal relationships at all: they would not be governed by law, but excluded from the scope of the legal system. See Simmonds, "Rights at the Cutting Edge" in M. H. Kramer, N.E. Simmonds and Hillel Steiner, *A Debate Over Rights* (Oxford 1998) pp.165–167.

Am I then committed to saying that something of moral importance is lost when judges fail to enforce wicked laws consistently? Is something of value sacrificed when the judge twists the law to allow the victim of oppression to escape his official persecutors? In the view of some critics, it will not be enough for me to say that the judge may do the right thing on balance by so departing from standards of legality: I must deny any moral force whatever to those standards, or I must stand condemned as a moral imbecile.

It was pointed out in Chapter 5 that there is a difference between a set of moral considerations being clearly outweighed, and their being inapplicable. When a law is so wicked that we cannot imagine any moral gain from enforcing it that would significantly counterbalance the immediate moral loss, we are inclined to deny that the law has any moral force whatever. Moral indignation is, however, a poor guide to the complexity of real life. The desire to give forceful expression to one's sense that the issue is clear cut is, here and elsewhere, a source of confusion: for the fact may remain that there *are* conflicting considerations in such cases, even if some are relatively insubstantial by comparison with others.

Philosophers are very fond of dreaming up hypothetical scenarios where all the circumstances and consequences of my actions are known, and we can say with certainty that no good will flow from my compliance with the law.[10] From these scenarios, they conclude that there is no general obligation to obey the law. In a similar way one might conclude that there is no general obligation to keep one's promises, or to tell the truth. Unfortunately, life is not so simple, nor are we ever so well-informed as in the examples of philosophers. We act under uncertainty, and the moral standards that guide us are intended for such conditions. Thus we must say that, even in the case of a wicked law, there is a moral cost in the deviation from standards of legality. The judge called upon to enforce an unjust curfew may feel that he sacrifices nothing of value by allowing the accused to escape punishment; but, by contributing to a situation wherein enforcement of the curfew cannot be relied upon, he may expose the author of subversive leaflets to hostile action of a kind sufficient to curtail his freedom.

---

[10] For example, traffic lights on red at a crossroads where one can easily see in all directions for miles, and one can easily see that no vehicle or pedestrian is coming.

RECAPITULATION AND RECONSTRUCTION

Fuller's argument is not an easy one to grasp, so it is worth taking a moment to recapitulate and reassemble the various ideas that compose his theory.

Fuller identifies eight features that must be exhibited to some extent by anything that we would count as a legal system. A society cannot be said to possess a legal system if it has no rules at all; or if all of its rules are retrospective; or if none of the rules are published; or if officials never act in compliance with the rules; and so forth. Notice very carefully that Fuller is *not* arguing that, to constitute a legal system, a regime must have *no* retrospective rules, or secret rules, or official deviations from the rules. He is well aware that all actual legal systems will exhibit features such as retrospectivity and official deviance to a greater or lesser extent. Such systems would certainly cease to constitute legal systems if there was a complete failure to comply with any one of the eight principles: in other words, if *all* of the rules were secret, or retrospective, or they were *never* followed by officials, etc. Short of such complete failure, however, the question of whether or not a social ordering constitutes a legal system depends upon how closely it approximates to the ideal that is represented by the eight principles.

When we take the eight requirements together, Fuller believes, we can see that they constitute an intelligible moral aspiration for legal systems. All actual legal systems will, to a greater or lesser extent, fall short of the ideal of total compliance with the eight principles. Nevertheless, an understanding of the ideal goal is important for two main reasons.

In the first place, the ideal of total compliance guides and informs the activities that compose the legal system: lawyers and law-makers are engaged in a purposive enterprise that aims, amongst other things, at achieving a higher degree of compliance with the eight principles. An understanding of the inner morality of law therefore enables us to comprehend the otherwise disparate features of legal thought and practice as a unified and coherent activity serving a recognisable goal: we come to understand the purpose of the practices in which we have unreflectively been engaged.

Secondly, a grasp of the ideal (represented by the eight principles) enables us to see that different legal systems exemplify that ideal to varying degrees. They are therefore better and worse approximations to the ideal of legality. The more closely a system approximates to the ideal, the better it is from the viewpoint of law's inner morality; but also, and by the same token, the better it is as an example of law. For Hart, to say that a social ordering is an instance of "law" is to make a morally neutral judgment. Furthermore (penumbral cases apart) a social ordering, for Hart, either constitutes a legal system or it does not. If there is a rule of recognition, accepted by officials, and if the primary rules are mostly obeyed by the bulk of the population, it is a legal system. Thus we understand the concept of "legal system" by reference to conditions that are either satisfied or not satisfied. For Fuller, however, we decide whether or not something counts as a legal system by its approximation to an ideal: to understand the nature of law, we must first understand the ideal goal that law serves, and we can then identify instances of law by their degree of approximation to the goal.[11]

Fuller's theory is not best interpreted as claiming that law will always be morally worthy or admirable. The law may exhibit serious failings with regard to the external morality of law even while exhibiting a high degree of compliance with the inner morality of law: that is to say, the law may be published, clear, prospective, consistently applied (and so forth) and yet be oppressive or unjust. Furthermore, a regime may rightly be regarded as a legal system even while exhibiting serious failures in relation to the *inner* morality of law. Fuller is not arguing that every regime that we will properly regard as a legal system will be morally good. Rather, the nub of his argument might be summarised in the following propositions:

(i)   our judgments about what counts as a legal system are guided by the ideal of compliance with the eight principles;

(ii) the more dramatically a regime departs from the eight principles, the more marginal it will seem as an example of a legal system;

(iii) this reflects the fact that governance by law is a purposeful enterprise, and we judge whether or not something is an instance of law by how far it approximates to the relevant purpose;

(iv) the concept of "law" is to be understood by reference to a

---

[11]   This idea should be compared with Finnis's notion of "focal instances" of law, where law serves the common good. See Chapter 4, and Introduction to Part 2, p.124.

purpose that finds expression in the eight principles;

(v) the purpose is one of facilitating our capacity and opportunity to choose and pursue projects, by means of the "subjection of human conduct to the governance of rules".

This argument (if successful) establishes a necessary connection between law and morality in so far as compliance with the eight principles is the central idea by which the concept of law is structured: instances of law count as such by virtue of their (greater or lesser) approximation to the ideal of total compliance.

The most popular objection to Fuller's theory claims that the eight principles do not represent a moral virtue in law, but a matter of efficacy, serviceable for good purposes or bad. Kramer's criticisms of my arguments (discussed above) exemplify this criticism. Kramer seeks to show that even a wicked regime might have good reason for following the eight principles. We saw, however, that Kramer's arguments failed in certain key respects. In spotting that failure, we saw that compliance with the eight principles *cannot* plausibly be explained as a matter of efficacy, instrumentally valuable for the pursuit of bad purposes as well as good. On the other hand, Fuller makes a decent job of showing how compliance with the eight principles serves the value that we place on human projective capacities. A traditional view turns out to be justified by theoretical reflection: the rule of law serves liberty.

OTHER WORLDS

This is not to say that liberty is the only, or the most important, value; nor is it to deny that the pursuit of the ideal of legality comes at a price. Consider, for example, a different approach to social ordering and the handling of disputes, of a kind that is exemplified by some pre-industrial societies.[12] To simplify matters, I will explain the point by means of an imaginary society, that I will call "New Monia".

In modern Britain, most of us occupy numerous different

---

[12] The discussion that follows draws very loosely upon the work of Max Gluckman. See M. Gluckman, *Politics, Law and Ritual in a Tribal Society* (Oxford 1971); Gluckman, *The Judicial Process Among the Barotse* (Manchester 1955); Gluckman, *The Ideas in Barotse Jurisprudence* (Manchester 1965). See also S. Roberts, *Order and Dispute* (London 1979) Chapter. 2.

social roles, and have many diverse relationships with different people. I sell my labour (very cheaply) to Cambridge University, buy my groceries at Sainsbury's, bank with Nat West, buy my cars from Dodgy Motors, and so forth. If I have a dispute with any of these, I will seek to discover my legal rights, and (if the matter is important) I may seek to ensure that my rights are enforced. I may not want to switch jobs, or banks, and so may accept some compromise rather than let the relationship break down; but, if necessary, I will go to court to seek enforcement of my rights.

When I get to court, the court will try to narrow down the issue in dispute as carefully as possible,[13] and will not investigate every aspect of the relationship between the disputing parties. Perhaps Dodgy Motors have sold me lots of dodgy motors in the past, for example, but I am *now* complaining about specific defects in this particular car. The court will try to determine, as exactly as possible, the rights and duties of the parties, and will then enforce those rights.

In New Monia, things are very different. For a start, the village elders in New Monia do not have police forces, prisons and armies at their disposal: consequently, there will be limits to the decisions that they can succeed in enforcing. Furthermore, whereas relationships in Britain are fairly narrow and specific (I bank with NatWest, but I do not buy my groceries there), relationships in New Monia were described by a visiting anthropologist as "multiplex": that is to say, they range across various aspects of life.[14] Thus, in New Monia, my neighbour might be related to me by marriage, and might supply me with water from the stretch of river where he lives, while I let him pasture some of his cattle on the meadow in front of my house. Because relationships have many different aspects, it is important for us not to let the relationship break down completely (where else can I get water? where else can he pasture his cows?). Because the tribal elders have limited enforcement mechanisms at their disposal, they will try to find a solution that is not wholly unacceptable to either party.

For these reasons, the elders in New Monia will try to get disputing parties to patch up their relationship and make a compromise of some sort. Fortunately, New Monian society

---

[13] This used to be the function of pleadings, before the "dumbing down" of litigation.

[14] Gluckman, *Judicial Process Among the Barotse* p.19.

tends to have rather complex kinship structures, so that wider kinship groups can often put pressure on intractable disputants to get them to accept a compromise. Because relationships with kin are themselves "multiplex" in character, disputants are unlikely to want to create a fundamental rift with their relatives, and the relatives therefore have considerable power available to them, which can be used to force a compromise upon the parties.

When the litigants appear in court, the elders who compose the court will not seek to define the issue in dispute as narrowly as possible: they will assume that the immediate matter in dispute is the tip of a large iceberg of bad blood between the litigants. This is because their objective is not precisely to define and enforce *rights* but rather to expel the bad blood and get the disputing parties to patch up their relationship.

New Monia has some general customary rules, governing a host of matters such as the pasturing of cattle, the extraction of water, kinship, marriage, the ownership of chattels, the prohibition of violence, and so forth. There is, however, no "rule of recognition". This does not mean that people do not disagree about the content of the rules. Hart is simply mistaken if he imagines that the only viable response to such disagreement is the establishment of a rule of recognition. In New Monia, disagreements about the content of the rules are treated as manifestations of a potential breakdown in a relationship. The elders do not aim to give precise definition to the content of the rules: they try to get the parties to make a compromise.

New Monia has much to be said for it. The approach to disputes adopted by the elders is a sensible one. The modern obsession with claiming one's "rights", even at the cost of valued and well-established relationships, is a potentially corrosive force that should be viewed with suspicion. But New Monia pays a price for its desirable features, and the price is paid in individual liberty.

Suppose that, in modern Cambridge, I erect an ugly steel construction in my garden. You, my neighbour, very much resent having to look at it, and you register your objections forcefully, by playing your records very loudly while I am trying to work. Suppose that we are unable to reach a compromise, and we wind up in court. The court will seek to decide who is and is not acting within their rights. This will be done by consulting, carefully defining, and applying legal rules; it will not be done by seeing how we can be forced to patch things up. Because the court will approach matters in this way, I know that I can behave in eccentric ways that my neighbours may object to: but, if I am acting within my legal rights, the law will protect me.

Now consider New Monia. Here I will know that, should anyone take exception to my eccentric behaviour, and should their objections lead to a serious dispute between us, I am likely to be forced into a compromise of some sort. My ability to stand foursquare within my established rights and to tell the world to go to the devil is severely reduced.

Clear, published, prospective rules that are meticulously enforced by officials therefore serve liberty. No matter how narrowly the content of the rules may constrain my freedom, the very fact that they are ascertainable rules, and are reliably enforced, is likely to give me certain areas of entitlement within which I will be free from interference. In the world of New Monian compromise, by contrast, I will never be wholly free to behave in a manner that my fellows consider unacceptable or obnoxious.

BASELINES FOR COMPARISON

Matthew Kramer has criticised arguments that ascribe intrinsic "moral worthiness" to law on the basis that law is an indispensable precondition for a viable and tolerable social order. He suggests that such arguments employ an inappropriate baseline for comparison, by comparing the situation of governance by law with a situation of anarchy. Compared to a situation of anarchy, even a wicked legal system may seem preferable: but this comparison does not succeed in demonstrating that any moral worthiness attaches to the wicked regime simply in virtue of the fact that it does not exhibit all the horrors of complete anarchy. Similarly, a brutal protection racket could not lay credible claim to any degree of moral worthiness by pointing out that they do not actually murder their victims, and even protect their victims from other thugs who might murder them.

The emptiness of a claim to moral worthiness such as that made by the protection racket can clearly be seen, according to Kramer, once we appreciate that the appropriate baseline for comparison in assessing moral worthiness should be determined by the moral entitlements of people, and the attainability of relevant states of affairs. If a state of affairs devoid of protection rackets is reasonably attainable, it clearly represents a matter of moral entitlement. Hence the non-murderous protection racket should be compared with a situation where no protection rackets at all are present, rather than being compared with a situation of even more murderous schemes. The upshot will be that the protection racket is judged to lack moral worth.[15]

Does my comparison with New Monia fall foul of this argument? Am I trying to show that legal systems of necessity, and simply in virtue of being legal systems, will exhibit a degree of moral worthiness by comparison with societies such as New Monia?

Let me emphasise first of all that I do not regard New Monia as an unattractive type of society: it has many virtues which are in large part absent from a modern liberal democracy. It does, however, lack some of the virtues of a developed legal system. To assess whether such features of a legal system are indeed virtues, we need to make a comparison with societies that lack those features; if possible, we need to make the comparison with other fairly attractive societies that lack those features. The difference between my present argument and the argument attacked by Kramer hinges on the fact that I am not seeking to ascribe any *general* moral worthiness to legal systems. My point is simply that certain features of those systems represent moral virtues.

The relevant rule-of-law virtues may well be exhibited by a legal system that is in other respects unjust and oppressive; and it may well be that, in such circumstances, a just and non-oppressive system is both attainable and represents the moral entitlement of people. Given such a situation, the authors of the unjust system cannot claim moral worthiness for their system by pointing out that it is better than some conceivable alternatives, for such conceivable alternatives do not represent the relevant baseline for comparison. This is Kramer's argument and I see in it nothing with which to disagree. If, however, we are asking a different question, different baselines become relevant.

Suppose that we are asking, not "Is this regime a morally worthy one?", but "Are the rule-of-law virtues genuine moral virtues?" Now the attainable situation where we have a regime that is both just and observant of the rule of law ceases to be a relevant basis for comparison: one cannot assess the virtue of the rule of law by comparing just and unjust regimes all of which observe the rule of law in equal degree. The baseline should now be a situation where the rule of law is absent. There are,

---

[15] Kramer, *op. cit.* pp.206–208.

however, many different scenarios where the rule of law is absent, including oppressive and unjust tyrannies, and situations of outright anarchy. The best baseline for comparison would seem to be a reasonably attractive society which is just and humane but which attaches little or no importance to the meticulous enforcement of clear, published and prospective rules. Hence, New Monia provides us with the perspective that we need.

GUIDANCE BY RULE AND BY ASPIRATION

Fuller emphatically rejects Hart's claim that law consists of rules emanating from a basic rule of recognition. We might at first find this suprising: for does not Fuller's theory (like Hart's) emphasise the public ascertainability of law? And is not the rule of recognition the means whereby law is rendered publicly ascertainable? Rejection of the idea of a basic rule of recognition is not required by Fuller's rejection of legal positivism, for Fuller could still claim that the eight principles constitute a necessary connection between law and morals, while acknowledging that the best way of giving effect to the eight principles is by means of a rule of recognition.

If Fuller's judges are not to be guided by a basic rule of recognition, what must they take as their fundamental guide in adjudication? The answer seems to be that they must be guided by the ideal aspiration of compliance with the eight principles. The activities of judges and lawyers are not to be understood by reference to a fundamental *rule*, but by reference to a fundamental aspiration that informs their practices and arguments and gives an overall point to what they do.

We do not always possess a full and transparent understanding of our own purposes. You may be unsure as to why you chose to study law or jurisprudence, for example; the attempt to articulate your purpose may require you to reflect more carefully on what it is about law (as a subject of study, or as a career) that you consider to be good and worthwhile.[16] Nor are purposes always simply the diverse purposes of individuals: social practices such as those that compose a legal system may be best understood by reference to aspirations that are integral to the

---

[16] Compare Finnis's argument that we discern the objective goods by reflecting upon our own engagements in practical reason. See p.101 above.

practices, rather than being reducible to the various reasons that individuals may have for engaging in the practice. Thus, even if a great many lawyers engage in legal practice in order to make obscene amounts of money, this does not make "getting rich" the purpose of law. Our practices may embody *shared* purposes, that can in some cases be articulated only with considerable experience and careful reflection.

Confronted with the very complex and varied phenomena of legal practice and argument, Hart seeks to make sense of it by postulating a fundamental rule of recognition in each system. Judges and lawyers are, most of the time, concerned to invoke and apply rules that stem from this basic rule of recognition. In some cases, their arguments take on a more open-ended character, perhaps invoking moral and political conceptions that cannot plausibly be analysed as the application of a basic rule: Hart explains such situations by saying that they concern "penumbral" cases, not regulated by the rule of recognition, or by the rules that flow from it.

Fuller proposes a different account. Judges and lawyers are not applying a basic rule of recognition: they are guided by a fundamental aspiration that is internal to the practices in which they are engaged. The aspiration is that of complete compliance with the eight principles. The pursuit of this aspiration, however, is far from straightforward. This is partly because the eight principles are themselves informed by broader moral conceptions (such as the need to "rescue man from the blind play of chance") that contribute to our understanding of the principles in inherently contestable ways; but it is also because the eight principles give rise, in the circumstances of real life, to cross-cutting demands that confront lawyers with moral (and therefore juridical) dilemmas. Frequently, respect for one principle will require some sacrifice of another principle; or a principle may in itself have conflicting implications when applied to a specific context. Much of Fuller's book *The Morality of Law*, and many of his other writings, are concerned with such problems, and they are presented with considerable insight and as the fruit of extensive legal experience. For present purposes, a comparatively crude example will have to suffice.

Suppose that, as a judge, I am confronted with a newly enacted statute that seems to be riddled with apparent contradictions and hopelessly vague formulations, to the point where it is hard to make much sense of it. Having studied Fuller carefully, I am aware that I should not regulate my conduct by a simple rule of recognition (*e.g.* "Enforce statutes") but by the ideal aspiration of compliance with the eight principles. The trouble is that it is not clear which course of action will best serve to advance that ideal. I might conclude that enforcing such an opaque and muddled statute cannot advance the ideal aspiration. To implement this view, I might devise and articulate a new doctrine, perhaps to the effect that the enactments of the legislature will be enforced as law only when they provide some intelligible guidance as to their requirements. On the other hand, I may feel that proposing such a doctrine invites the courts to pick and choose amongst statutes, enforcing some and refusing to enforce others: perhaps this will do more to undermine the ideal goal (represented by the eight principles) than would be done if I simply did my best to make *some* sense of the statute and then enforced it as law.

Where else have we come across the idea of judges being guided by an ideal aspiration, rather than being guided by a basic rule of recognition? The answer is, of course, in Dworkin's theory of law. For Dworkin, judges are to be guided by the ideal of "integrity", understood as the internal moral coherence of the law. There can surely be little doubt that Dworkin has been influenced by Fuller's work,[17] but whereas Fuller links the aspiration of law to somewhat conservative values of liberty and order, Dworkin's emphasis is upon notions of equality and community. Dworkin's approach also suffers from a degree of implausibility, since we may well doubt whether modern legal systems can really be expected to exhibit much moral coherence,[18] and can even be accused of aiming at an anti-democratic form of intellectual "closure".[19] Fuller's view, with its emphasis upon the dilemmas with which law's goal confronts its practitioners, may well seem considerably more interesting and less problematic.

Both Dworkin and Fuller seek to make sense of legal practices by proposing a shared goal or aspiration. Hart, by contrast, seeks to make sense of the practices by proposing a basic rule, specific to each system. This contrast is linked to another important difference. Hart sees legal theory as an entirely different intellectual enterprise from the business of engaging in legal argument or seeking to ascertain and apply the law. Dworkin (explicitly) and Fuller (implicitly) regard the questions of legal

---

[17] The influence does not seem to be acknowledged by Dworkin.
[18] See the position of the "internal sceptics", above p.204.
[19] See Unger's criticisms, above pp.218–219.

theory as entering into, and forming a part of, the practice of law. Which view is better?

Consider my example of the Fullerite judge and the muddled statute. Such a judge might feel himself torn, in the first instance, between a simple rule ("Enforce statutes") and a more complex aspiration (represented by the eight principles). To decide between these two approaches, he would have to decide what his duty to apply the law requires of him. Does his duty to apply the law require him to enforce the statute? Is the temptation to do otherwise simply a wish to implement his own preferences, while overriding the law's requirements? Or is Fuller correct that, in enforcing the statute *simply* because of its source, and without reference to the ideal aspiration, the judge would be exhibiting "subservience to authority" rather than "fidelity to law"?

Lawyers who regard legal theory as an important and valuable form of intellectual inquiry assume, I suspect, that it is intended to help answer such questions as those raised by the judge in our example. What exactly does the duty to apply the law require? Is law just a body of rules laid down in statutes and cases? Or should we think of it more in terms of Fuller's ideal aspirations? Or is it more like the conception of justice implicit in the enacted rules, so that legality requires the rules always to be applied in the light of underpinning considerations of justice?

These questions are not occasional aberrations within legal practice: they pervade its every aspect. For example, should statutory provisions be construed on the assumption that they embody some intelligible general principle? Or should the judge confine himself to the wording and layout of the statutory provision, avoiding reliance upon principles that were not stated in the statute itself? The answer to such questions depends upon what we take law to be, and it is partly in order to address such questions that we study jurisprudence.

Defenders of the Hartian view of legal theory will view these remarks as manifestations of confusion. In their eyes, I am confusing questions concerning the nature of "law" with questions concerning the content of "the law" within a particular jurisdiction. Questions of the former type are philosophical questions calling for analysis of the concept of "law"; questions of the latter type are not philosophical questions at all, and are to be resolved by applying the basic rule of recognition of the system (or, in penumbral cases, by reliance upon wider moral or political considerations).

Such an accusation of confusion, however, simply begs the question. *If* the practices of law are best understood by reference to a basic rule of recognition, *then* the questions of legal theory are to be distinguished from questions about the applicability of that basic rule of recognition. But if the practices of law are best understood by reference to ideal aspirations (whether or not conceived along the lines proposed by Fuller or Dworkin), the debates of legal theory may best be thought of as attempts to construe and formulate those aspirations.

Selected reading

L. Fuller, *The Morality of Law* (revised ed., 1959).
L. Fuller, *Anatomy of the Law* (1971).
H. L. A. Hart, Book Review (1965) 78 *Harvard Law Review* 1281. (also printed in Hart, *Essays in Jurisprudence and Philosophy*, Essay 16).
M. Kramer, *In Defense of Legal Positivism*, (1999) Chap. 3.
R. S. Summers, *Lon L. Fuller* (1984).

PART 3: RIGHTS

Chapter 8

THE ANALYSIS OF RIGHTS

It is common to see a distinction drawn between "analytical jurisprudence" and "normative jurisprudence". Analytical jurisprudence is concerned with the formal analysis of concepts, in an effort to exhibit their logical structure and to reveal and refine conceptual distinctions. Normative jurisprudence is concerned to offer a theory about what is morally right and just, and therefore about the criteria by which the law should be evaluated. Thus the analytical jurisprudence of rights aims to answer the question of what it is to have a right: what exactly do we mean by "a right"? The normative jurisprudence of rights seeks to explain the moral foundation of rights and to answer the question "what rights do we actually have?"

This distinction is a conventional one and it is not without value, but its value can be overestimated. In Part 2 of this book we encountered theorists (such as Dworkin) who question the division between analytical and normative jurisprudence in relation to debates concerning the nature of law, and similar questions can be raised about the distinction in the context of the debate over rights.

Normative theories of justice (of the type that we studied in Part 1) seek to inform us of the moral rights that we actually possess, and the foundation from which they are to be derived. Thus Nozick derives our rights from the idea of self-ownership; Rawls from his two principles of justice; Finnis from the notion of objective goods; and so forth. More detailed inquiry, however, is likely to reveal that each theorist has a slightly different conception of what a right actually *is*. Conversely, rival analyses of the concept of "a right" are frequently connected with different normative theories about which rights we actually possess. This chapter will examine some "analytical" theories about the nature of rights: these theories are not aimed at telling us what rights we actually possess, but rather what it is to possess a right. The choice between different conceptions of "a right", however, cannot in all cases be detached from rival (normative) views about the content of our rights. So the analytical/normative division must be regarded as a provisional one only: more a matter of emphasis than a fundamental intellectual watershed.

The reason for this complex situation of mutual dependence between the analytical and normative inquiries is not far to seek, for *both* forms of inquiry try to interpret the significance of some fundamental ideas that structure and give point to our invocations of "rights" in both legal and moral contexts. We will begin by identifying some of those fundamental ideas, and explaining how their significance can be construed in different ways, suggestive of different accounts of both the nature and basis of rights.

SOME FUNDAMENTAL IDEAS

When one asserts a right to act in a certain way, one does both more and less than claim that the action is a good or admirable one to perform. One claims *less* than that, insofar as we generally believe that people may have the right to perform actions that are foolish, unworthy or even bad. Perhaps smoking cigarettes is a stupid thing to do, but I have a right to do it. Watching lots of T.V. game shows may be unworthy of an intelligent human being, but you act within your rights in so choosing to spend your time. To say that my action is one that I was entitled to perform is not to say that the action was worthy or admirable, or that it was a good thing that I did it.

Actions that exercise rights need not be good actions that it is desirable to perform. Yet, in claiming a right to perform those actions, I make a claim that in some respects goes beyond the mere assertion of desirability. Perhaps it would be good for everyone to be given holidays with pay: we might have different opinions about this and debate the matter at length. If, however, people have a *right* to holidays with pay, these deliberations pro and con must be set aside. For rights seem to possess peremptory force: they seem to cut short debate and preclude the balancing of various considerations one against another. Suppose that I think that watching T.V. game shows *is* a good activity: it provides innocent pleasure, and even some intellectual exercise. Nevertheless, the fact that watching T.V. game shows does have these good features does not in itself entail that I ought to be allowed to watch them: for these good features would have to be weighed against *other* goods that could be attained by spending my time in other ways (studying Shakespeare) and against the associated *bads* that are inseparable from watching T.V. (consumption of electricity, for example). Asserting the existence of a *right* to watch game shows, by contrast, seems to leave no room for further debate about the permissibility of my action: if I have a right to do it, the action is permissible regardless of the balance between competing goods and bads.

The peremptory force of rights sets the agenda for the philosophical debate, for rights seem to exclude as irrelevant considerations that might otherwise be regarded as possessing an obvious relevance. If you have £100, the fact that you can do more good by giving it to charity than by giving it to me seems to have an obvious and important bearing upon what you should do. Yet, if I have a right to the money (let's say that you promised to give it to me), the desirability of giving to charity should not influence your decision. Why then should such considerations be set on one side as irrelevant? What is a "right", that it should so require us to disregard important facts of human welfare in our deliberations on what is to be done?

The notion of an individual right appears to embody a jurisdictional frontier between distinct sets of considerations: on the one hand are questions about the good or bad nature of the actions I choose to perform; and on the other hand are questions about my entitlement to perform those actions. In asserting a right to act, I make no claim about the goodness or desirability of my action: rather I claim that all such considerations must be set aside in the face of my entitlement.

Jurisprudential theories vary in the significance that they attach to this jurisdictional frontier. Some theories see the prominence of the notion of "rights" in modern political thought as reflecting the division (noted in Part 1) between ancient and modern approaches to politics, with ancient approaches seeking to encourage and inculcate excellent and valuable ways of life, and modern approaches seeking to provide a framework of entitlements within which diverse "conceptions of the good" may be pursued. We will in due course examine the notion of "a right" that is to be found in the Kantian tradition of jurisprudence, and will find that this notion builds very directly upon the idea that "rights" mark out a fundamental distinction between considerations of justice and freedom, on the one hand,

and considerations of virtue or "the good", on the other.

Other approaches, by contrast, attach a less far-reaching significance to the special force of rights. Utilitarians, for example, accept no fundamental distinction between "the right" and "the good" (they define right conduct as that which maximises good consequences). Those utilitarians who find the notion of "a right" to be valuable tend to regard rights as conferred by *rules*. Rules (legal or moral) are selected for their good consequences, and actions are required to comply with rules.[1] A rule may serve overall utility even though not every action complying with the rule does so. Consequently, many of the considerations that are relevant at the stage of choosing and establishing rules should be disregarded at the stage of applying and enforcing those rules.

For example, a utilitarian might regard the establishment of rules of property and contract law (of the kind necessary for the operation of a market) as justified by the fact that markets operate, in the long run, to maximise human welfare. This is not to say, however, that utilitarians would permit property owners and contracting parties to exercise their contractual and proprietary rights only in ways that advance the general welfare. For to permit only those actions that can be shown to maximise welfare would replace the market with a governmentally controlled economy (officials would have to decide, in each situation, what should be done with your property) thereby sacrificing the benefits to welfare that flow from the operation of a market.

When actions are performed within the scope of the entitlements established by the rules governing the market, the actions must be permitted, even if they are actions that will not in fact serve to maximise welfare. The considerations that led to the establishment of the rules (considerations relating to the maximisation of welfare) must be excluded from consideration when the rules are to be applied and actions are to be judged permissible or impermissible.

We find in the utilitarian view of rights no fundamental division between "the right" and "the good", but merely a division between the considerations that justify the rules, and the values served (or disserved) by the actions that comply with the rules. We deliberate upon multifarious considerations of welfare when we are deciding which rules to establish. Once we have

---

[1] See above p.35.

established some rules (*e.g.* in legislation), such general arguments pro and con must not be reopened every time the rules have to be applied: otherwise the whole point of having rules will be defeated. Hence, the rules must be treated as conferring certain entitlements, and imposing certain duties, that have the effect of settling issues relating to the permissibility of conduct while excluding the general utilitarian calculus of costs and benefits. For utilitarians, therefore, assertions of rights claim *more* than assertions that the relevant action is good, insofar as they invoke rules that are already established and regarded as justified: they therefore have "peremptory force". But such assertions also do *less* than claim that the relevant action is good, in so far as not all actions complying with a rule will instantiate the values that actually justify the rule. Essentially the same explanation of the peremptory force of rights might be employed by anyone who rejects a basic divison between "the right" and "the good': thus, adherents to the natural law position defended by Finnis might take a broadly similar view.

Not all theorists accept the idea that rights have the power to exclude conflicting considerations. We have seen that the peremptory force of rights can be treated as a manifestation of a very fundamental distinction between different areas of moral concern (frequently referred to as "the right" and "the good") or as manifesting a distinction between established rules and their underpinning reasons. Both of these views ascribe to rights genuine peremptory force. That is to say, they take the view that rights are not simply *very weighty* considerations that are to be balanced against conflicting factors: rights operate to exclude some otherwise relevant considerations from our deliberations upon the permissibility of action. Where the two approaches differ is in how they explain the point and significance of this peremptory force. It is important to appreciate, however, that a third group of theorists argues that the alleged "peremptory force" of rights is nothing more than the great *importance* of those individual interests that may be represented by rights. Even while acknowledging that importance, they would say, we nevertheless have to *weigh* rights against conflicting considerations. Thus (they might say) people have a very strong and important interest in judging for themselves what will best advance their own welfare. When people decide to smoke (for example) the interest that we all have in being allowed to judge for ourselves must be weighed against the gains to human health that might be achieved by prohibiting smoking. The "right to smoke" (as a specific manifestation of the broader "right to judge for oneself") does not really *exclude* as irrelevant the possible benefits of prohibition. When such a right does indeed give the impression of possessing "peremptory force", this is not because it operates to exclude conflicting factors as irrelevant, but because the right *clearly outweighs* those considerations.

One reason which persuades some theorists to adopt this view is the difficulty of sticking in all circumstances to the austere line of treating conflicting considerations as irrelevant to the permissibility of actions licensed or prohibited by the right.[2] Suppose, for example, that I promise to meet you at the pub this evening. As a result of my promise, you have a right that I should meet you there, and I am under a duty to keep my promise. My duty gives me a reason for meeting you at the pub. But this is not *simply* a reason to meet you, for reasons must be balanced against countervailing reasons; and we do not feel that my promise is merely one factor that I should take account of in deciding whether to meet you at the pub. Rather, having promised to meet you, I can no longer feel free to spend my evening in whatever way I think best. Perhaps, after making my promise, I realise that I have a chapter about rights to write, and would be better getting on with that instead of going to the pub. My promise seems to *exclude* such considerations as irrelevant: you have a right that I should meet you, and that is that.

But suppose that I suffer a serious accident after making my promise. It would still be possible for me to meet you in the pub, but only at great personal inconvenience and perhaps even some risk to my health (I will have to limp from my hospital bed on crutches). Are these considerations also to be excluded as irrelevant to what I should do? Are we still to say that you have a right that I should meet you, and that is that?

We are all, at first, inclined to say that people's rights should

---

[2]   Also, there are undoubtedly certain contexts where we speak about rights being "balanced" against other factors. This tends to be the case where the right serves to protect some interest which is identified only by a general description. Such situations are best analysed as attempts to define the precise scope of the legitimate interest protected by the right, rather than as attempts to "balance" the right against other considerations.

Some legal scholars believe that the balancing of rights against other considerations is more characteristic of the European legal and political tradition than the American. See Mary Ann Glendon, *Rights Talk: The Impoverishment of Political Discourse* (New York 1991).

not be encroached upon simply because the encroachment will fractionally increase aggregate welfare (consider a suggestion that the occasional use of torture would reduce the costs of law-enforcement, for example). But will we stick to the austere line of excluding welfare considerations as irrelevant when respect for rights seems to require some very serious sacrifice? Even some of the most ardent defenders of rights feel the need to build into their theories provision for cases of this general type. Dworkin, for example, suggests that rights operate to "trump" considerations of utility; but he does not deny that it is in principle possible for *sufficiently large* welfare gains to override rights. Nozick claims that rights operate as "side-constraints", prohibiting us from encroaching upon the right-holder's integrity regardless of the values that may be served by such encroachment: but he allows that in "catastrophic situations" where the costs of respect for rights will be very high, rights may justifiably be overridden.

It is therefore not surprising that some theorists are inclined to reject the view that rights require us to exclude conflicting factors from consideration, and to conclude that rights only appear to possess special "peremptory" force because they are *very weighty* considerations, always open to being outweighed if the gains from encroachment upon the right are sufficiently large.

Joseph Raz has offered an analysis of the binding force of rules and duties that appears to let us have our cake and eat it; for the analysis suggests that a binding requirement may exclude certain conflicting factors from consideration, while still admitting room for us to balance the binding requirement against other considerations in appropriate circumstances. Raz's analysis treats rules and duties as "exclusionary reasons": a duty (for example) is not only a reason for acting in a certain way, but is also a reason for disregarding certain reasons *against* acting in that way. Thus, if I promise to meet you at the pub this evening, I am under a duty to keep my promise. My duty gives me a reason for meeting you at the pub. Raz, however, considers that the special force of the duty is captured only when we see that my promise has not only given me a reason to meet you, but also a reason for *disregarding* certain countervailing reasons (reasons for *not* meeting you). The fact that I have promised to meet you at the pub is not just a weighty consideration that I should balance against considerations of personal preference and convenience, for example. For the fact that I have promised should lead me to exclude such factors as personal preference and convenience from my consideration.

The idea that my duty should exclude conflicting considerations does not, of course, represent an original contribution to the debate: rather it represents the basic focus of the debate, long-familiar to all participants although explained by them in different ways. Raz's own contribution comes with a further claim that he makes, a claim that is aimed at showing how rules and duties may have exclusionary force while not being conclusive of what we should do: for exclusionary reasons, according to Raz, require me to exclude certain *kinds* of countervailing consideration from my deliberations (which kinds depends upon the precise content of the particular exclusionary reason) while leaving other countervailing reasons in play, to be balanced against the requirements of rule or duty. Thus, the duty created by my promise to meet you at the pub does not operate to exclude *all* possible reasons against meeting you at the pub. The promise need not be a *conclusive* reason for meeting you, for it is always possible that certain non-excluded countervailing reasons may outweigh the duty to keep my promise. Suppose that I am asked to help at an emergency where I could save many lives; unfortunately I have promised to meet you at the pub. Perhaps my promise excludes from consideration normal reasons of personal convenience (when the evening arrives, I feel tired and do not really want to go out) but not exceptional reasons of the kind created by the emergency. Hence, the duty created by my promise would have to be balanced against the conflicting considerations arising from the emergency, because these considerations escape the scope of the promise's exclusionary force.

According to Raz, an exclusionary reason excludes "by kind" not "by weight". My duty to meet you at the pub is an exclusionary reason in that it prohibits me from balancing my reasons for meeting you against conflicting reasons *of certain types*. But there may be other, non-excluded, types of reasons that I must still balance against my duty to meet you. Which reasons are excluded and which are not excluded will depend upon the circumstances and the content of the exclusionary reason in question. Many have concluded that this analysis enables us to capture our sense that my promise to meet you is not simply a reason for meeting you, for it requires me to disregard certain conflicting reasons (such as reasons of personal convenience); yet, equally, my promise is not conclusive of what I should do, nor does it exclude consideration of *all* countervailing factors (for some conflicting reasons may be non-excluded).

There is surely room for considerable scepticism regarding the distinction between "kind" and "weight" on which this analysis turns, for the distinction seems too pliable to be a load-bearing part of any structure of argument. Reasons are not divided by nature into different kinds, and it is always open to us to regard more weighty countervailing reasons as different "in kind" from less weighty reasons. In the case of the promise, for example, we might say that my promise excludes reasons of personal convenience from consideration. But what if (as events turn out) I would find going to the pub *very* inconvenient (after making the promise I have an accident and now find myself on crutches, for example). Can I not say that countervailing reasons such as these are really a different *kind* of reason from ordinary reasons of personal convenience, and so are *not* excluded from consideration? And if I *can* say that, what prevents that answer from being available whenever my reasons for not going to the pub are sufficient to outweigh the reasons created by my promise?

For present purposes we need not decide whether Raz's analysis of exclusionary reasons is to be accepted. At a later point in the chapter, however, we will need to consider whether the analysis can be used to provide Raz with an acceptable account of the "peremptory force" of rights.

LEGAL AND MORAL RIGHTS

Since utilitarians tend to treat the special force of rights as reflecting the special force of established rules, it is not uncommon for them to deny the existence of rights that are not recognised by established rules. Indeed, some utilitarians, on this basis, deny the existence of any rights not established in law. Most non-utilitarian theorists, however, recognise the existence of both legal and moral rights, and this recognition gives rise to some questions concerning the relationship between the two ideas.

Theories of the nature of law (discussed in Part 2) raise the question of whether legal rights are a specific kind of moral right: are they moral rights that we enjoy in consequence of the existence of certain legal institutions? Or are legal rights and moral rights linked by more structural analogies?

Legal positivists such as Hart tend to view the concepts of "right" and "duty" as devices whereby we can express conclusions about the applicability of rules, without necessarily evincing thereby our moral approval of the rules, or our belief that the rules are binding. One may have various types of rights just as there are various types of rules: legal rules, moral rules, and rules of the game of chess, for example. We saw, however, that not everyone regards this aspect of Hart's theory as successful. Hart concedes that concepts such as "right" and "duty" are appropriately used only from an "internal point of view", and some of his critics believe this to be indistinguishable from a point of view of moral approval.

Those who reject a positivist view of legal rights may say that law cannot be spoken of as conferring rights and imposing duties unless it has some moral claim on our conduct. This does not mean that law can only confer rights if it is just. Even if the law is unjust there may be strong moral reasons for complying with it: organised society needs publicly ascertainable rules which are not at the mercy of each individual's personal views of justice, and we should therefore be prepared to comply with such rules even when we consider them to be unjust. Similarly the requirement of formal justice, that like cases be treated alike, may confer on individuals a right to a certain decision from a court of law even if that decision would be wrong as a matter of abstract justice. On this type of approach, therefore, legal rights may be thought of as a variety of moral rights: they are the moral rights that we have as a result of the existence of legal institutions such as bodies of publicly ascertainable rules and courts committed to the principle of formal justice.

Most theorists tend to assume that an adequate analysis of the concept of a right should fit both moral and legal rights (perhaps with some modifications). To take the opposite view (that legal and moral rights are not open to a common analysis) would suggest, somewhat implausibly, that "right" in the two contexts is a mere homonym. But the assumption that a common analysis must be found tends to raise a question of strategy. Is it best to begin by reflecting upon legal rights, and then see how far the resulting analysis can be adjusted to fit moral rights? Or is it better to begin with moral rights, and then analyse the law in terms of a concept of right derived from morality?

One good reason for starting with legal rights is that the law is much more firmly established than are ideas about morality. In particular, there is a rich and articulate tradition of thought about legal rights that we can draw upon in trying to produce an adequate analysis. With morality, by contrast, very little is uncontested, and the principal ideas are sufficiently amorphous to rob us of firm ground from which to work.

It is sometimes assumed that, if we hold legal rights to be a species of moral right, we must begin our analysis from moral rights and then fit legal rights to it: an analysis of the broader category (moral rights) must precede and inform the analysis of the sub-category of legal rights (being moral rights enjoyed by virtue of the law). This assumption, however, is incorrect: there is no reason why the greater determinacy of the sub-category cannot be relied upon to inform and structure our analysis of the broader idea. Indeed, one could argue that some of the key moral ideas in this area only attain a determinate expression when worked out in the detailed form of legal institutions. Thus, in developing an account of rights from the idea of principles of equal freedom governing the justifed use of coercion, Kant informs us that "positive laws can serve as excellent guides" to the relevant principles.[3] Presumably, this is because we only comprehend the real content and significance of the idea of "equal freedom" when we have reflected upon detailed attempts to demarcate the legitimate bounds of conflicting freedoms in the context of the real world, the accumulated results of such attempts being expressed in the body of legal doctrine.

Just as one might believe that the notion of equal freedom finds its clearest and fullest expression in the body of legal doctrine, so one might think that it is in the context of law that the notion of "peremptory force" finds its true home and its most satisfactory concrete expression.[4] It is some such thought that lies behind the occasional suggestion that legal rights are the only genuine rights, and that the notion of "a right" lacks any substance or significance if detached from the availability of mechanisms for enforcement.[5] Whether or not we believe in the existence of non-legal rights, we should concede that the otherwise puzzling notion of the "peremptory force" of rights

---

[3]   I. Kant, *The Metaphysics of Morals* (Cambridge 1991) translated by Mary Gregor, p.55.

[4]   Hart tells us that "the word 'peremptory' in fact just means cutting off deliberation, debate or argument and the word with this meaning came into the English language from Roman law, where it was used to denote certain procedural steps which if taken precluded or ousted further argument." H.L.A. Hart, *Essays on Bentham* (Oxford 1982) pp.253–254.

[5]   See, for an excellent example, R. Geuss, *History and Illusion in Politics* (Cambridge 2001) pp.131–152.

finds an admirably precise and substantial articulation in the context of law. The peremptory force of legal rights could be thought of as their capacity conclusively to settle certain questions relating to the legal permissibility of action. Thus, if I have a right not to be assaulted by you, my right is conclusive as to the impermissibility of your assault; if I have a right to smoke a pipe, my right is conclusive of the permissibility of my act of pipe-smoking.

If, therefore, we focus our analysis upon legal rights, we can attach a clear and determinate meaning to the idea of the peremptory force of rights: peremptory force can, in this context, be construed as conclusory force: the power to settle issues of permissibility[6] conclusively. If, on the other hand, we seek to elucidate the sense in which *moral* rights possess a special peremptory force, we will face far more intractable problems. An account of moral rights must explain how rights are to be fitted into a broader field of moral and practical reasoning, encompassing reasons that are potentially in conflict with individual rights (such as the urgent demands of collective welfare); and it is precisely this task that makes it hard to explain what "peremptory force" might amount to in the case of moral rights (as we have seen above).

The strategy of analysis that begins by considering moral rights, and then seeks to offer an account of legal rights on that basis,[7] is therefore very misguided. For to base one's understanding of legal rights upon an analysis of the moral realm threatens to import the uncertainties surrounding moral rights into the context of law. The law equates the peremptory force of rights with conclusory force: legal rights conclusively resolve issues relating to the legal permissibility of action, for example. An account of "peremptory force" constructed in the problematic context of moral rights, however, is unlikely to treat rights as conclusive in this way.

In the bulk of this chapter, we will concentrate upon legal rights, making only passing reference to moral rights. This will enable us to focus upon questions concerning the role of legal

---

[6] When, later in this chapter, we examine the Hohfeldian analysis of rights, we will see that some rights bear upon (and conclusively resolve) issues concerning the permissibility of actions, while other rights bear upon (and conclusively resolve) issues concerning the exercise of legal powers.

[7] Such a strategy is advocated by J. Raz, *Ethics in the Public Domain* (Oxford 1994) Chapter.11.

rights within legal reasoning, and the relationship between legal rights and other specifically legal concepts, such as legal duties and powers. We will be able to set on one side the much more intractable question of how rights (and duties) should be fitted into our moral and practical reasoning generally. Thus we will not be asking such questions as whether moral rights are goals or side-constraints; whether they can be outweighed by considerations of the general welfare; whether they are to be set aside in situations of moral catastrophe; and so forth.

Of course, at some point, law must be reconnected with our practical and moral reasoning generally. That which is decisive of my legal duty may not be decisive of my moral duty: we may decide that we have a moral duty to ignore certain legal rights (and we may take that view even if we believe legal rights and duties to be themselves a species of moral right and duty). There may be circumstances (of national emergency, for example) where legal rights and duties and the rule of law in general may be abrogated or overridden, just as there may be situations of "moral catastrophe" where normal moral requirements lose their force. But this does nothing to undermine or cast doubt upon the decisiveness that legal rights may exhibit within the context of legal institutions and legal reasoning. It does not suggest that the peremptory force of legal rights is unreal, or that its clearest manifestation might not be in the enforceable requirements of a legal system.

HARD ATOMS AND SOFT MOLECULES

We have seen that the special peremptory force of rights (and the associated distinction between the desirability of an action and the entitlement to perform it) can be explained in different ways. It might be treated as reflecting the distinction between the invocation of general considerations of utility (or the common good), and the invocation of established rules (which are themselves to be justified by their utility, or by the extent to which they serve the common good); or it might be treated as a manifestation of a far deeper distinction, emphasised by those theories that give "priority to the right over the good" (see Part 1). Those who adopt the former view are likely to think of the notion of "a right" as useful primarily in contexts where we report the applicability of well-established and univocal rules, and as being of little value in contexts where we are deliberating upon conflicting arguments of justice or policy. Advocates of the latter view, on the other hand, are unlikely to accept such a restricted view of the nature and role of rights.

Sometimes we invoke relatively settled or agreed moral or legal principles and apply them to a specific situation. On other occasions, we debate the rival claims of alternative principles, being uncertain which ones should be accepted as valid. Some theorists regard the notion of a right as a valuable device for reporting the way in which established legal or moral principles apply to the situation of specific individuals; but they see the notion as of little help when we are debating the rival merits of alternative principles at a more abstract level. On occasions of the latter type, it is felt, we need to structure our debate in terms of a rather different set of concepts, such as the maximisation of welfare (if we are utilitarians); or "the common good" (if we adopt a position closer to that of Finnis); or the urgency and importance of individual needs.

Other theorists see the notion of "a right" as pointing to an entirely distinct type of consideration that should feature in our moral and legal deliberations, and that will be overlooked if those deliberations are framed in terms of such ideas as need, aggregate welfare, or the common good. In their view, "rights" are not simply a device whereby we may report the implications of settled principles: rights have a unique and irreducible importance, which should be incorporated into our deliberations upon rival moral and legal standards.

The debate between these rival views of rights has assumed considerable importance with the rise of the judicial protection of human rights. When judges act to protect human rights, their actions are in general legitimated by appeal to a fundamental document guaranteeing those rights (Bill of Rights, European Convention, etc). In such documents, the relevant rights are usually defined in terms of great generality, and the detailed implications of the proclaimed rights must be ascertained from the case law, rather than from the document itself.

How should we understand this increasingly common situation? Are the relevant documents best seen as offering very vague formulations, that place only the loosest possible constraints upon what the judges do in "interpreting" them? When judges come to apply such highly general provisions, are they of necessity thrown back upon questions concerning the general welfare, public policy, and the common good? Or is there some sense in which they could honestly claim to be working out the "implications" of this or that abstractly stated right? Is there, as it were, an internal logic to the notion of "a right", that would enable the judges to pass from abstract formulation to concrete result, without simply falling back upon open-ended political questions of the kind that any intelligent citizen might be equally competent to assess?

In this chapter we will first consider the views of theorists who ascribe to the notion of "a right" a high degree of internal complexity: they regard rights as complex molecular structures serving as intellectual nodal points in our legal and moral deliberations, and from which diverse concrete conclusions may be drawn. Legal reasoning can be understood, on this view, as the working out of a kind of logic of rights: each right entails a diverse range of juridical consequences, which can be deduced from the assertion that the right obtains; and the totality of rights forms a system of domains of liberty, the system as a whole making possible the realisation of equal freedom.

These views will be contrasted with those of theorists who view rights as lacking such internal complexity, but as being simple atomic elements that supply us with a precise terminology whereby we may report the settled requirements of law or justice, but which do not play a central part in our deliberations upon contentious legal or moral issues.

The idea that rights possess "peremptory force" will play a significant part in the analysis offered by this chapter. For it will be suggested that the debate over rights has passed through three main stages, that can be represented as follows:

1. One view of rights, derived from Kant, ascribed to rights both internal complexity and peremptory force. The internal complexity of a right consisted in the fact that possession of a right entailed the permissibility of actions exercising the right, duties on other people not to interfere with that exercise (inviolabilities), powers of waiver over such duties, and other juridical consequences. The peremptory force of rights consisted in the fact that rights were not simply reasons for recognising such permissibilities and inviolabilites, liable to be outweighed by other conflicting reasons. Rather, rights *entailed* their various juridical consequences, so that my possession of a right was *conclusive* of the existence of certain permissibilities and inviolabilities.

2. The analysis of rights offered by the American jurist Hohfeld

demonstrated that no conception of rights as possessing both internal complexity and peremptory force could fit the existing legal doctrines and institutions. This was because the various permissibilities, inviolabilities and powers of waiver associated by the Kantian conception were, in the actual legal rules, frequently found in separation rather than in conjunction. It was consequently impossible plausibly to treat them all as entailed by the single notion of "a right". Rather, Hohfeld concluded, the appearance of internal complexity in the concept of "a right" had been produced by the fact that the word "right" is in fact ambiguous between four *different* ideas (which Hohfeld distinguished in his analysis, and which will be examined below).

Hohfeld treated the various types of "rights" as simple atomic elements, lacking in internal complexity and therefore providing no basis for understanding legal reasoning as the working out of a logic of rights. On this view, one type of right cannot be inferred from the existence of another type, and very abstract formulations of rights are likely to be simply ambiguous rather than being fertile nodal points for legal reasoning. On the other hand, Hohfeld's account of rights treats them as conclusively settling those issues to which they are indeed relevant: their significance is limited and highly specific, but utterly reliable.

3. Finally, a more recent analysis of rights (developed by Raz and MacCormick) endeavours to restore the idea that rights possess internal complexity. The features of legal doctrine encountered by Hohfeld (suggesting that various permissibilities, powers, and inviolabilities are entirely separable concepts, rather than facets of a single concept) are accommodated within this new analysis by saying that a right does not *entail* permissibilities and inviolabilities: rather, it provides a reason (to be balanced against conflicting reasons) for recognising such. Situations where permissibilities, powers or inviolabilities are found in isolation rather than conjunction are explained by saying that the reasons for recognising some or all of these consequences of the right were outweighed by conflicting considerations.

We may summarise by saying that the Kantian view ascribed to rights both internal complexity and peremptory force; the

Hohfeldian view ascribed to rights peremptory force without internal complexity; and the Raz/MacCormick view tries to restore to rights their internal complexity, but does so by sacrificing their peremptory force. This is so, at least, if we equate "peremptory force" with "conclusory force", understood as the ability of legal rights conclusively to resolve specific issues of the permissibility of action. In the latter part of the present chapter we will need to consider whether an alternative, less stringent, interpretation of the peremptory force of rights might in fact be superior, and we will conclude that it is not.

If we assume that the Kantian view is incorrect,[8] we are therefore left with a choice between a view of rights as internally complex but lacking in peremptory force, and a view of rights as lacking internal complexity but possessing peremptory force.

On the one hand we might think of rights as occupying a central role in legal reasoning, informing much of the development of the law and providing fertile premises from which diverse conclusions of general principle can be drawn. This view, however, comes at a price; for it seems to be the case that, when thought of in this way, legal rights are of only limited reliability when we need to invoke them. On the other hand, rights can be thought of as useful concepts in which the applicability of the law to concrete circumstance may be reported, but which will prove to be somewhat vacuous if we look to them for guidance on issues concerning the law's reform or development. Rights on this view, however, prove to be very dependable when we possess them and need to rely upon them. Rights, it seems, can be thought of as either soft molecules or hard atoms.

RIGHTS AS COMPLEX AND PEREMPTORY

It is appropriate for us to begin by considering the view of rights that was characteristic of the Kantian tradition in jurisprudence. This is so for a number of reasons. A set of ideas derived from Kant's "Doctrine of Right" in his *Metaphysics of Morals* exerted

---

[8]   By no means everyone shares that view. For a very able defence of a Kantian view of rights (arguing that I am wrong to see Hohfeld's analysis as inconsistent with Kant) see Hillel Steiner, "Working Rights" in Kramer, Simmonds and Steiner, *A Debate Over Rights* (Oxford 1998). See also Hillel Steiner, *An Essay on Rights* (Blackwell, Oxford 1994).

considerable influence upon European legal thinking in the nineteenth century, and it continues to receive significant, if rather muted, echoes in the contemporary debate. Moreover, the Kantian view formed the backdrop for the analysis of rights offered by Hohfeld, whose work is of seminal importance, and to which we will turn shortly. Finally, the Kantian account of rights gives an interesting example of how analytical claims about the concept of "a right" may be intimately bound up with broader theories of justice and law.

Kant's view is grounded in the features of rights noted above: claims of right appear to possess peremptory force, and to exclude considerations relating to the worthiness or value of the entitled action. Kant inferred, from the peremptory force of rights, that rights were essentially linked to the justified use of coercion. To assert the existence of a right to free speech (for example) is to claim that coercion to prevent me from speaking would *not* be justified, and that coercion to prevent others from interfering with my freedom of speech *would* be justified. As authorisations for the use of coercion, the content of rights could be derived from the principles governing the legitimate use of coercion. Coercion, in Kant's view, is wrong insofar as it interferes with freedom; it is justified when it serves to maintain equal freedom. Rights, therefore, constitute a set of domains of equal liberty. Kant believed that it was possible to delineate principles which would demarcate these domains of entitlement. Such principles would be concerned solely with the extent to which my pursuit of my objectives could interfere with your pursuit of your objectives: they would be wholly independent of considerations relating to the virtue or desirability of the purposes for which the various liberties were exercised.

The Kantian analysis treats rights as possessing a certain internal complexity. That is to say, possession of a right has a variety of implications, stemming from the fact that rights represent domains within which the individual will should reign supreme. Thus, actions performed within the scope of a right are *permissible*: if I have a right to act in a certain way, my action must be permitted, even if the action is unworthy or undesirable. Actions performed within the scope of a right are also juridically *inviolable*: if I am acting within the scope of my right, you may not interfere with my action, and the law should step in to prevent you from doing so. Moreover, legal rights entail further consequences: I possess a power to waive my entitlements, together with immunities against having my rights abridged by the say-so of others.

To establish that an individual possesses a legal right is therefore, according to the Kantian view, to provide the basis for a number of inferences relating to the permissibility and inviolability of actions, the existence of immunities, and powers of waiver. Legal rights therefore function, on this view, as significant nodal points within legal reasoning, enabling lawyers and judges to draw complex conclusions from apparently simple premises.

An example is provided by some of the remarks in the judgment of Lord Lindley in *Quinn v. Leathem.*[9] In this case, Leathem was a butcher who employed some non-union workers. Quinn tried to force Leathem to sack his non-union workers and employ only union members. He threatened a strike at the shop of one of Leathem's customers unless the customer would stop doing business with Leathem. Leathem sued Quinn. At one point in his judgment, Lord Lindley offered the following observations:

"As to the plaintiff's rights. He had the ordinary rights of a British subject. He was at liberty to earn his living in his own way, provided that he did not violate some special law prohibiting him from doing so, and provided he did not infringe the rights of other people. This liberty involved liberty to deal with other persons who were willing to deal with him. This liberty is a right recognised by law; its correlative is the general duty of every one not to prevent the free exercise of this liberty, except so far as his own liberty of action may justify him in so doing."[10]

Lord Lindley's argument can be reconstructed in terms of the Kantian analysis of rights. Leathem had a right to run a butcher's business; therefore, his action in running such a business was permissible. As the exercise of a right, Leathem's action should be juridically inviolable: that is, it should be protected from actions aimed at interfering with the exercise of the right. Quinn had tried so to interfere with the exercise of Leathem's right, and (in the absence of any justification for the interference) had thereby violated Leathem's right, committing a legal wrong.

---

[9] [1901] A.C. 495.
[10] [1901] A.C. 495 at p.534.

A SLIGHT DIGRESSION

It might be of some interest to see in a little more detail how Kantian notions of right can be played out in the context of a specific case. For that reason, I will allow myself a small digression from the main line of argument in this chapter, in order to say a little more about *Quinn v. Leathem.*

Lord Lindley had studied in Germany and had translated works of German jurisprudence. It is not at all unlikely that he may have been influenced by the conception of right dominant in German Kantian jurisprudence.[11] This is not to say that his judgment in *Quinn v. Leathem* is a straightforward *application* of Kantian ideas, however. The Kantian view tends to assume a juridical space divided into non-overlapping domains of liberty: the enforcement of rights consists in policing the boundaries between distinct domains. As I have pointed out elsewhere,[12] the rise of industry and of corporate and labour organisation created a host of new ways (unregulated by any existing practice) in which the actions of one individual could impact upon those of another. Not all such situations could be treated as involving a legal wrong, and the courts had to recognise the prevalence of *damnum absque injuria* (the causing of loss without any legal wrong having been committed). This was hard to reconcile with a view of rights that ascribed to the actions of the right-holder both permissibility and inviolability. Lord Lindley wrote his judgment in a context informed by these tensions, and they structure the approach adopted in his judgment.

Thus, his judgment wrestles with two main ideas, which are not easy to reconcile. On the one hand, in the passage quoted above and elsewhere in his judgment (*e.g.* at p.537), Lord Lindley takes the view that Leathem's right to run a butcher's business places every other person under a duty not to interfere with that liberty "except so far as his own liberty of action may justify him in so doing." On the other hand, Lord Lindley tells us that "an act otherwise lawful, although harmful, does not become actionable by being done maliciously in the sense of proceeding from a bad motive, and with intent to annoy or harm another".[13] It is hard to reconcile the principle that all interferences require

[11] See Simmonds, "Rights at the Cutting Edge" in Kramer, Simmonds and Steiner, *A Debate Over Rights* (Oxford 1998) at pp.168–171.

[12] Simmonds, *op. cit.* pp. 187–195.

[13] [1901] A.C. 495 at p.533.

justification with the principle that the presence of a malicious motive should not rob an action of its legality.

Under the first principle, when A's action interferes with B's liberty it must be shown to be justified if it is not to be a breach of duty. Under the second principle, however, malice or intent to harm should not render an otherwise lawful action unlawful. When A's action interferes with B's liberty, A must show that his action had some legitimate justification. Would not the presence of malice be enough to deprive the action of any such justification? The requirement of justification would seem to be without real content if it did not exclude purely malicious actions from the realm of legitimacy. We might, of course, say that the principle treating malice as irrelevant is restricted to actions that interfere with no one: but such an interpretation would obviously rob the principle of any substance.

In spite of their mutual incompatibility, each of these two structuring ideas is of a Kantian lineage. The notion that the actor's motive should not render an action wrongful reflects the Kantian view that justice and right are concerned with how my actions impact upon your freedoms, and *not* with the good or bad motives with which I act. This view assumes that it is possible to demarcate the legitimate bounds of liberty without reference to the actor's motives. On the other hand, the idea that Leathem's entitlement to run his business entails a duty on others not to interfere is drawn from the Kantian notion of a right as involving both permissibility and inviolability. The tension between the two ideas is generated by the realisation that, in a complex society, actions tend quite pervasively to interfere with each other. The "duty not to interfere" must therefore be reconstrued as a "duty not to interfere without legitimate reason"; this revised idea then comes into conflict with the exclusion of the relevance of motive.

HOHFELD'S ANALYSIS

The most important and influential modern analysis of the notion of a legal right was put forward by W.N. Hohfeld. Hohfeld died young and wrote only a handful of essays. Partly in consequence of this, we know very little about the broader significance that he himself attached to his work. It is fruitful, however, to consider his analysis in relation to the Kantian view of rights that we sketched above.

On the Kantian view of rights, rights possess a degree of internal complexity. That is to say, possession of a right has a number of diverse consequences: it renders action permissible, inviolable, confers certain powers (such as powers of waiver) and so forth. On Hohfeld's view, however, rights are not internally complex in this way: rather, the appearance of internal complexity is the product of *ambiguity* in the word "right".

Hohfeld pointed out that, when lawyers talk about "rights", they use that term to refer to a number of quite different notions. These various types of "right" are ultimately reducible to four: (a) claim-rights (Hohfeld calls these simply "rights"); (b) liberties (Hohfeld used the term "privileges"); (c) powers; and (d) immunities. Other types of rights, such as the right of ownership,[14] can be broken down by analysis into a combination of the four basic notions, which Hohfeld called the "lowest common denominators of the law". Each type of right is one aspect of a legal relationship between two persons. Claim-rights, liberties, powers and immunities are distinguished by what they entail for the legal position of the other party to that relationship. A claim-right is correlative to a duty in the other party; a liberty is correlative to a "no-right" (being the absence of a claim-right); a power is correlative to a liability in the other party; and an immunity is correlative to a disability.

The various Hohfeldian "jural relations" are represented by the following table, in which the top row consists of the four types of legal right identified by Hohfeld, while the lower row indicates the legal position entailed for the other party by each of those types of right:

claim-right	liberty	power	immunity
duty	no-right	liability	disability

To say that X has a claim-right against Y entails that Y owes a duty to X. Thus if X has a claim-right that Y should pay him £100, this means that Y has a duty to pay X £100; if X has a claim-right that Y should not assault him, this means that Y has a duty not to assault X.

---

[14] The right of ownership, in Hohfeld's view, is really a complex bundle of claim-rights, liberties, powers and immunities. An owner of land, for example, typically enjoys (*inter alia*) the claim-right that others should not trespass on his land, the liberty to walk upon his land, the power to transfer title to others, and an immunity against having his title altered or transferred by the act of another.

A liberty differs from a claim-right in a number of ways. Claim-rights held by X concern the actions of the *other* party to the jural relationship, since they entail a duty on the part of that other party. Liberties, by contrast, are concerned with the right-holder's own actions: they establish the permissibility (as against some other party) of the right-holder's action. Thus X has a liberty to wear a hat, as against Y, when X owes Y no duty *not* to wear a hat. The liberty consists *solely* in the absence of a duty owed to the other party, and the other party's consequent lack of any claim-right against the right-holder. A liberty in X does not entail any duty owed by Y: we cannot infer from X's liberty to wear a hat that Y is under a duty not to prevent X's hat-wearing. Even in the absence of such a duty not to prevent hat-wearing, Y may find it hard lawfully to stop X wearing a hat: but this will be because Y owes a duty to X not to assault X or commit a trespass upon his goods. These duties, however, are not correlative to X's liberty but to separate claim-rights possessed by X. X's claim-right (correlative to Y's duty) not to be assaulted helps to protect X's liberty to wear a hat: but the claim-right cannot be *deduced* from the liberty: whether or not such a claim-right should exist is a matter of justice and policy, not of logic.

It should be carefully noted that all of the basic Hohfeldian rights (*i.e.* claim-rights, liberties, powers and immunities) must be thought of as rights against a specific person. Thus it can be misleading simply to speak of X having a liberty to wear a hat, for he may have such a liberty as against Y but not as against Z. If, for example, X has entered into a contract with Z whereby X promises not to wear a hat, he owes a duty to Z not to wear a hat, and Z has a claim-right that he should not wear a hat. But X still has a liberty as against Y, with whom he has no contract, and Y has no claim-right that X should not wear a hat.

Thus, each Hohfeldian right resolves one issue only, as between two parties only. My liberty, as against you, to wear a hat does not in itself resolve the issue of whether you should be permitted to interfere with my wearing a hat: that issue can be settled only by establishing what claim-rights I possess against you (what duties you owe to me), and no particular answer to this latter question is entailed by my possession of a liberty. Similarly, the fact that I possess a hat-wearing liberty as against you does not settle my situation *vis-à-vis* your mother, the Duke of Edinburgh, or the man who supplies me with hats (for I may have made contracts with them whereby I undertake certain duties not to wear a hat, or not to wear particular hats). The

Hohfeldian analysis of rights is intended to supply us with a precise vocabulary for reporting the *effect*, in specific circumstances, of legal rules and transactions; it is not intended to assist us in reaching conclusions about what, in cases of uncertainty, the legal rules are or should be.

Note carefully that each Hohfeldian right, although resolving only one issue as between two parties, does indeed *resolve* that issue. Thus, X's claim-right is not simply a reason, to be balanced against other reasons, for recognising Y to be under a duty: X's claim-right *entails* that Y is under a duty (Y's duty follows from X's claim-right as a matter of logic). Similarly with all the other Hohfeldian jural relations.

Students are often confused by the fact that, in the Hohfeldian scheme, X's liberty does not entail any duty on the part of Y not to interfere. The fact that X has a liberty (as against Y) to wear a hat does not entail that Y has a duty not to interfere with X's hat-wearing. Y may be doing nothing wrong in stopping X from wearing a hat, *e.g.* if Y monopolises the world supply of hats and refuses to sell one to X. X may then be *unable* to wear a hat, but this does not mean that he possesses no *liberty* (in the Hohfeldian sense) to wear one. A Hohfeldian liberty is not a general factual ability or opportunity to perform an action: it is simply the absence of a duty *not* to perform the action.

Failing monopolistic control over the world supply of hats, most of the ways in which Y might seek to prevent X from wearing a hat will involve an assault on X, and Y is under a duty not to assault X. The general laws prohibiting assault and trespass have therefore been said to provide a "protective perimeter" for liberties.[15] The duties imposed by such laws, however, are not the correlative of X's liberty, but of separate claim-rights enjoyed by X, such as the claim-right not to be assaulted by Y. The importance of distinguishing between X's liberty to wear a hat and his claim-right not to be assaulted can easily be seen if we consider a situation where X's claim-right has been extinguished while his liberty has survived. Suppose that X and Y were playing a game where X had to try to wear a hat while Y had to try to knock it off. X would then be waiving his normal claim-right not to be the victim of a (minor) assault: but his liberty to wear a hat would survive unimpaired, in that he still has no duty not to wear a hat, and Y has no claim-right that X should not wear a hat.

---

[15] H.L.A. Hart, *Essays on Bentham* (Oxford 1982) Chap.7.

Rights such as the claim-right not to be assaulted provide a perimeter of protection for Hohfeldian liberties. One of the law's most important and difficult tasks is to determine the forms and extent of that protection. For example, people have the liberty to operate commercial enterprises and to make profits. If X and Y have businesses which are in direct competition with each other, each will be seeking to expand at the expense of the other, and even to drive the rival out of business. The law must draw the line between legitimate competition and illegitimate interference. But there remains an area of free competition within which the liberties of X and Y are allowed to conflict. It is therefore a fallacy to argue that if X has a right to run a business, Y has a duty not to interfere with him. The argument would be valid only if by "a right" we meant a claim-right; but X enjoys only a liberty to run a business, and such a liberty does not entail any duty on Y's part. A claim-right is the correlative of a duty in the other party, but when we say that someone has a liberty to do an act we mean only that he is not doing anything wrong in performing the act: he violates no duty and infringes no claim-right.

Lawyers sometimes speak of rights when they mean neither liberties nor claim-rights, but what Hohfeld called "powers". A power is the ability to alter legal rights and duties, or legal relations generally. Thus one might have the power to make a will or to conclude a contract, each of these being an act that alters legal relations. Powers differ from claim-rights because they are not correlative to a duty in someone else: Hohfeld describes them as being correlative to a "liability" in the other party, by which he means that the party is liable to have his legal situation altered by an exercise of the power. Powers differ from liberties also. I may have the "power" (in Hohfeld's sense) to perform an act and yet not have the liberty to do so. In certain cases, for example, a non-owner can pass a good title to a bona fide purchaser for value. In such a case, the non-owner has the power to transfer title, since his acts will be legally effective in making the purchaser the owner of the goods. But the exercise of that power may still be a breach of duty: although effective in transferring title, it may still be a legal wrong. Since a liberty is the absence of a duty not to do the act, it is clear that the non-owner in such a case has the power to transfer, but not the liberty to do so. Imagine how confusing it would be if we did not possess the Hohfeldian vocabulary, but had to refer to both powers and liberties as rights. We would then have to say that the non-owner has the right to transfer, but does not have the right to transfer!

Immunities are essentially a matter of not being under a liability to have one's legal situation altered by the act of another. If X has a power, then Y is under a liability to have his legal position changed by (for example) having duties imposed on him, or rights conferred. Where X has no such power (Hohfeld speaks of the absence of a power as a "disability"), we may describe Y as enjoying an immunity. Once again we must remember that Hohfeldian relations are specific to pairs of individuals. Thus, as against you, I enjoy an immunity in relation to my liberty to wear a hat. That is to say, not only do I enjoy the liberty to wear a hat, but you are unable to deprive me of that liberty by imposing upon me a duty not to wear a hat. As against Parliament, however, I enjoy no such immunity: it is within the power of Parliament to enact a statute depriving me of the liberty to wear a hat.

Thus Hohfeld's analysis gives us four types of right, each of which is to be understood as one side of a jural relationship obtaining between a pair of individuals. We understand the nature of each type of right by seeing what it entails for the other party to the relevant relationship. Thus, claim-rights are correlative to duties; liberties to "no-rights"; powers to liabilities; and immunities to disabilities. But claim-rights, liberties, powers and immunities are logically independent of each other, in the sense that my possession of a liberty does not entail a claim-right not to be interfered with in the exercise of that liberty; my possession of a power does not entail a liberty to exercise the power; and so forth.

KANTIAN AND HOHFELDIAN RIGHTS COMPARED

On the Kantian view, rights are internally complex in so far as possession of a right entails a number of different consequences. For example, if my action is an exercise of a right, it is both permissible and inviolable: that is to say, I violate no duty in performing the action, and others are under a duty not to interfere with my performance of the action.

On the Hohfeldian view, by contrast, the permissibility of my action amounts to the possession of a liberty; while any legal protection against interference that I enjoy will amount to the possession of certain claim-rights. Liberties, however, do not *entail* claim-rights. For Hohfeld, it does not follow from the fact that I have a legal right to wear a hat that you are under a duty not to interfere with my hat-wearing. To the extent that you are under a duty not to interfere, it will be in consequence of certain distinct claim-rights that I possess against you, such as the right not to be assaulted. It is important to distinguish these claim-rights from the liberty, for several reasons. In the first place, the claim-rights may be extinguished while the liberty remains in place (or vice versa): see the example above of the game where you have to knock off my hat. Secondly, it is misleading to suggest that the mere permissibility of an action entails a general duty on others not to interfere with the action: it is permissible for you to make a profit by running a shop, but I may permissibly interfere with your doing so, by opening up a rival business next door.

The Kantian analysis portrays a right as a complex molecular structure, consisting of a number of different components (permissibilities, inviolabilities, powers, etc). On the Hohfeldian analysis, rights are discrete and atomic: each type of right has one facet only, and each type of right is entirely distinct and separable from the other types. Thus, a Hohfeldian liberty entails the permissibility of an action as against the other party to the jural relationship (you have no-right that I should not wear a hat) but it does not entail any duty on that other party, or on anyone else. A Hohfeldian power entails a liability on the other party, but it does not entail a liberty to exercise the power (I may have a power to transfer title but a duty not to do so); etc.

Hohfeld's analysis enables us to see that the Kantian approach cannot accommodate the complexities of actual legal doctrines and institutions. Situations where the various facets of the Kantian "right" come apart (powers without liberties, liberties without inviolabilities, etc.) are too numerous for the Kantian view to remain plausible as an analysis of legal rights.

The internal complexity of the Kantian notion of a right was important in sustaining the idea that legal reasoning is a matter of working out the internal logic of rights. Hohfeld's analysis exposes the hollowness of this belief, and reveals that any appearance to the contrary results from equivocations between distinct senses of the word "right", rather than from deductive reasoning. Lord Lindley's judgment in *Quinn v. Leathem* provides an apt example, which is discussed by Hohfeld.

As we saw above, Lord Lindley's argument proceeds from the idea that Leathem had a right to run a butcher's business, to the conclusion that Quinn had a duty not to interfere with the exercise of that right. The argument appears on the face of it to flow smoothly from premises to conclusion. In the light of Hohfeld's analysis, however, we can see that the term "right" is being employed in two different senses in Lord Lindley's argument. When it is said that Leathem has a right to run a butcher's business, this can only mean a Hohfeldian liberty: Leathem is doing nothing wrong in running such a business; his action is legally permissible. No duty incumbent on other people can be inferred from a liberty, however. So, when Lord Lindley concludes that Leathem's right entails certain duties on Quinn, a claim-right must be contemplated.

This is not to say that the decision is wrong; but the belief that a single concept of "right" can entail both permissibilities (liberties) and inviolabilites (duties on other parties) serves to conceal the issue raised by the case. This was whether Leathem's liberty ought to be protected by a claim-right against interference and (if so) how that claim-right should be formulated (given that not *all* forms of interference should be prohibited, for fear of outlawing reasonable competition). Leathem's rights in the established law did not seem to dictate a clear answer to this question; but Lord Lindley's deployment of a Kantian notion of "right" made the result appear to be dictated by logic, rather than by broad considerations of justice or social policy.

Hohfeld demonstrates that the internal complexity of legal rights is an illusion produced by the fact that the word "right" is used to refer to four distinct ideas: claim-rights, liberties, powers and immunities. On the Kantian account, by contrast, these various notions are specific features of a single concept: possession of a right *entails* a variety of claim-rights, liberties, powers and immunities. The decisive consideration in favour of the Hohfeldian view of legal rights is the frequency with which the various facets are separated by the law: their regular separation makes it impossible to regard them as various entailments of a single concept, if that concept is to be widely applicable to the law.

While rejecting the idea that rights possess internal complexity, the Hohfeldian analysis endorses the view that rights possess peremptory force, and construes the peremptory force of rights as *conclusory* force: a matter of each right *entailing* certain jural consequences. Thus, X's claim-right against Y is not simply a reason for recognising a duty incumbent upon Y, for such a reason might have to be balanced against other countervailing reasons: X's claim-right against Y *entails* the existence of Y's duty towards X, and so is conclusive of the existence of that duty. If X demonstrates to the judge that he has a right that Y should pay him £100, X will not expect the judge to treat the right as a reason that will be taken into account (along with other conflicting reasons) when he is deciding whether to hold that Y is under a duty. X will regard his right as conclusively settling the issue of Y's duty. Similarly, X's possession of a liberty to wear a hat (as against Y) entails that Y has no right that X should *not* wear a hat; X's power entails Y's liability; and so on.

We noted earlier the legal origins of the idea of "peremptory force", and the sense in which it is within the law that the idea receives its clearest expression (avoiding the problems that characterise the alleged special force of rights in the context of morality). One very appropriate way to interpret this idea, therefore, is in terms of the consequences of rights for the permissibility of action, or the effect of purported exercises of legal power. Rights are peremptory, for Hohfeld, in so far as their juridical consequences are directly entailed by the content of the right, rather than (for example) the right being merely a non-conclusive reason for recognising or giving effect to those consequences.

INTERNAL COMPLEXITY RESTORED?

John Finnis has observed that "The modern language of rights provides . . . a supple and potentially precise instrument for sorting out and expressing the demands of justice. It is often, however, . . . a hindrance to clear thought when the question is: What *are* the demands of justice?"[16]

Hohfeld might well have agreed with these sentiments, for the Hohfeldian analysis provides us with a very precise vocabulary for reporting the detailed implications of established and univocal legal (and, by extension, moral) standards. By destroying the illusion of internal complexity in the notion of a right, however, the analysis also suggests that the notion of a right has little to contribute when we are seeking to adjudicate between various conflicting accounts of the relevant legal and moral standards. To see this point, one need only reflect once again upon *Quinn v. Leathem*. On a Kantian view, we can infer

[16] John Finnis, *Natural Law and Natural Rights* (Oxford 1980) p.210.

Leathem's claim-rights against Quinn from his entitlement to run a butcher's business: reflection upon the concept of a right leads us from the permissibility of Leathem's action to the duty upon Quinn. On the Hohfeldian view, no such inference is valid. The permissibility of Leathem's business operations does not entail the impermissibility of all interference with those operations: otherwise trade competition would be impossible. The question raised in *Quinn v. Leathem* was whether Leathem's liberty ought to be protected by a claim-right against the type of interference that Quinn had organised. This question cannot be answered by thinking about the concept of "a right", but only by addressing a host of complex issues of justice and social policy. For Hohfeldians, the language of rights gives us a precise way of identifying the issue to be decided in the case, and a precise way of describing the law-making effect of the decision: but the concept of a right does not help us to *decide* the case.

Once they have grasped this implication of the Hohfeldian view, many lawyers dislike it. For it seems to undermine the belief that legal reasoning in innovative cases is a matter of working out the implications of legal rights. It suggests that these cases turn upon issues with which lawyers have no special expertise or insight: questions of policy or the common good, on which any intelligent citizen might feel qualified to express a view. This matter has become especially important with the domestic and international protection of human rights: for the law of human rights is aimed, in large part, at removing issues concerning rights from the agenda of democratic politics and placing them in the hands of elite groups of judges and lawyers. This transfer of power is effected by the enactment or ratification of documents listing various rights, formulated in the broadest possible terms. The working out of the detailed implications of such rights is viewed as a matter for legal experts, rather than ordinary citizens. The suggestion that such questions are in fact not governed by any particular logic of rights is therefore a troubling one: for the Hohfeldian view suggests that lawyers are not in fact working out the consequences of possession of this or that right, but deciding a series of political issues relating to justice and the common good. This does not, of course, in itself condemn the judicial protection of human rights as wrong: but it forces upon its defenders some intractable questions which they would rather avoid.

Whether for this reason or for other reasons, Hohfeld's analysis met some influential opposition in the closing decades of the twentieth century. The most important line of anti-Hohfeldian argument seeks to restore a notion of rights possessed of internal complexity, by suggesting that Hohfeld misconceives the relationship between rights and the duties, liabilities and disabilities to which they are correlative. In Hohfeld's analytical scheme, claim-rights are correlative to duties in a very strict way. When we say that X has a claim-right of a certain kind, a part of what we mean (according to Hohfeld) is that Y owes a duty of some kind to X: the claim-right is, as it were, simply the duty viewed from the perspective of the party to whom it is owed. Liberties are not correlative to duties: they are correlative to the absence of a claim-right, or what Hohfeld calls a "no-right" (thus if X has a liberty to wear a hat, Y has "no-right" that X should not wear a hat). Powers are correlative to liabilities (being liable to have one's legal position changed by the act of another) and immunities are correlative to disabilities (*i.e.* the inability to change another person's legal position).

According to critics such as Raz and MacCormick, however, the idea of correlativity obscures the fact that duties are imposed in order to protect rights: the existence of a right is a justifying reason for imposing a duty. The claim that rights are strictly correlative to duties obscures this point, it is suggested, because it involves holding that part of what we mean by saying that X has a right is that Y already has a duty: thus the rights cannot be a reason for imposing a duty on Y. Indeed, in the Raz/MacCormick analysis, rights can be protected in other ways than by the imposition of duties. They may be protected by the conferment of Hohfeldian liberties or powers, or by the imposition of Hohfeldian disabilities on other persons. A follower of Hohfeld would insist that, when we speak about rights, we should make it clear whether we mean claim-rights, liberties, powers or immunities. But, according to Raz and MacCormick, we may speak of rights without this kind of discrimination because, at their most basic level, rights are the justifying reasons for the creation of Hohfeldian claim-rights, liberties, powers and immunities: the latter concepts represent various legal devices for the protection of rights. Hence, Hohfeld is wrong to treat the word "right" as being ambiguous between four different notions, each of which is the correlative of either a duty, a no-right, a liability, or a disability. The true situation, Raz and MacCormick suggest, is that a right is a weighty interest which may be protected, in appropriate circumstances, by an array of Hohfeldian claim-rights, liberties, powers and immunities: in effect, Hohfeld confuses "rights" with the specific modalities whereby they are protected.[17]

MacCormick produces some examples of legislation which he believes expose the inadequacy of the Hohfeldian view. He argues that statutes may sometimes confer rights without imposing duties on anyone. One example that he offers[18] is section 2(1) of the Succession (Scotland) Act 1964, which provides that an intestate's children shall have the right to the whole of the intestate estate. Here there is no duty on anyone until an executor has been appointed; vesting of the right is therefore temporally prior to vesting of the duty. Moreover, a child of the intestate has a preferential right to be confirmed as executor by virtue of his right to the estate. In MacCormick's view, this statutory provision is an example of (1) a right being temporally prior to a duty; (2) a right being the reason for imposing a duty (*i.e.* the child's right is a reason for his being appointed executor); and (3) a duty being borne by the bearer of the "correlative" right.

At first this example does seem to pose intractable problems for the Hohfeldian correlativity thesis! But on reflection, the difficulties will be seen to be less formidable. After all, we are quite familiar with the idea of the duties of an office, and we do not think of such duties as springing in and out of existence each time the office holder changes. We think of the duties as attaching to the continuing office, not the changing holder of the office. Thus we may think of the right created by section 2(1) of the Succession (Scotland) Act 1964 as being correlative to the duty borne by the office of executor. The right is thus not temporally prior to the duty. Similarly there is nothing odd in speaking of an office holder owing a duty to himself in his private capacity: a wages officer might have the duty of paying all the firm's employees, including himself. Nor does MacCormick's example present an instance of a right being the reason for imposing a duty: the child's right is a reason for appointing the child to an office that carries a duty, not a reason for creating the duty.

---

[17] Matthew Kramer has done much to undermine the key premises of this argument. See Kramer, "Rights without Trimmings" in Kramer, Simmonds and Steiner, *op. cit.* pp. 36–42.

[18] His other example is analysed in Simmonds, "Rights at the Cutting Edge" *op. cit.* pp. 158–165.

The Raz/MacCormick view has been widely regarded as highly persuasive. One reason for this is that it seems to capture what we might describe as the "dynamic" aspect of legal rights, while the strict correlativity view (that we find in Hohfeld) appears to deny that dynamic aspect. If rights are strictly correlative to duties, then a person has established legal rights only insofar as there are established duties corresponding to those rights. The law on this account may seem to have a static appearance: it could be represented as a long list of duties.[19] If, on the other hand, it makes sense to talk of established rights without established correlative duties, we may think of the law as imposing duties, and perhaps creating new duties, in order to protect established rights. On this account, there may at any one time be established legal rights which are inadequately protected by legal duties: such rights provide a legal reason for creating new legal duties. Seen from this perspective, the law is not static but has an inner dynamic of its own. It is not a long list of duties that is added to whenever moral and policy considerations make this desirable: new duties may be recognised as a response to specifically legal considerations, in the attempt to give better legal protection to established legal rights.

In fact this apparent contrast between the dynamic anti-Hohfeldian view, and the static Hohfeldian view, is overly simplistic. For nothing in Hohfeld's analysis commits us to a denial of the idea that the recognition of one type of legal right may sometimes give us good reason for recognising another type of legal right bearing upon the same area of conduct: thus, having recognised that butchers have a liberty to run butchers' businesses, we may have a good reason for protecting the exercise of that liberty by certain claim-rights against specific forms of interference. What Hohfeld's analysis *does* suggest is that such decisions are never dictated by the *concept* of "a right": they are always matters of judgment, informed by many diverse considerations of justice and the common good.

Once again, the example of *Quinn v. Leathem* will help to clarify the point. A Hohfeldian would see Leathem's liberty to run a business as entailing the permissibility of his action, and the absence of a claim-right (possessed by others) that he should not do so. The liberty would *not* entail a claim-right possessed by Leathem, that he should not be interfered with in the running of his business. Nevertheless, the existence of Leathem's liberty to

---

[19] See, however, Kramer, *op. cit.* pp. 41–42.

run a business might provide us with a good reason for *conferring* upon Leathem certain claim-rights against specific forms of interference. Whether or not such claim-rights should be conferred (and what their content should be) is a question that would demand complex and open-ended reflections upon matters of justice and social policy. When we reason from Leathem's liberty to the desirability of giving him an appropriate claim-right, therefore, we must draw upon a host of diverse considerations. When, by contrast, we reason from Leathem's claim-rights to the correlative duties, we need engage in no such wide-ranging reflections: indeed, such reflections are excluded by the peremptory force of the rights in question.

Hohfeld's analysis therefore marks a contrast between significantly different forms or phases of legal reasoning. When we reason from a Hohfeldian right to its jural correlative (the legal position of the other party to the "jural relation"), we need engage in no reflection upon justice or policy, for the right *entails* its jural correlative. When, by contrast, we reason from one type of Hohfeldian right to another (from Leathem's liberty to the need for a protecting claim-right, for example), we engage in an intellectual exercise involving the balancing of many diverse moral and political considerations. The anti-Hohfeldian "dynamic" view of rights has a tendency to obscure this important distinction, for it suggests that rights are non-conclusive reasons for recognising liberties, duties, liabilities, and so forth, in appropriate circumstances: being non-conclusive, such reasons will always tend to invite open-ended deliberations upon possible countervailing considerations. The anti-Hohfeldian view also tends to suggest that deliberations on justice and policy, in the context of law, will be in large part a matter of reflecting upon the significance of our rights. The Hohfeldian analysis, by contrast, is quite compatible with the claim that the notion of "rights" is a relatively unhelpful concept to employ in such deliberations. Casting light as it does upon important distinctions within legal reasoning, while avoiding any commitment to a highly contestable view of justice and policy, the Hohfeldian view seems clearly preferable to more fashionable alternatives.

IS THE ABSENCE OF A DUTY A RIGHT?

Hohfeld's analysis rejects the idea that the concept of a right exhibits internal complexity. Possession of a particular right does not entail possession of various permissibilities (liberties), inviolabilities (claim-rights), powers and immunities. A right is not a complex molecular stucture of different components. Rather, according to Hohfeld, assertions of rights are frequently ambiguous as between these different atomic elements. Once the ambiguity is shed, each specific type of right is essentially simple, and is to be understood in terms of what it entails for the other party to the relevant juridical relationship. The various Hohfeldian atomic rights are mutually independent: one cannot infer the existence of claim-rights from liberties, for example; or liberties from powers.

The superiority of the Hohfeldian view as an analysis of legal rights is demonstrated by the frequency with which the various Hohfeldian elements are separated by the legal doctrines of most developed systems. It is, for example, relatively unusual for liberties to be protected by general claim-rights obtaining against all forms of interference with the liberty: the liberty to run a butcher's business is not accompanied by a claim-right against being interfered with in that business, but by specific claim-rights against specific forms of interference. Liberties receive a degree of protection from the general claim-rights against assault and trespass, and further claim-rights (such as claim-rights against forms of unfair trade competition) may be recognised to provide additional protection. The proper extent of such protective claim-rights is a matter for policy judgment in relation to each type of liberty: it is not the case that the protective claim-rights are entailed by the liberty.

Defenders of the anti-Hohfeldian position are inclined to respond by claiming that liberties unprotected by claim-rights, or powers not combined with liberties, would not be spoken of as "rights": only when we find someone in possession of a cluster of related Hohfeldian atomic elements do we speak of them as possessing a right. Hence, it is argued, the Hohfeldian view is quite misguided in suggesting that individual claim-rights, liberties, powers and immunities constitute, in themselves, individual rights.

Numerous examples of this type of argument are to be found in the literature, and I have considered some of them elsewhere.[20] For the present I will take only one example, which I choose because it exemplifies perhaps the commonest fallacy of

---

[20] See Simmonds, "Rights at the Cutting Edge" Kramer, Simmonds and Steiner *op cit.* pp.153–158.

this type, and one of the commonest sources of confusion:

> "The absence of a duty does not amount to a right. A person who says to another 'I have a right to do it' is not saying that he has no duty not to or that it is not wrong to do it. He is claiming that the other has a duty not to interfere. It is not necessarily a duty not to interfere in any way whatsoever. It is, however, a claim that there are some ways of interference which would be wrong because they are against the interest of the right-holder."[21]

Let us begin by examining the assertion made in Raz's first three sentences: that the absence of a duty (a Hohfeldian liberty) is not a right, so that when someone claims a right to act in a certain way, they are not asserting the absence of a duty on their part but the presence of a duty (incumbent upon others) not to interfere. To see that Raz is mistaken, we need only imagine a context where others are under no duty not to interfere with my action, and where the suggestion has been made that I am under a duty not to perform the relevant act.

Suppose, for example, that in the context of a ball game, someone erroneously suggests that it is a foul deliberately to kick the ball into touch. A player might well reply to this suggestion by saying that the rules confer a right to kick the ball into touch. Such an assertion would not, however, constitute a claim that others are under a duty not to interfere with such a kicking into touch: the position would be that each player has a right to kick the ball into touch, and there is no duty not to prevent such a kicking into touch.

Assertions of a right to perform an action may, in some situations, be shorthand ways of asserting a claim not to be interfered with in performing the action. Or, alternatively, they may be ways of resisting a suggestion that one violates one's duty in so acting: they may, in other words, be assertions of a Hohfeldian liberty (the absence of a duty not to perform the action). The Hohfeldian view, that such claims are potentially ambiguous (until clarified by use of the Hohfeldian terminology)

---

[21] Joseph Raz, *Ethics in the Public Domain* (Oxford 1994) p.259.

The type of argument put forward by Raz and others could easily be confused with a much more subtle and powerful claim offered by Hart, but which I do not regard as inconsistent with Hohfeld's analysis. See Simmonds, *op. cit.* pp.165–168.

therefore seems to be correct. The Razian view, that such claims are invariably assertions of a duty not to interfere, seems obviously unsound.

The very common belief that the absence of a duty cannot constitute a "right" unless the liberty is protected by a claim-right (a duty on others not to interfere) requires its defenders to spell out the content of the relevant protective duties. The proper extent of any such protective duties will be a matter for political judgment, however, requiring consideration of a great multiplicity of values and concerns. Defenders of the anti-Hohfeldian view are therefore inclined to resort to vacuous handwaving at this point in their arguments, thereby concealing the impossibility of inferring the relevant claim-rights from the liberty. In *Quinn v. Leathem*, for example, Lord Lindley treats Leathem's liberty to run a butcher's business as entailing a duty on Quinn, and others, not to interfere; Quinn's duty is said to be one of non-interference "except so far as his own liberty of action may justify him in so doing."[22] This seems remarkably uninformative, for it amounts to telling us that Quinn does no wrong in interfering, except in so far as he *does* do wrong in interfering; or, conversely, that he does wrong in interfering, except in so far as he is entitled to interfere.

INTERNAL COMPLEXITY WITHOUT PEREMPTORY FORCE?

Given that the modern anti-Hohfeldian view seeks to restore an understanding of rights as internally complex, how does that position explain the frequency with which the various Hohfeldian elements are separated by the law?

The answer is that rights, on the analysis offered by Raz,[23] do not possess *conclusory* force: they do not *entail* their various consequences, or provide conclusive reasons for recognising those consequences. Possession of a right does not in itself ensure the existence of any particular duties, liberties, powers and so forth. Rather, the right provides a sufficient but non-

---

[22] [1901] A.C. 495 at p. 534.
[23] In what follows I will focus on Raz's version of the anti-Hohfeldian position, as being somewhat more extensively developed than MacCormick's version.

conclusive[24] reason for recognising such forms of protection. If I have a right to free speech, for example, my right provides a sufficient but non-conclusive reason for recognising others to be under a duty not to interfere with my free speech; it may also provide a reason for conferring upon me certain powers, or recognising certain liberties. The right corresponds to an important individual interest, and its implications in any concrete set of circumstances depend upon the best way of protecting that interest, when all things are taken into account (including countervailing considerations). Hence, situations where a right is protected in law by some but not all of the Hohfeldian elements can easily be reconciled with Raz's theory by the simple expedient of saying that they represent situations where the interest was adequately protected without the full gamut of protective claim-rights, powers, liberties and immunities; or, alternatively, by saying that the reasons for providing this or that form of protection were outweighed in the circumstances by countervailing considerations.

Suppose that I have been injured, and that it is agreed that I have a right to be compensated for my injury. On the Razian view the right is a sufficient reason for imposing on someone a duty to compensate me. But it is not a *conclusive* reason, and it may always be outweighed by countervailing considerations. Whenever I seek to enforce my right against some specific defendant, it will be open to that defendant to argue that, while they acknowledge the validity of my right, they should not be placed under a correlative duty because my right is only a non-conclusive reason for recognising such a duty, and in this case it is outweighed by countervailing considerations.

In abandoning the idea that rights *entail* their juridical consequences, however, has the Razian analysis not abandoned the idea that rights have peremptory force? We argued above that the idea of rights possessing a special or "peremptory" force receives its clearest expression in the law, where the peremptory force of rights may be thought of as their power conclusively to determine the permissibility of action: my claim-right conclusively determines the existence of your duty (the impermissi-

---

[24] According to Raz, a right is a sufficient reason, "other things being equal", for recognising or imposing a duty. A reason that is "sufficient other things being equal" is non-conclusive, because it admits the possibility that, in this instance, other things are not "equal": in other words, it admits the possibility of countervailing considerations that may outweigh the otherwise sufficient reason.

bility of acts that would breach the duty); my liberty conclusively determines the permissibility of my action (your "no-right" in relation to that action).[25] Rights cannot conclusively determine such issues, and cannot possess peremptory force in this sense, if they are merely non-conclusive reasons for particular conclusions on permissibility, needing to be weighed against other competing considerations.

Two distinguishable lines of argument seem to be open to Raz in response to the accusation that his theory abandons the peremptory force of rights. One line of argument would concede that his theory does not preserve the peremptory force of rights in the strong sense of *conclusory* force: that is, rights do not entail, or provide conclusive reasons for, juridical conclusions of permissibility. Nevertheless, it would be argued, the theory preserves a genuine (albeit weaker) form of peremptory force of the kind that we might attribute to moral rights.

A second, and more ambitious, line of argument (not incompatible with the first line) might also be attempted. This would claim that Raz's theory can preserve the peremptory force of rights (in the strong Hohfeldian sense of conclusory force) in all of those situations where it would be recognised by Hohfeld; the Razian theory would differ from Hohfeld's (on this view) insofar as it also recognised a more general type of right, not possessed of peremptory force in the strong conclusory sense, but possessing peremptory force in a weaker yet still genuine sense.

Raz's views on these matters are far from clear, and we are therefore left with little choice but to consider a variety of ways in which his position might be construed. Once we separate distinct lines of argument, it will become clear, I think that Raz's analysis holds little appeal. In the meantime, we are faced with considerable complexity and uncertainty, going far beyond anything that one might reasonably expect to find in an introductory work of this kind. Readers who are already growing tired of rights, their peremptory force or lack of it, and perhaps of jurisprudence as a whole, may wish to skip the next few pages on Raz, and go straight to p.304 where I turn to the "will" and "interest" theories of rights. Gluttons for punishment who are determined to persevere have only themselves to blame.

---

[25] A slightly more complex formulation would be required to cover powers and immunities, which concern the validity of legal transactions, rather than the permissibility of actions.

RIGHTS AGAINST NOBODY?

Suppose that I sue you for some legal wrong, claiming that you owe me a duty to compensate me for loss. The judge hears the arguments, and concludes that I have established the existence of a legal right to be compensated by you. He then goes on to explain that, while my right constitutes a sufficient reason for imposing a duty on you other things being equal, the reason is not a conclusive one, because it must be weighed against other conflicting considerations. In this case, he holds, the reasons against imposing liability upon the defendant outweigh my right. So, although I have a right to be compensated by you, you do not have a duty to compensate me.

We must assume, I think, that Raz does not intend his theory to license this way of speaking about legal rights. For it is surely normally assumed by lawyers that, if I possess a valid right to be paid compensation by you, your duty to pay the compensation follows as a matter of logic. My right is *not* simply a non-conclusive reason for recognising the duty. If Raz's theory of rights would permit judges to reason in this way, it would conflict fundamentally with the ordinary assumptions structuring our grasp of the concept of a "legal right". Yet how would Raz *avoid* speaking in this way of rights? After all, he takes the view that a right is a non-conclusive reason (a sufficient reason "other things being equal") for recognising a duty: so what is wrong with our imaginary judge's statement?

Razians will feel confident that they have a response easily available, for they are likely to say that I have begged the entire question in assuming a right that obtains against a specific individual. Let me formulate their objection in the following way:

"Simmonds imagines a situation where X has demonstrated that he has a right against some specific Y. He then assumes that any reasons against the recognition or imposition of a duty will kick in after the right has been established but before the duty has been recognised. This, however, is a confusion. Raz envisages rights that identify important interests. The interests may be protected in various ways, including the imposition of duties on individuals. We may know that someone has a right without knowing the identity of the person against whom the right obtains: the content of the right is separable from the modalities whereby it is appropriately protected. Deciding upon the identity of the person against whom the right obtains is precisely a matter of deciding who is subject to a duty owed to the right-holder. There is no stage at which I have a right against you, but it is unclear whether you owe me a duty: the reason being that my having a right *against you* is precisely a matter of you owing me a duty in consequence of my right."

For this argument to succeed, we would have to distinguish the content of the right from the modality whereby it is protected. X would have, for example, a right to be paid £100, rather than a right to be paid £100 by Y. The decision to impose the duty upon Y would be the choice of a particular modality for protection or enforcement of the right, rather than a logical consequence of the content of the right. Such a view is not impossible: but it would commit Raz to a very contentious and problematic theory of private law. The duty placed upon the tortfeasor to compensate the tort victim (for example) might have to be explained as the best way of enforcing a general right to be compensated in the abstract. Nor could we say that the tortfeasor's duty was the "best" way of enforcing the victim's right because of some inherent moral appropriateness in receiving compensation from the wrongdoer: such a view would strongly suggest that the entitlement is one to receive compensation from the tortfeasor, and not simply an entitlement to be compensated in the abstract. The choice of the tortfeasor as the appropriate duty-bearer would therefore have to be explained by instrumental or efficiency considerations. The problems that dog such analyses of tort law are well-known.[26]

The content of such private rights as those found in tort law is such that it makes no sense to separate identification of the right's content from identification of the party against whom the right obtains. There is no gap here into which the defeasibility of the right's power to generate a duty can be fitted. If such an element of defeasibility exists, it must be fitted into the moment between the recognition of my right against the defendant, and the recognition of the defendant's duty to me.

[26] See Jules Coleman, *Markets, Morals and the Law* (Cambridge 1988) Chapter. 8; Ernest Weinrib, *The Idea of Private Law* (Harvard 1995).

RIGHTS AGAINST SPECIFIC PERSONS

Raz is careful to note that a right which is *permanently* defeated by countervailing considerations and *never* succeeds in grounding a duty cannot be regarded as a genuine right.[27] He also notes that some rights (such as contractual rights) can obtain only against a specific individual. In these cases, Raz might possibly claim that the right does entail a duty on the other party, since genuine rights must succeed in justifying duties on someone (see above), and a right of this type has only one opportunity for success. Let us, once again, imagine what the defender of Raz might say:

> "Suppose that we accept Simmonds' claim that, in private law, the content of a right cannot generally be separated from the identification of the party against whom the right obtains. Nothing detrimental to Raz's theory follows from that. For Raz points out that, from the existence of a genuine right, we can infer the existence of a duty incumbent upon *someone*, even if we cannot identify that person. If the content of the right is such that it could be protected *only* by a duty incumbent upon one particular person, and we know that a right must give rise to a duty on someone, we know that the right must give rise to a duty upon the one person who is the only possible bearer of the duty. On Simmonds' view about private rights, Raz's theory would yield the happy conclusion that private rights *entail* correlative duties. This entailment would not, however, be a general conceptual feature of rights generally: it would be the result of applying the general Razian theory to the special context of private rights. Thus Raz's theory would *explain* the features of private rights that misled theorists such as Hohfeld, but would explain them by reference to a theory that possesses far greater generality, and is well able to accommodate rights that do not entail duties in this way."

The trouble with this approach would be that it detaches Raz's claim (that every right must succeed in establishing a duty on someone, somewhere) from the most plausible reasons for making that claim. If I claim to be a very good boxer, having fought many fights and lost all of them, my claim may be

[27] Joseph Raz, *The Morality of Freedom* (Oxford, 1986) p.184.

discounted as obviously false. Similarly, if a right potentially obtains against many people but never succeeds in establishing a duty on any of them, it is probably spurious. If, on the other hand, I claim to be a very good boxer having fought only once and lost, my claim may well be true: perhaps I went the distance with Mike Tyson and lost on points. By analogy, a right that, by its content, can obtain against only one individual is not shown to represent an unreal or insubstantial interest simply because, in the only circumstances in which the right could come into play, it was outweighed by some countervailing factor of unusual power (the Mike Tyson of countervailing factors).

LEVELS OF ABSTRACTION

A further difficulty is inherent in Raz's claim that a genuine right must succeed in establishing a duty on someone. For that claim could be construed in a way that would simply collapse his theory into that of Hohfeld. Rights may be stated at various levels of abstraction. People have a right to compensation from those who have negligently damaged their property. I have a right that you should compensate me for negligently breaking my tea-pot. When Raz tells us that a genuine right must succeed in imposing a duty on someone, he does not explain how that thesis is to be related to these differing levels of abstraction in the formulation of rights.

Presumably, the genuine nature of the (abstract) right to be compensated for negligent damage is demonstrated by the fact that, as a result of that right, particular individuals are sometimes found to have a duty to pay compensation to those that they have negligently injured. But what of my (concrete) right to be compensated by you for the breaking of my teapot? Can one show that this is a genuine right by showing that the abstract right from which it is derived sometimes succeeds in justifying a duty? Or can the genuineness of this concrete right only be established by showing that it gives rise to duties at the same level of concreteness?

Suppose that I fail to establish that you are under a duty to compensate me for the loss of my teapot. Does this failure show that I have no genuine right? Or can I show that the right is genuine (in spite of the absence of anyone who bears a duty to compensate me) by treating it as a specific application of the (abstract) right to be compensated for negligent injury, which does sometimes justify the imposition of a duty?

The first view (call it "option 1") requires genuine rights to establish duties at the same level of abstraction. The second view (call it "option 2") permits us to treat concrete rights as derivatives of abstract rights, and so to demonstrate their genuine nature by reference to the occasional success of the abstract right in justifying the imposition of a duty.

If Raz adopts option 2, he must then accept that I may have a genuine right to be compensated by you, for the damage you caused to my teapot, while you are under no duty to compensate me for that damage. This conclusion seems to be wholly at odds with the way in which we would ordinarily think about legal rights.

If, on the other hand, Raz adopts option 1, he is not disagreeing with Hohfeld's correlativity thesis. For, on option 1, a genuine right *does* entail a correlative duty. The right to be compensated entails a duty to be compensated. The right to be compensated by the person who caused the damage entails a duty to compensate on the person who caused the damage. My right to be compensated by you for the damage to my teapot entails your duty to compensate me.

PEREMPTORY FORCE: EXCLUSIONARY OR CONCLUSORY?

I suggested above that Raz might be committed to saying that the plaintiff's right to be compensated by the defendant does not entail the defendant's duty to pay the plaintiff. We then considered various ways in which Razians might seek to resist that suggestion, and we discovered that the possible responses would involve Raz in considerable additional complexities of a kind that he does not address. Let us now set that issue on one side, and return to Raz's general thesis that a right is a sufficient but non-conclusive reason for recognising a duty.

Raz claims, from time to time, that his theory preserves the "peremptory force" of rights. At one point, for example, he says that "According to our account the special features of rights are their source in individual interest and their peremptory force."[28] Yet how can a non-conclusive reason be spoken of as possessing "peremptory" force? Such a reason seems on the face of it to be no more than a (possibly very weighty) consideration that is to

[28] J.Raz, *The Morality of Freedom* (Oxford, 1986) p.192.

be balanced against other conflicting factors. It is clear that Raz does not regard the right as conclusive of the duty, so he cannot intend to equate "peremptory force" with "conclusory force".[29] We must, however, consider the possibility that rights in Raz's theory could be said to possess "peremptory force" in some other acceptable sense.

It will be remembered from the earlier part of the present chapter that there is a general problem in explaining the "peremptory force" of moral rights and moral duties. We feel that moral rights are more than simply weighty considerations that must be balanced against all other factors; yet we feel equally uncomfortable with the suggestion that they are absolutely overriding considerations that are conclusive of what we should do. We saw, for example, how even ardent advocates of moral rights such as Nozick feel compelled to acknowledge certain situations where rights must be set aside in the light of other countervailing factors.

Raz, it will be remembered, proposes an analysis of "exclusionary reasons" that seems to help us understand this problem: for the analysis explains how exclusionary reasons may exclude some conflicting reasons from consideration, while allowing others to enter into our deliberations on what is to be done. Raz also takes the view that an analysis of legal rights should proceed from, and be informed by, a prior analysis of moral rights. Is it possible, therefore, that Raz intends to explain the peremptory force of legal rights by saying that rights are *exclusionary* reasons for recognising duties? Hart tells us that "peremptory" means "cutting off deliberation, debate or argument".[30] While exclusionary reasons do not *conclude* the debate (since they can leave non-excluded countervailing reasons still in play) they do at least "cut off" one *part* of the debate, precisely by excluding *certain* reasons from consideration. There would therefore seem to be some justification for analysing "peremptory force" as "exclusionary force" rather than as "conclusory force".

Such a strategy of analysis would manifest an error that was criticised earlier in this chapter. That is to say, it would import into the context of law and legal rights the considerable uncertainties that characterise claims of right in the moral realm, and it might with ample justification be rejected for that reason.

---

[29] I speak of a right possessing "conclusory force" when it gives us a conclusive reason for recognising a duty.

[30] Hart, *Essays on Bentham* (Oxford 1982) p.253.

There are, however, a host of other difficulties that the analysis would have to face, as we shall see.

EXCLUSION UPON EXCLUSION

On this interpretation of Raz, therefore, he is arguing that rights are exclusionary reasons for recognising duties. But duties are themselves (according to Raz) exclusionary reasons. Can exclusionary reasons be piled one upon another in this way? The principle known to philosophers as "Ockham's razor" prohibits us from multiplying entities beyond necessity. We might well wonder whether this interpretation of Raz's view generates a superfluity of exclusionary reasons, in violation of Ockham's razor.

To focus clearly upon this question, we should I think ask whether there might be (non-excluded) reasons against imposing or recognising a certain duty that would not also be (non-excluded) reasons against performing the duty-act. Alternatively, might there be (non-excluded) reasons against performing the duty-act that would not be (non-excluded) reasons against recognising a duty? If there are such reasons, then the double layer of exclusionary reasons, that is (on this interpretation) integral to Raz's account of rights, exhibits no redundancy. The right and the duty might both be exclusionary reasons, but they might establish different boundaries between excluded and non-excluded first-order reasons.

If, however, every genuine and non-excluded reason against the recognition of a duty would also be a genuine and non-excluded reason against performing the duty-act (and vice versa), the double layer of exclusionary reasons seems redundant: for there is little point in reproducing the same intellectual structure if, in its second manifestation, it captures nothing that was not already captured the first time around.

When we are dealing with *legal* rights it is easy to see how there might be reasons against imposing a duty that would not also be reasons against performing the duty-act. For example, should the duty to feed hungry children be placed solely upon their parents and guardians, or should some such duty be placed on citizens generally? One reason against imposing such a duty on citizens generally would be that any such duty would have to framed in rather vague terms (When a child starves are we *all* guilty of a breach of duty, or only those who could have helped easily? What does "easily" mean?). Yet the vagueness of any such legal duty is not a reason for me, now, to refuse to feed this particular starving child. Therefore, there can be reasons against imposition of a legal duty that would not also be reasons against the performance of the duty-act.

Raz would have considerable difficulty, however, in showing that the separation between "reasons against imposing a duty" and "reasons against performing the duty-act" traces in some convincing way the distinction between rights (as exclusionary reasons for imposing duties) and duties (as exclusionary reasons for performing certain acts).[31] Certainly he says nothing whatever that could be construed as an attempt to demonstrate the correspondence between these ideas. The absence of any such attempt on his part must cast doubt upon the interpretation of Raz that we are currently considering.

ONE SET OF REASONS; TWO PERSPECTIVES

To say that rights are exclusionary reasons for recognising duties, and duties are exclusionary reasons for acts, seems therefore to duplicate exclusionary reasons without good reason. Suppose, however, that Raz were to say that the concepts of "right" and" duty" are two different ways of speaking about the *same set* of reasons.

Raz might say that talk of rights and duties is one way in which we refer to the reasons (ultimately grounded in considerations of the "good") that bear upon our conduct. Rights and duties operate at a median level of discourse, between the level of particular prescriptions (*you* ought to do *this, now*) and the ultimate reasons that ground those prescriptions. They describe the bearing of reasons upon conduct; and the notions of "right" and "duty" have distinct descriptive roles,

---

[31] Even if he succeeded in doing this, he would still have to explain how the analysis could be applied to moral rights, given that the justification for his general approach is precisely that it bases the analysis of legal rights upon that of moral rights.

It is of course possible to speak of "morality" in a way that analogises it to law. Thus, when Bentham employs the principle of utility as a guide to "morals and legislation", he means the principle to guide us in our adoption of general social rules to be enforced by informal sanctions: the decision is, as it were, a quasi-legislative one. When Raz offers a theory of moral rights, however, he does not seem to have this view of morality in mind.

even though what they are describing is the same set of reasons. Thus talk of rights serves to identify the important interests that are at stake, without necessarily specifying the act that is required to protect those interests; while talk of duty specifies the required act, without identifying the interest that explains the need for that act. There are certain exclusionary reasons bearing upon our conduct. When we focus upon the acts required by these exclusionary reasons, we speak of them as "duties"; when we focus upon the individual interests which these exclusionary reasons serve to protect, we speak of them as "rights".

This position, however, strongly suggests the kind of correlativity of rights and duties espoused by Hohfeld and ably defended by Kramer. For it suggests that talk of rights is one possible way of referring to a set of reasons bearing upon an act, while talk of the duty is simply an alternative way of referring to the same set of reasons. Kramer employs the example of a man who creates a slope in his garden: we can choose to focus upon the up-slope that he has created, or we can focus on the down-slope; but the alternative perspectives do not alter the fact that an up-slope logically entails a down-slope.[32] Suppose then that Raz regards "rights" as enjoying peremptory force not because they are exclusionary reasons for recognising duties, but because they are the exclusionary reasons that *constitute* duties, viewed from the perspective of the individual interest thereby protected. He would then be unable to deny correlativity, because his theory would logically presuppose it.

A final line of argument might be invoked by Razians, to the effect that the relationship between right and duty is not like that between up-slope and down-slope, insofar as we may meaningfully talk of rights even when we cannot identify the bearers of any relevant duties. We could not, by contrast, be able to describe the existence, length or inclination of the up-slope without being able to convey the same information about the down-slope. When we cannot identify the duty bearer, talk of the right gives us the information that there is an interest that would justify a duty other things being equal; and when we have identified the duty bearer, talk of a right still functions to give us the additional information that the duty is justified by the right-holder's interest. Thus talk of the right gives us, in the first type of case (where the duty-bearer is not yet identified) an incomplete specification of reasons for action (we are not told

[32] Kramer, in *Kramer, Simmonds and Steiner op, cit.* p. 39.

whose action, or what action precisely); while in the second type of case (where the duty is specified) talk of the right specifies the reason more fully (a statement about the duty tells us that there is a reason to perform an action, but not what the reason is).

This reply fails, however, to distinguish Raz's theory (on the present interpretation) from the Hohfeldian correlativity thesis, for it concedes that, when we can speak of rights without knowing the corresponding duties, the relevant reasons that are being described in the language of rights are incompletely specified. Hohfeld would surely say that the correlativity of rights and duties enables us to infer the precise content and location of a duty from the existence of a right only when the right is completely specified. If someone asserts a "right to be compensated", for example, Hohfeld would say that the right remains incompletely specified until we have been told against whom it obtains.

EXCLUSION ABANDONED

If Raz is construed as treating rights as exclusionary reasons, therefore, his analysis would face substantial problems. In fact, it is reasonably clear that Raz does not adopt this view.[33] From time to time, he describes rights on his theory as possessing "peremptory force", and he tends to equate the word "peremptory" with the notion of an exclusionary reason. Yet his most scrupulous formulations of his analysis of rights are careful to avoid these equations, preferring to adopt a more circumspect approach:

> "[R]ights have a special force which is expressed by the fact that they are grounds of duties, which are peremptory reasons for action."[34]

In this statement, it will be noted, duties are said to possess peremptory force but rights are not so described: rights are said to possess "special" force in being grounds of duties. I can find no passage where he treats a right as an exclusionary reason for recognising a duty: he invariably speaks of the right as a

---

[33]   I have discussed the view that treats rights as exclusionary reasons only because I have heard Raz's followers confidently assert that this *does* represent his position.

[34]   J.Raz, *The Morality of Freedom* (Oxford 1986) p.249.

sufficient but non-conclusive reason for recognising the duty.

The abandonment of peremptory force by Raz's theory therefore seems to be open and acknowledged, for a sufficient but non-conclusive reason possesses "peremptory force" in no recognisable sense.

THE "WILL" AND "INTEREST" THEORIES

Debate about the nature of law is often thought of as a long-running battle between "legal positivists" and "natural lawyers". Similarly, debate about the nature of rights is often thought of as a battle between the "will" and "interest" theories of rights. We have avoided mention of this debate until a late stage in our chapter on rights in order to emphasise the fact that many important issues concerning the nature of rights have no substantial connection with the will/interest division.

In its classical form, the disagreement between the will and interest theories bears out our earlier observations about the intimate connections between analytical jurisprudence and normative jurisprudence. For the rival theories did not simply offer different analyses of the "concept" of a right: they offered sweeping theories of the nature of law, its role in the political community, and the basis of its legitimacy; the rival accounts of right formed an integral part of these broader investigations.

Kant's theory of right provided the most influential version of the will theory. Kant viewed law as essentially a body of principles capable of justifying the use of coercion: judges invoke propositions of law, not as neutral statements of fact, but as a basis for ordering coercive measures against individual defendants. Given law's capacity to justify coercion, it followed that, even in a system of wholly posited laws, one would still require a basic natural law establishing the moral authority of the law-maker: without such authorisation, the decrees of the law-maker would lack the power to justify coercion.[35] In the light of this need for moral authorisation, Kant believed that one could determine the possible scope and necessary structure of law by reflecting upon the conditions in which coercion can be justified. Without such reflection, the jurist may easily state what is laid down as right in each jurisdiction; but he cannot determine

---

[35] Kant, *The Metaphysics of Morals*, translated by Mary Gregor (Cambridge 1991) 51.

whether it is truly right without reflecting upon "the immutable principles for any giving of positive law".[36]

Coercion is in general wrong, Kant held, because it interferes with freedom; but if freedom is used to interfere with the equal freedom of others, one may coercively restrain that exercise of freedom and, in doing so, act justifiably because consistently with equal freedom. By delineating principles which flesh out the notion of equal freedom, therefore, we determine the necessary structure of genuine (because legitimate) law. The relevant principles will define domains of entitlement within which the individual will is supreme. It is for this reason that rights, in Kant's view, possess a degree of internal complexity: for the supremacy of the individual will within the relevant domain entails that certain actions of the right-holder are permissible; and are also inviolable (interferences with the relevant actions will violate equal freedom); the right-holder enjoys power to waive his entitlement, and so forth.

The interest theory, by contrast, was grounded in the view that the notion of "equal freedom" was empty, and that it was impossible to derive any principles or rights from the bare idea of a realm where individual wills were jointly compatible. Exponents of the will theory, such as Ihering and Bentham, abandoned the unhelpful notion of equal freedom in favour of the idea that individuals have interests which frequently conflict. It is necessary for law to step in in order to *create* boundaries between different interests. The creation of such boundaries is the result of a legislative or judicial choice, after deliberation upon which are the most weighty interests, and how best they may be protected. There are, as it were, no natural boundaries between interests waiting to be discovered by reason, comparable to the rationalistic principles envisaged by the theory of equal freedom.

In the twentieth century, the debate between the will and interest theories of rights became detached from the ambitious and sweeping claims about justice and legitimacy in which the older views were grounded. The debate is now thought of (in line with the conventional division between "analytical" and "normative" inquiries) as an attempt to "analyse" or "clarify" the concept of "a right", without involving any questions of justice or legitimacy.

---

[36] Kant, *op. cit.* p.55. Kant adds that positive laws serve as "excellent guides" to the underlying principles of right.

The modern debate is most easily explained by reference to Hohfeld's analysis. Hohfeld, it will be remembered sees claim-rights as correlative to duties: X's possession of a claim-right against Y entails a duty owed by Y to X. What Hohfeld does not tell us is this: what exactly is involved in owing a duty *to* a specific individual? Suppose that I am under a duty to install certain items of safety equipment in my factory: to whom do I owe this duty? How would we tell? To answer this question, should we look at the content of the duty itself? Or at the reasons for its imposition? Or at the powers of enforcement that exist in relation to the duty?

Another question left unanswered by Hohfeld concerns the relationship between the various Hohfeldian types of right: claim-rights, liberties, powers and immunities. The word "right" is ambiguous between these various notions: but, presumably, the word is not a mere homonym. There must be some general reason why these four different notions are all referred to as "rights". What is it that they have in common, explaining our treatment of them as rights?

The answer given to this latter question by our two rival theories is relatively straightforward. According to the will-theory, the various Hohfeldian rights are linked by the fact that they all protect choices: liberties leave me free from duty so that I may act as I choose; powers make it possible for me to alter legal relations if I choose to; immunities ensure that my legal position will not be altered otherwise than by my own choice; claim-rights (as we shall see) make the falling due or the enforcement of another's duty dependent upon my choice.

The interest theory, by contrast, regards the various Hohfeldian rights as linked by the fact that they are all, in general, advantageous to their possessor: they all serve the right-holder's interests. A slightly different version of the will theory (offered by Raz) sees the various Hohfeldian "rights" as mechanisms whereby the right is protected, the latter "right" representing a weighty interest of the right-holder.

In what follows, we will concentrate upon the first question, concerning the relationship between claim-rights and duties.

The interest theory tells us that a claim-right is an interest protected by a duty. To identify the person to whom I owe my duty (the holder of the correlative claim-right) we need to work out whose interest is protected by my duty.

The will-theory, by contrast, tells us that the duty is correlative to a claim-right only when the duty (or its enforcement) is made conditional in some way upon an exercise of will by another party. Thus, if you make a contractual promise to pay me £100, your duty to pay is owed to me, and is correlative to my claim-right, because and insofar as the duty (or its enforcement) is conditional upon my will: I could waive your duty entirely if I wished, and it is my choice whether or not you will be sued for any breach of it.

Some duties appear on the face of things to fit neither model. Take, for example, a duty to hoist the Union Jack on the Queen's birthday. Here, there may be no-one who has the power to waive the duty, and perhaps no one who can choose to sue to enforce it: hence it does not seem to fit the will-theory. On the other hand, it is far from obvious whose interest is protected by the duty: the Queen's? does she really care?

In relation to such duties, the will-theory is happy to concede that there is no-one who possesses a claim-right correlative to the duty. The will theory holds that every claim-right entails a duty, but not every duty entails a claim-right. Duties imposed by contract, or by the law of tort, for example, can generally be waived by the parties to whom the duties are owed. Duties imposed by the criminal law, on the other hand, cannot be waived in this way: if you steal from my house, and I decide not to prosecute, other people (such as the police) may nevertheless decide that you should be punished and may proceed to prosecute you. Duties in private law entail correlative claim-rights; but duties in public law quite often do not do so, for there may be no one who has the power to waive the public duty, or to sue for its enforcement. Will-theorists see their analysis as drawing attention to important structural differences between private law and public law, with the strict correlativity of duties to claim-rights obtaining only in private law.

Interest theorists, by contrast, are anxious to avoid such complex distinctions. When duties do not protect *individual* interests, they are regarded as protecting *collective* interests, and the correlative rights are assigned to the state. Hence, interest theories regard the correlativity of claim-rights and duties as strict and universal: for them, all claim-rights entail duties, *and* all duties entail claim-rights.

Will-theorists can identify rights on their analysis simply by examining the content of the legal rules. Some versions of the interest theory, by contrast, can identify legal rights only by entering into an inquiry into the *purposes* of the rules.

The problem arises when we ask what exactly it is for a duty to "protect" an interest. A law does not confer rights on me simply because I stand to benefit from that law: the manufacturers of motorcycle crash helmets no doubt benefit from a law compelling the wearing of helmets, but the law confers upon them no rights. Consequently, interest-theorists have been inclined to say that the right-holder must be the *intended* beneficiary of the law imposing the duty: it must be the object of the law to benefit the right-holder. However, it is not always easy to determine who the intended beneficiaries of a duty are, and this inevitably introduces a degree of uncertainty into the language of rights. For example, parents are under a duty to send their children to school. Is this law intended to benefit the children? Or is it perhaps, intended to benefit all of us, by ensuring a well-educated population and workforce? Or is it perhaps intended to benefit householders, by ensuring that there are fewer children roaming the streets in the middle of the day, with ample opportunity to burgle houses?

The theory of rights offered by Raz and MacCormick, and discussed earlier, is itself a version of the interest theory. Raz, it will be remembered, rejects the view that a right is the correlative of a duty: he regards rights as representing weighty interests that might justify the imposition or recognition of various duties, liabilities, and other juridical consequences. Thus, my right of free speech may be the basis of various duties imposed on others, liberties possessed by me, powers enjoyed or disabilities borne by local authorities or policemen. The fragmentation of legal relations portrayed by the Hohfeldian analysis is viewed here as a superficial appearance only: beyond the level of Hohfeldian relations is a deeper level of "rights" where the coherence of the law is made clear.

There is nothing wrong with this way of speaking when it is understood as a shorthand way of talking *about* the law's content, and its relationship with various human concerns. If, however, the concept of a legal right is to function as a means whereby we can precisely report the content and applicability of the law, the analysis has serious flaws. In the first place, and as we have already seen, it undercuts or denies the peremptory force of rights. Equally seriously, the Razian approach seems calculated to make the identification of legal rights highly contestable and uncertain. If we assume that the law is the implementation of a single and very integrated moral vision, we may expect it to embody some identifiable array of Razian legal rights. If, however, the law is in large part the residue of our attempts to deal, in an entirely pragmatic manner, with conflicts between a great diversity of human interests, we may expect Raz's analysis to present as legal rights practically all of the interests that have commonly played a part in those conflicts. Such an analysis will be found congenial by those who wish to present every interest in the form of an assertion of "rights", but it hardly seems conducive to clarity of thought or to a cool assessment of conflicting interests.

Kramer has offered a sophisticated version of the interest theory which avoids these difficulties. In his view, Y's duty is correlative to X's claim-right when one way in which we might establish that Y is in breach of his duty is by showing that X has suffered a set-back to his interests at the hands of Y. Thus, Y's duty to pay X £100 is correlative to X's claim-right in so far as we could establish that Y had failed in his duty by showing that X's interest (in receiving the money) had received a set-back at Y's hands (*i.e.* Y had not paid).[37]

Kramer's approach neatly avoids any need to address questions concerning the intentions underpinning the law; nor does it require us to identify interests that are served by diverse legal protections, on the Razian model. It does, however, encounter certain problems of its own. For, when a legal duty is created in order to protect certain individual interests, the content of the duty may have a purely contingent connection with the interest that it is intended to protect: thus, the integrity of the home may be protected by a law prohibiting possession of skeleton keys and jemmies. In the case of such laws, however, it will not be possible to identify the individual interests protected simply by reference to the conditions sufficient to establish a breach of the duty. We noted above that, where a duty does not seem to protect any *individual* interest, Kramer maintains the thesis of universal correlativity between duties and claim-rights by locating the correlative claim-right in the state. But it follows from this that he will have to ascribe many claim-rights to the state. For, whenever the duty is connected to the relevant individual interests in a contingent way (as in the above example), the duty will register in Kramer's theory as one that protects no individual interest: it will therefore fall into the residual category of duties that are correlative to claim-rights possessed by the state.

---

[37] See Kramer, *op. cit.* pp.80–98.

MACCORMICK'S CRITICISMS

MacCormick has offered some influential arguments against the will-theory which merit consideration at this point. The first argument concerns restrictions on the power of the right holder to waive or alienate his right, and the second argument concerns the difficulty that the will theory has in accommodating children's rights.

The will theory considers the essence of a right to be a power of waiver over someone else's duty. But, MacCormick argues, the law sometimes restricts powers of waiver, and such restrictions are not usually regarded as limiting or abolishing our rights: more commonly they are seen as attempts to strengthen our rights. Two types of cases should be distinguished:

1. In some cases an act continues to be unlawful even though the "victim" consents to it, *e.g.* murder and grievous bodily harm. In other cases, consent is a good defence, *e.g.* minor assaults in the course of a game.

2. In some cases people are given rights and are deprived of the power to contract out of the right. This is commonly the case with rights conferred on employees.

MacCormick argues that in both types of case, the will theory leads to paradoxical conclusions. In the first type of case, the will theory requires us to say that we have rights not to be assaulted in a minor way (since here we have a power of waiver) but no right not to be grievously assaulted (since here we have no power of waiver). In the second type of case, the will theory requires us to say that legislation preventing employees from contracting out of their rights restricts those rights, by restricting the scope of the power of waiver. But such legislation would obviously be thought of as strengthening the employee's rights.

The second type of case can be dealt with relatively easily. MacCormick here confuses the power of waiver over the enforcement of the duty (which, according to the will theory, is the essence of a right) with the power to alienate the right. The right itself is a power to demand that the employer performs his obligations, including the power to sue or not as the employee chooses. By prohibiting the employee from contracting out of his rights, we do not restrict his power of waiver: we merely ensure that he continues to possess it.

The first type of case is more complex as it hinges on the view that we take of the criminal law. In relation to my private law rights, the duty not to assault is waivable by the victim, whether the assault be major or minor. Only in relation to the criminal law does the victim's waiver cease to be relevant to the legality of a major assault. The criminal law (unlike the civil law) is not usually thought of as conferring rights. Of course, part of the object of the criminal law is the protection of rights, but these rights are conferred either by morality (*e.g.* in the case of the right not to be assaulted) or by civil law (in the case of property rights). It is not at all clear, however, that the protection of rights is the predominant concern of those areas of criminal law to which MacCormick directs his attention. Laws punishing acts of violence perpetrated on consenting adults are not best seen as protecting the rights of those adults. In some cases they are concerned to punish activities which are regarded as immoral but not as violating anyone's rights, *e.g.* MacCormick uses the example of the flagellation of (or by) a prostitute, which is illegal irrespective of the "victim's" consent. In other cases, the acts are punished in a paternalistic spirit, to protect the "victim" from his or her own folly in consenting to the illegal act, *e.g.* euthanasia. It is doubtful if paternalism of this kind is best interpreted as a protection of the party's rights.[38]

So much for MacCormick's argument concerning restrictions on the power of waiver. His other principal argument concerns the rights of children.

According to the will theory, a right is an option or power of waiver over the enforcement of a duty, and the right-holder is the person who can demand performance or waive the duty, who can choose to sue or not sue. Such powers are not generally exercised by children. Where duties are owed to children, the enforcement of those duties is not left at the discretion of the child. In the case of legal rights, the power of waiver or enforcement rests in the hands of the child's parent or guardian. MacCormick argues that these facts should lead exponents of the will theory to conclude that children do not have any rights. But that conclusion, MacCormick suggests, would be preposterous: we know that children have rights, therefore the will theory must be false.

H. L. A. Hart defended the will theory in a number of

[38] See also Simmonds, *op. cit.* pp.225–232.

important papers which preceded MacCormick's work. Hart appreciated the problem with children's rights and draws the following conclusions. So far as moral rights go, Hart accepted that it is a mistake to ascribe rights to small babies, at least. The moral requirements on our conduct towards such infants are not based on respect for the infant's will, and therefore are not a matter of respect for rights (presumably Hart believed that, with older children, there are some areas of life where the child's will is controlling and where, therefore, the child can be spoken of as having rights). This conclusion should not be dismissed too quickly. Respect for rights is not the only possible basis for morality: there are duties of humanity, and moral requirements of love and compassion, to which the notion of "rights" is irrelevant.

In relation to legal rights, Hart adopted the conventional view that, in exercising powers of waiver, the parent or guardian is exercising the child's rights on behalf of the child. The fact that the parent or guardian is exercising the child's rights and not his own is borne out, Hart argues, by two features of the situation: (i) what the parent or guardian can do in exercising the power is determined by what the child could have done if *sui juris*, and (ii) when the child becomes *sui juris* he can exercise the powers without any need for an assignment of them. These features show that the powers are regarded as belonging throughout to the child, though exercised by another during the period of immaturity.

Selected reading

W. N. Hohfeld, *Fundamental Legal Conceptions* (1919).

G. Williams "The Concept of Legal Liberty" in R. S. Summers (Ed.), *Essays in Legal Philosophy* (1968).

H. L. A. Hart, *Essays on Bentham* (1982), Essays 7 and 8.

M. Kramer, N.E. Simmonds, H.Steiner, *A Debate Over Rights* (1998)

N. MacCormick, *Legal Rights and Social Democracy* (1982), Chapter. 8.

N. MacCormick, "Rights in Legislation" in P. M. S. Hacker and J. Raz (Eds.), *Law, Morality and Society* (1977).

J. Raz, The Morality of Freedom (1986) Chap. 7.

INDEX